Back to the Future and Philosophy

ALSO OF INTEREST
AND FROM MCFARLAND

Skateboarding and Philosophy: Essays Concerning the Life of the Grind (edited by Joshua Heter and Josef Thomas Simpson, 2025)

Back to the Future and Philosophy

Essays on Traveling Through the Space-Time Continuum

Edited by Joshua Heter *and* Richard Greene

McFarland & Company, Inc., Publishers
Jefferson, North Carolina

This book has undergone peer review.

LIBRARY OF CONGRESS CATALOGING-IN-PUBLICATION DATA

Names: Heter, Joshua editor | Greene, Richard, 1961– editor
Title: Back to the future and philosophy : essays on traveling through the space-time continuum / edited by Joshua Heter and Richard Greene.
Description: Jefferson, North Carolina : McFarland & Company, Inc., Publishers, 2026. | Includes index.
Identifiers: LCCN 2025048395 | ISBN 9781476696089 paperback ∞
  ISBN 9781476657400 ebook
Subjects: LCSH: Back to the Future films—History and criticism | Philosophy in motion pictures | Ethics in motion pictures | Time travel in motion pictures | BISAC: PERFORMING ARTS / Film / Genres / Science Fiction & Fantasy | PHILOSOPHY / General | LCGFT: Film criticism | Essays
Classification: LCC PN1995.9.B26 B34 2025
LC record available at https://lccn.loc.gov/2025048395

ISBN (print) 978-1-4766-9608-9
ISBN (ebook) 978-1-4766-5740-0

© 2026 Joshua Heter and Richard Greene. All rights reserved

No part of this book may be reproduced or transmitted in any form or by any means, electronic or mechanical, including photocopying or recording, or by any information storage and retrieval system, without permission in writing from the publisher.

Front cover image: © Shutterstock AI Generator

McFarland & Company, Inc., Publishers
  Box 611, Jefferson, North Carolina 28640
  www.mcfarlandpub.com

Acknowledgments

Working on this project has been a pleasure, in no small part because of the many fine folks who have assisted us along the way. A debt of gratitude is owed to Dré Person and everyone at McFarland, the contributors to this volume, the School of Humanities at Jefferson College, and the Department of Political Science and Philosophy at Weber State University. Finally, we'd like to thank those family members, students, friends, and colleagues with whom we've had fruitful and rewarding conversations on various aspects of all three of the beloved *Back to the Future* films.

Table of Contents

Acknowledgments   v

*If You're Going to Publish a Philosophy Book,
Why Not Do It with Some Style?!*
Joshua Heter *and* Richard Greene   1

I. All About Time Travel

Driving in Fourth Gear Through the Fourth Dimension
Nikk Effingham   4

Cinematic Determinism and the Grammar of Storytelling
Ryan Falcioni   18

McFly Meets McTaggart
John M. DePoe   29

Back to a New and Improved Future
Taylor W. Cyr *and* Grace Scott   36

II. Knowledge and Belief in Hill Valley

Following Your Heart to the Future
Kate C.S. Schmidt   46

Time Travel and Knowledge of the Future
Kristie Miller   52

Was Marty Just Dreaming?
David Kyle Johnson   61

III. Right and Wrong Across Time (and Space)

Quit Hitting Yourself!
    Daniel Malloy   72

On Keeping People in the Dark About the Future
    Don Fallis   81

Back to Morality
    Xuanpu Zhuang   89

Betting on the Past
    Zack Garrett   96

IV. Matters of Value

Nostalgia and Mimesis
    S. Evan Kreider   106

The Punch That Changes Everything
    John Garcia   114

The Flux-Series of Time
    Dennis M. Weiss   123

Doc Brown and the Erotic Ideal
    Justin Kitchen   132

V. Sex and Gender in *Back to the Future*

"Regress" to the Future
    Catherine Villanueva Gardner   142

The Feminist McFly
    Leigh E. Rich *and* Michael N. Robinson   151

Making Sense of Masculinity in the Past, Present, and Future
    Ben Almassi   161

VI. Issues of Personal Identity

Past, Present, and/or Alternative Selves
    Jeremy C. DeLong   170

From Density to Destiny
    Casey Rentmeester   180

Does Marty Commit Temporal Manslaughter?
   JOE SLATER   187

VII. Traveling Through (the) History (of Philosophy)

Back to the Future ... of an Illusion
   LEONARD KAHN   198

A Sartrean Time Machine
   ELAD MAGOMEDOV   208

"*Nobody* calls me chicken": How Should Marty Respond to Insults?
   JON ROBSON   215

VIII. Doc Brown and the Philosophy of Science and Technology

Doc Brown's Paradox and Dr. Frankenstein's Plight
   JOHN P. IRISH   222

Great Scott! The Logic of Certain Scientific Discovery
   KEITH BEGLEY *and* AADIL KURJI   231

Doc Brown's Techno-Ethical Journey
   KENNETH R. PIKE   240

The Pinheads   249

Index   255

If You're Going to Publish a Philosophy Book, Why Not Do It with Some Style?!

JOSHUA HETER *and* RICHARD GREENE

Back to the Future was born out of a simple, if odd, question: "Would I have been friends with my dad if we'd gone to high school together?"

Sometime during the summer of 1980, screenwriter Bob Gale was visiting his parents at his boyhood home in St. Louis, when he stumbled upon one of his father's old high school yearbooks (from the same high school he attended nearly 30 years later). To his astonishment, Gale learned that his father had been president of the 1940 graduating class. A respectable, prim and proper sort, he wasn't exactly the type of guy Gale would've seen himself palling around with in the more rebellious 1960s. It was at this point that the inciting question about a theoretical teenage friendship with his own father popped into his head. This was followed almost immediately by the thought, exhilarating for any screenwriter, "That's a movie!"

When he returned to California, Gale pitched the idea to his writer and director friend Robert Zemeckis, who was immediately floored. The two got to work fleshing out further narrative details and pulling together an impressive collection of storytellers who would go on to make three of the most beloved science-fiction films of all time.

Indeed, the story of the McFlys and the broader world of Hill Valley have struck a chord with moviegoers around the globe for decades. Beyond the allure of time travel and a slew of memorable comedic moments, *Back to the Future* invites us to reflect on the relationships that matter most to us and to realize that were it not for the inevitable generational impediments, we might be able to more easily make meaningful connections with those we love.

As it turns out, the films that were born out of Gale's unscheduled peek into his father's adolescence—beyond delivering a great deal of memorable entertainment—have given rise to a great number of additional questions, many of them philosophical in nature. Perhaps it should be no surprise that a story about time travel, family dynamics, and the litany of issues that arise during the journey from youth to adulthood should raise a host of interesting, at times confounding questions.

Is time travel even possible? If so, could it pose a threat to the space-time continuum? What obligation (if any) do parents have to divulge (or hide) details about their youthful indiscretions to their children? Do we have free will? How would free will work in a universe in which time travel occurs? What exactly is a "chicken," and should Marty care if he is one? After all is said and done, can Marty really *know* that he didn't just dream his time-travel adventure? What's the deal with Jocasta / Oedipus complexes? These, and a great deal of additional issues, can't help but linger for anyone who spends even a modest amount of time reflecting on *Back to the Future* and the story therein. And it is just these questions that the authors of this book (and the all-too-fortunate editors who were able to bring them together) attempt to answer here in these pages.

So, for all of these reasons, we published a philosophy book about one of the most beloved sci-fi comedy franchises of all time. Hopefully, we did it with some style. At the very least, it's our aim that through these pages, you'll gain a deeper appreciation of *Back to the Future*, its themes, and the thought-provoking questions they raise. You might even learn a bit of philosophy along the way. With that in mind, we hope you keep reading, that is, if you've got the time.

I
All About Time Travel

Driving in Fourth Gear Through the Fourth Dimension

Nikk Effingham

A simple Google search will return multiple theories attempting to make sense of the time travel in *Back to the Future*. I do not believe any of them are successful. What follows is my own attempt, one which draws upon contemporary philosophical treatments of time travel.

First Gear

Consider the start of the first film: Marty has never been in 1955, his *father* was run over by Sam Baines (Marty's grandfather), and the McFlys seem to be struggling financially. But during the film, we see things play out differently. Marty arrives in 1955, it is *Marty* who is hit by his grandfather, and the events of the film lead to the McFlys being wealthy in 1985.

In *Part II*, Doc Brown helpfully explains how all of this is possible: when time travelers go to the past, they arrive in "offshoot universes" budding off from the original universe.[1] Marty begins in one universe, U_1; see Figure 1. When he travels back to 1955, he creates

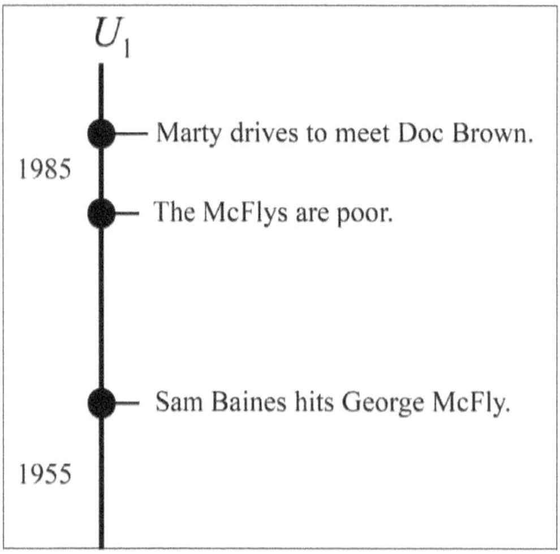

Figure 1: Marty's "original timeline."

an "offshoot universe," U_2. In U_2, Marty is hit by a car (and so on). See Figure 2.

While Marty both does and does not get hit by his grandfather's car (and the McFlys both are and are not rich, etc.), this is not contradictory because these things are true in different universes. In the same way that it can rain in Hill Valley while *not* raining in San Francisco, there is no contradiction in Marty getting hit by a car in 1955 in U_2, but not in U_1.

The DeLorean is obeying the following rules:

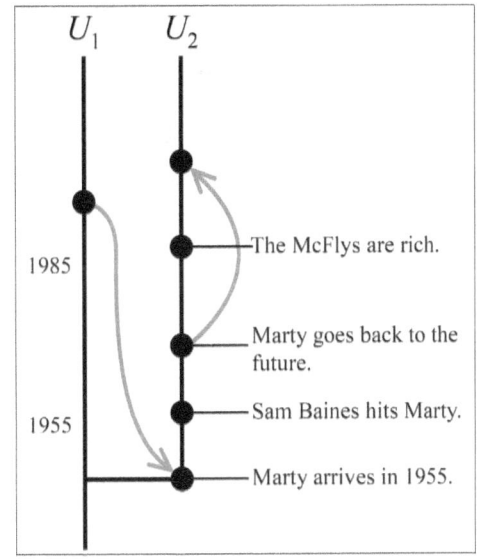

Figure 2: The events of *Part I*.

First Gear Rules of Time Travel

If a time machine (from universe U) travels to the past (arriving at time t), then it arrives at t in an offshoot universe budding off from U.

If a time machine (from universe U) travels to the future (arriving at time t), then it arrives in the future of U at time t. No offshoot universe is created.

Given these rules, in U_1 Marty vanishes without a trace! His family never sees him again; presumably, they think he's dead. Along similar lines, consider the Marty born and raised in U_2. At the end of the first film, this "Other Marty" uses the DeLorean to travel back to 1955. In the films, we never see him again—and now we know why! When he travels to 1955, he arrives in an offshoot universe, U_3. Assuming Other Marty manages to get back to the future, he arrives in the future of U_3, not U_2, hence why he disappears. See Figure 3.

You might ask why traveling to the future doesn't create an offshoot universe. Doc tests the DeLorean by sending Einstein to the future. If Einstein arrived at an offshoot universe, then the Doc Brown of U_1 would never see him again. Presumably, Doc loves his dog too much for that, so he would never use Einstein if those were the rules the DeLorean played by.

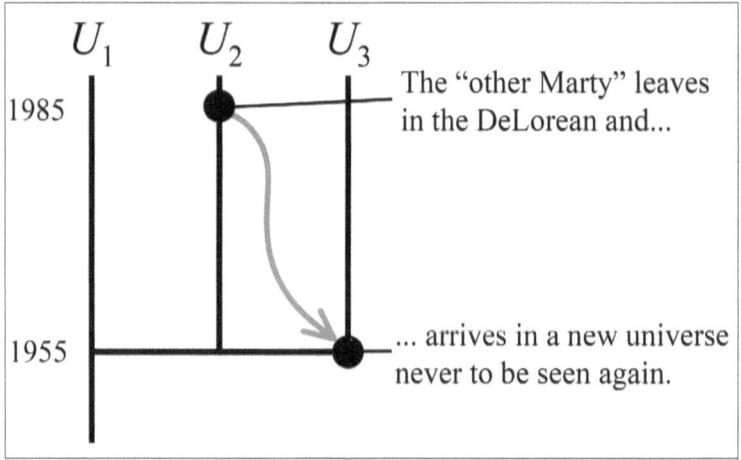

Figure 3: Why "Other Marty" vanishes.

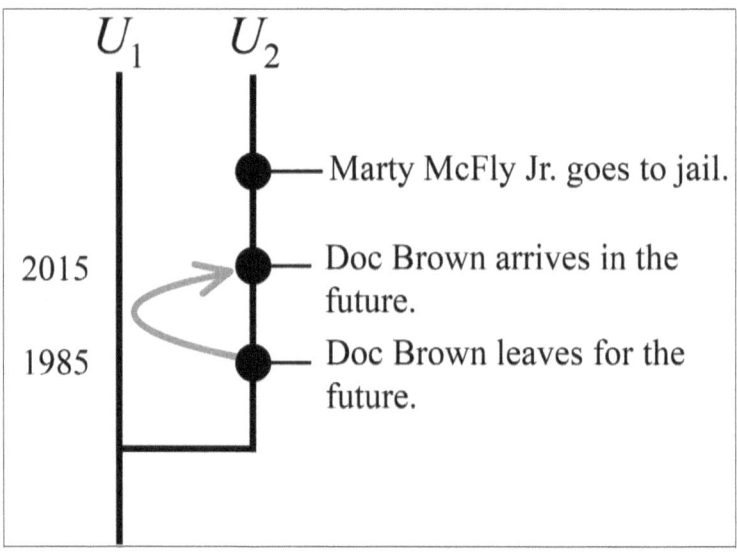

Figure 4: Doc Discovers Marty Jr. goes to jail.

Second Gear

At the end of the first film and the beginning of *Part II*, Doc travels to 2015, arriving in the future of U_2 to discover that Marty's son goes to jail. See Figure 4. Doc then leaves 2015 for 1985, recruiting Marty and Jennifer and creating an offshoot universe, U_4. See Figure 5. All of this is in line

Driving in Fourth Gear (Effingham)   7

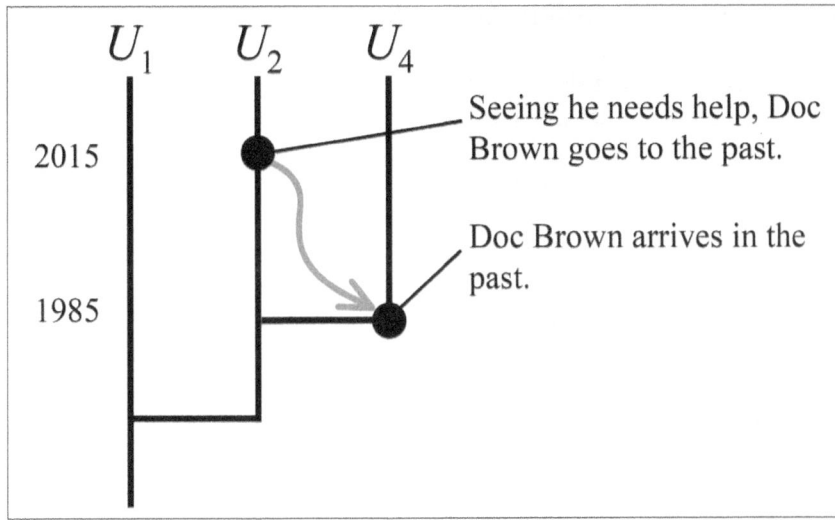

Figure 5: The end of *Part I* / beginning of *Part II*.

with the first gear rules. However, what happens next fails to obey those rules. In U_4, Doc, Marty, and Jennifer return to 2015. The "first-gear rules" say they should arrive in the future of U_4—but they don't! If they arrived in the future of U_4, they would arrive in a future where, back in 1985, Marty and Jennifer flew off in a car, never to be seen again (or not until 2015!),

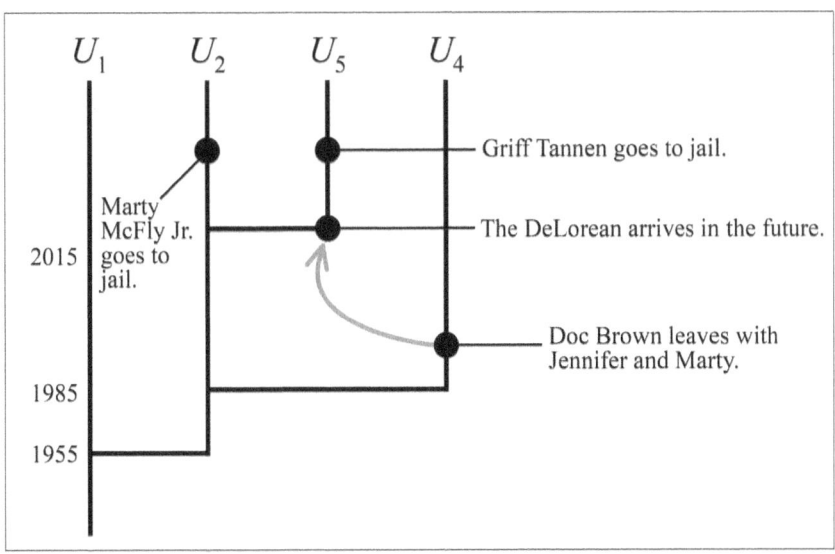

Figure 6: Griff Tannen goes to jail instead of Marty Jr.

rather than a future where they live with their kids in Hilldale. (You might think otherwise, believing that they could always travel *back* to 1985, but this is wrong-headed since, given the first-gear rules, they would travel back to a *new* offshoot universe, rather than U_4.)

Instead of arriving in the future of the universe they are currently in (i.e., U_4), they must have arrived in the 2015 of another universe. The natural suggestion is that they arrive at an offshoot universe budding off from the 2015 of U_2; call it U_5. In the 2015 of U_2, Marty McFly, Jr., goes to jail while, because of our protagonists, he avoids that fate in the 2015 of U_5. See Figure 6.

Clearly, the DeLorean is not following the first-gear rules. It must have different gears that obey different sets of rules! When the DeLorean travels to U_5, it obeys the following rules:

Second Gear Rules of Time Travel

If a time machine (from universe U) travels to the past (arriving at time t), then it arrives at t in an offshoot universe budding off from U.

If a time machine leaves U and travels to the past (arriving at U) and then travels back to the future, it arrives (at t) at an offshoot universe budding off from U.

The DeLorean's flux capacitor is also in second gear when "Old Biff" takes the Sports Almanac back to 1955. By going to 1955, Old Biff creates a universe, U_6, which buds off from U_5. See Figure 7. U_6 is the "dark timeline" in which George McFly is murdered and Biff rules with an iron fist. When Old Biff returns to the future, the second gear rules entail that he returns to the future of U_5 and creates an offshoot universe, U_7. See Figure 8. (This means that, in U_5, neither Old Biff nor the DeLorean returns, marooning the Marty, Jennifer, and Doc Brown of U_5 in 2015. We don't see that on-screen because the "viewpoint" of the movie instead follows the Marty, Jennifer, and Doc Brown of U_7.)

Third Gear

When our heroes return to 1985, the DeLorean must again switch gears. Given either set of rules, they should return to the 1985 of U_7 (which is also the 1985 of U_2 and U_5) and create an offshoot universe. But this isn't what we see. Instead, they arrive in a dystopian 1985 where Biff runs the show. While there's no contradiction in thinking that they arrive in U_6, I will instead make the rules of time travel as similar to one another as I can

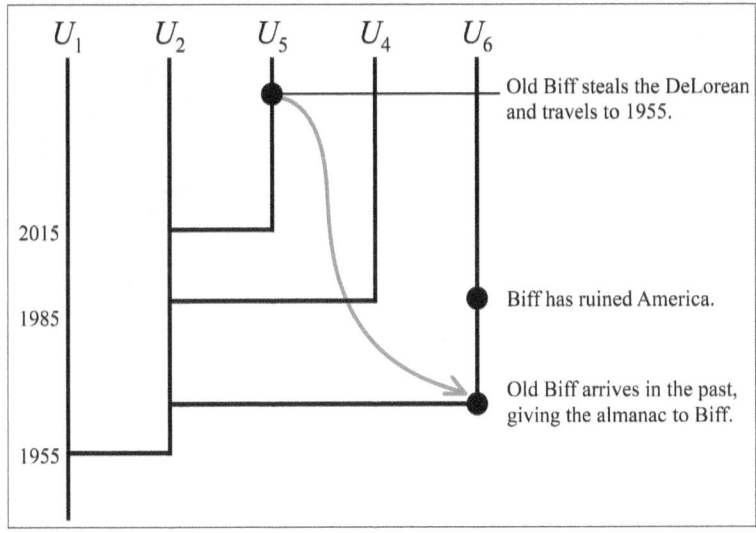

Figure 7: Biff creates the "dark timeline."

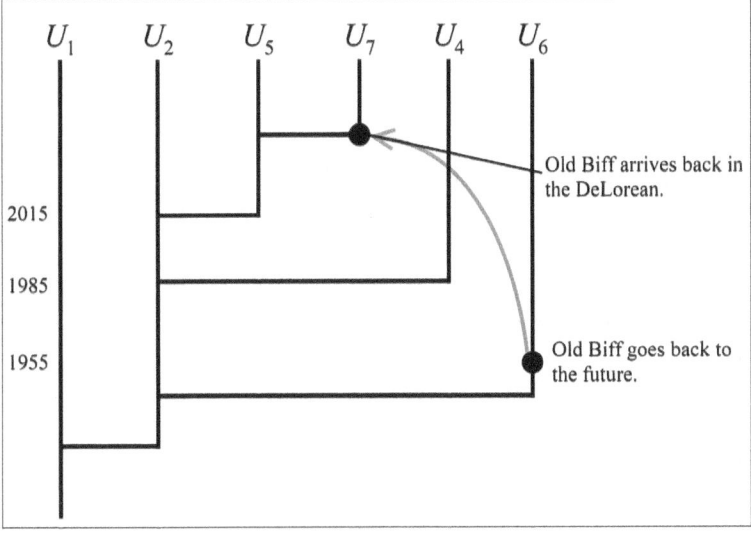

Figure 8: Biff returns to 2015.

by assuming that they arrive in an offshoot universe, U_8, budding off from U_6. See Figure 9.

This means that the rules must have changed again; Old Biff must have accidentally shifted gears when he clambered out of the DeLorean! The new rules are:

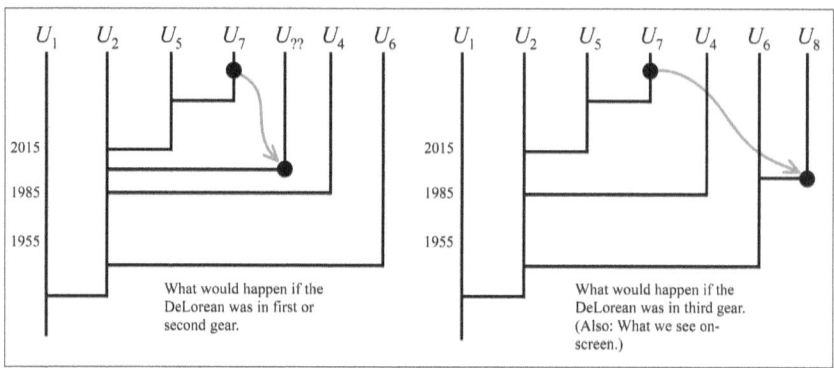

Figure 9: Why the DeLorean must be in third gear.

Third Gear Rules of Time Travel

If a time machine (from universe U) travels to the future (arriving in universe U') and then travels again into the past (arriving at time t), then it arrives at t in an offshoot universe budding off from U.

(The third-gear rules say nothing about how time travel to the future works since that isn't settled by the movies.)

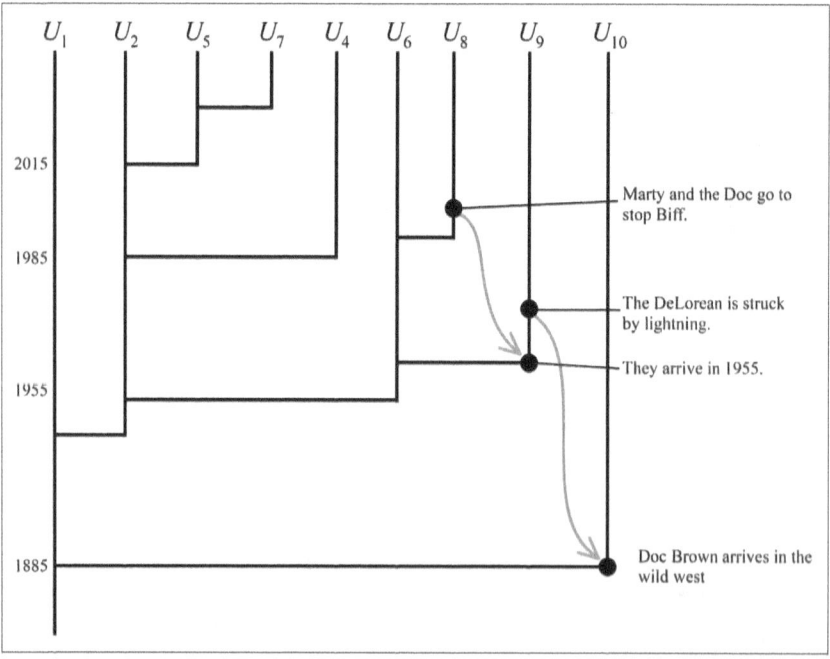

Figure 10: The end of *Part II*.

In the 1985 of U_8, Doc and Marty decide to foil Biff by traveling to 1955. They arrive at a new offshoot universe, U_9. They change the future of U_9 so it is no longer a dystopia. After lightning unexpectedly strikes the DeLorean, Doc Brown then travels to 1885, creating a new universe, U_{10}. See Figure 10.

We then come across a new problem. Marty receives the letter that the Doc left with Western Union (way back in the Old West) and eventually stumbles across his grave from 1885. But both things appear to be impossible. U_9 shares its 19th-century history with U_1, and in U_1, Doc never arrived in the past, never left a letter, never died, etc., so Marty should not receive the letter in U_9 and should not be able to find the grave.

To solve this problem, keep focusing on U_{10}. In U_{10}, "Mad Dog" Tannen kills Doc Brown in 1885, and the future carries on as it otherwise would have, playing out roughly as it did in U_1. In U_{10}, Doc Brown is born sometime in the 20th century; in 1955, Marty's Grandfather runs over George McFly; in 1985, Marty goes back in time to 1955 after the Libyans kill Doc, creating a new universe, U_{11}. U_{11} is exactly the same as U_2, except that Doc Brown died in 1885 (and left a letter with Western Union, etc.). Just as Marty's arrival in U_2 ultimately led to the creation of more universes, U_4-U_9, Marty's arrival in U_{11} does the same, leading to U_{12}-U_{18} coming into existence. See Figure 11.

In U_{10} to U_{16}, the Western Union representative turns up in the soaking rain looking for Marty, only to find no one there. In U_{17}, things are different. In U_{17}, the DeLorean is struck by lightning, goes back to 1885 (creating a new offshoot universe, U_{18}, from which the same series of universes repeat *ad infinitum*!), and Marty manages to receive the letter—just as we see on-screen! Then, he stumbles across the grave (which, again, exists in each of U_{10} to U_{18}, even though it did not exist in any of U_1 to U_9)

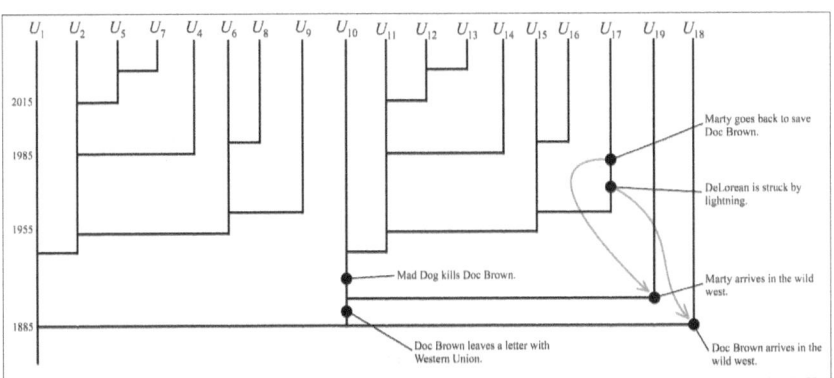

Figure 11: How to explain the delivery of the Western Union Letter.

and settles on going back in time to save Doc. In doing so, Marty creates a new offshoot universe, U_{19}.

This means that *when we are watching the first movie*, we are unwittingly watching events taking place in U_{10}. During the finale of the second film, we are watching the events taking place at U_{17}, while in the third film, we are watching events taking place in U_{19}. At the start of the original film, we are *not* seeing "the original timeline" of U_1, but are instead watching a world where time travel has already taken place (which is not an uncommon twist in time travel fiction—see, e.g., *Primer* or *Time and Time Again*).[2,3]

Hypertime

The offshoot universe model helps us understand *Back to the Future*'s narrative. But it is not perfect. The model appears to contradict what Doc tells Marty about why he cannot "fix" the dark timeline by returning to the future and preventing Old Biff from time traveling to 1955. Doc says: "We *can't*, because if we travel into the future from this point in time, it will be the future of *this* reality, in which Biff is corrupt and powerful—and married to your mother." This makes no sense given the offshoot universe model. Doc and Marty are in U_8. If Doc sticks the car into third gear, he can return to a future that offshoots from U_7. That universe would share its 1980s history with U_2—which was lovely and nice in 1985—and it wouldn't be horrible, like the dark timeline. Given that this is *precisely* what Old Biff has just done, why can't Doc pull the same trick?

We might fudge the issue. We might say that the vagaries of time travel mean that only certain gears can be used in certain situations. Or, perhaps Doc doesn't know what he's talking about in the above quote—after all, Doc says at one point that Jennifer meeting herself might destroy the space-time continuum, and he was wrong about *that*, so maybe he's wrong about *this*?

But I suggest a different route. When Doc says "this reality," maybe he doesn't mean "this universe" or "this timeline." Rather, he means the entire collection of universes. While Doc can escape the dark timeline by creating some nice new offshoot universe, the dark timeline would remain. Marty and Doc can escape to a future that is nice *for them*, but it will still leave (in the past) a world that is dystopian (in $U_6/U_8/U_{15}/U_{16}$). Doc does not want to *escape* the dark timeline; he wants to *eliminate* it. He doesn't just want to not be in it anymore; he wants it to *never have come into existence*.

The offshoot universe model doesn't allow for the "elimination" of timelines; indeed, in a sense, the model doesn't allow for history to change in any way whatsoever. Rather than changing history, the creation of offshoot universes merely "supplements" history by adding another universe containing different events. If time travel in *Back to the Future* only involved offshoot universes, Doc could never hope to eliminate the dark timeline—he could never hope to change things so that Biff never inflicted terrible suffering upon so many people.

However, we can capture the elimination of the dark timeline by adding in extra theoretical machinery. We can combine the offshoot universe model with another model of time travel that has found favor with many philosophers: the "hypertemporal model of time travel."[4]

First, we need to get a grip on what "hypertime" is meant to be. Normally, we think time has only one dimension. But, just as space has *three* dimensions, time might have two dimensions. Call that second temporal dimension the "hypertemporal dimension" (which extends into the "hyperpast" and "hyperfuture").

A hypertemporal model deals with time travel differently from the offshoot universe model. Consider an example of how the hypertemporal model would work. Imagine it is AD 2025. Given the model, it is also some hypertime (e.g., it is hypertime T_1). I use my time machine to go back in time and kill Hitler in 1930. What happens is that I go *back in regular time* but *forwards in hypertime*, arriving at the 1930 of hypertime T_2. There, I kill Hitler, making history at T_2 different from how it hyperwas at T_1. Just as things differing between regular times counts as change (e.g., if it's raining in the morning and not raining in the afternoon, we say it has changed from raining to not raining), when histories differ between hypertimes, that also counts as a type of change (e.g., I have changed history from having Hitler being alive in 1930 to having Hitler be dead in 1930).

Hypertime allows for the elimination of unwanted historical events in a way that the offshoot universe model does not. Admittedly, given the hypertemporal model, killing Hitler in 1930 leaves him alive in 1930 *at the hyperearlier hypertime*. Nothing can stop that being the case, and you might suspect that I haven't really changed time at all. But compare this situation to a regular temporal situation. If I accidentally put my hand on a red-hot stove, I am motivated to change things by taking my hand off the stove. Taking my hand off the stove does nothing to change the fact that my hand was still being burned at an earlier time, but what of it? I am motivated to bring about that change because it's in my interests to make it *presently* the case that my hand isn't burning. Similarly, it is rational to prefer for Hitler to have hyperpresently died in the 1930s. By killing Hitler in 1930 at T_2, I "eliminate" Hitler and the evils he brought about, in just the same way that I "eliminate" my hand being in pain.

I suggest that we take this hypertemporal model and meld it with the

14   I. All About Time Travel

offshoot universe model.[5] Usually, the DeLorean is *not* traveling through hypertime; usually, it moves back in time but stays at the same hypertime. When it does this, it creates an offshoot universe (as per the first-, second-, and third-gear rules). But having seen how bad the dark timeline is, Doc Brown shifts the DeLorean into fourth gear, which allows it to move through hypertime and allows him to set about eliminating historical details he doesn't like:

Fourth Gear Rules of Time Travel

If a time machine (at hypertime T) travels to the past (and arrives at time t), then it arrives at t at the hypertime immediately later than T. The time machine can arrive at any universe the pilot chooses. No offshoot universe is created upon arrival.

Assume *Back to the Future* starts at hypertime T_1. In 1985 at U_8, Doc shifts the DeLorean into fourth gear, traveling to the 1955 of the shared past of U_6/U_8, but at the hypernext hypertime, T_2. There, Marty and Doc stop Biff, changing history. The futures of U_6/U_8 are (hyper)now much nicer, having more or less the same history as U_2. While U_6 and U_8 have horrible histories at the earlier hypertime, they now have a nice history at the hyperpresent hypertime. Thus, Marty and the Doc have succeeded in eliminating the evils that Biff brought about!

Adopting this mixed model means tweaking some of the details discussed above. Consider three such tweaks.

Tweak one: Because Doc and Marty have moved in hypertime, they no longer create U_9 when they go back to 1955 to burn the Almanac. Instead, things appear as they do in Figure 12.

Tweak two: at hypertime T_2, Old Biff still travels from the 1955 of U_6 to 2015, and so still creates U_7. In the 2015 of U_7 (at T_2), Doc, Jennifer, and Marty still make their way back to 1985. Just as at T_1, they end up creating U_8 but (unlike hypertime T_1) the 1985 of U_8 is quite pleasant, being more

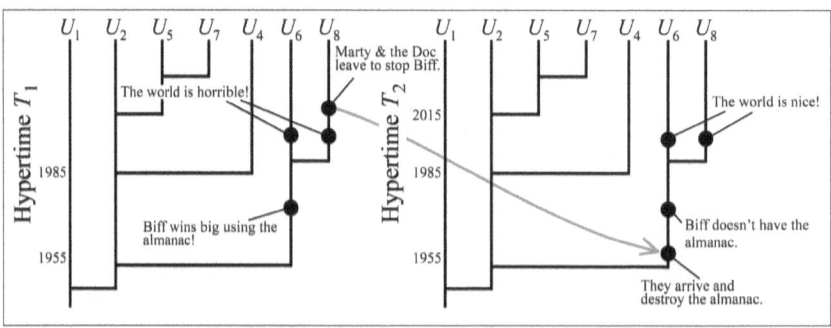

Figure 12: How hypertime helps eliminate the "dark timeline."

or less the same as the 1985 of U_2. This means that, when they arrive at U_8, they arrive in a world where (unlike U_4, where the Doc had expected to land) Doc has not taken Marty and Jennifer to the future to prevent Marty Jr. going to jail. There are thus two Martys and two Jennifers at U_8 (at T_2) in 1985, so our time travelers cannot simply settle back down into their lives. Like the Other Marty who went to U_3 (and the Marty, Jennifer, and Doc Brown of U_5), we don't see any of this on-screen. The events that take place at U_8 at T_2 must be left for the inevitable fan-fiction that will no doubt be inspired by this essay.

Tweak three: We might also modify what happens when the DeLorean is struck by lightning. Rather than being in third gear and creating universes U_{10}-U_{18}, it might be in fourth gear. In that case, when struck by lightning, the DeLorean leaves hypertime T_2 and goes to the 1885 of hypertime T_3. The Marty of T_2 is left, marooned in the past of U_6/U_8, unable to leave. The history of T_3 is then such that Doc Brown is killed by Mad Dog Tannen in 1885. The Marty of T_3 then gets the Western Union letter (in the 1955 of U_6/U_8). Doc Brown would presumably then also want to eliminate his 19th-century death, and so, when Marty goes to 1885, he stays in fourth gear, moving forward to hypertime T_4. In doing so, when Marty saves the Doc in the Old West, he eliminates Doc's death in the same way that the dark timeline (hyper)was eliminated.

Why Bother Mixing?

Let's end by considering three reasons why we must mix the models, and why we cannot just use the hypertemporal model alone.

First reason: Doc Brown is adamant that time travel works using offshoot universes. It would be hard to see how we could do justice to the trilogy if they were not included.

Second reason: Second-gear rules were introduced to explain Doc taking Jennifer and Marty to a future where they didn't vanish without a trace years earlier. I cannot see a way to make that work given the hypertemporal model alone. (The same applies to Old Biff going to 1955, and then somehow returning in the DeLorean rather than vanishing forever into the hyperfuture.)

Third reason: Imagine we used a hypertemporal only model. At every hypertime, T_n, there would be a different Marty born in the 1960s; call them "Marty$_n$" to distinguish them. At T_1, Marty$_1$ is poor. At T_2, Marty$_2$ grows up rich because Marty$_1$ has changed the past at T_2. Indeed, at every subsequent hypertime, the Marty from the previous hypertime turns up in 1955 and ensures that the McFlys become rich. That means that the *only* poor Marty is Marty$_1$. This makes it impossible to explain the delivery of the Western Union letter. Assume T_9 is the hypertime at which lightning blasts the DeLorean to 1885. Marty$_1$ would then be stranded in the 1955 of T_9 and would never meet the Western Union deliveryman. Aping the above trick, we want to say that, throughout the trilogy, we have instead been following the antics of Marty$_{10}$ (who *does* meet the Western Union deliveryman). But, at T_{10}, Marty$_9$ (who was born in the 1960s of T_9) arrived in 1955, making the McFlys rich and successful. Thus, Marty$_{10}$ grew up rich, not poor. He cannot be the Marty we see on-screen in *Part II*!

One might object that Marty$_9$ might just have *failed* to make the McFlys rich and successful at T_{10}. For instance, Farmer Peabody might have shot Marty$_9$ dead when he arrived in 1955 and Marty$_{10}$ would have grown up poor. But, throughout this essay, I have assumed that chains of events play out exactly the same way, except when an external time traveler interferes with them, which cannot be true if Peabody shoots Marty$_9$. To drop that assumption is to allow for a "butterfly effect," whereby the same events play out differently at different hypertimes even when no time traveler directly interferes. And it is implausible that a butterfly effect is at play in *Back to the Future*! Consider the hypertime at which Marty and Jennifer live in Hilldale with their kids. Were there a butterfly effect, then when Doc takes them to 2015, there's no reason to think history would play out as it hyperpreviously did, and every reason to think that Jennifer and Marty might not get married and move to Hilldale. Moreover, there's every reason to think that different sperm would fertilize different eggs and produce different children, none of whom would end up getting bullied by Griff. Since this is not what we see on-screen, there cannot be a "butterfly effect"; thus, my assumption holds, Marty$_{10}$ must be rich, and the hypertemporal model alone cannot capture the narrative. To fully capture the narrative, we must mix the two models of time travel.

Out of Time

This concludes my attempt to give a consistent understanding of *Back to the Future*. Admittedly, it does not explain *every* element of *Back to the Future*. Specifically, it doesn't explain "fading cases," e.g., Marty's family fading from the photograph, Marty's hand fading away, or the disappearing ink on Jennifer's fax (or, if we count deleted scenes, Old Biff petering out of existence). It's incredibly difficult to explain "fading," and I cannot do it justice here—however, elsewhere I have given it a go.[6]

Notes

1. This theory of time travel has also been discussed by physicists; see Deutsch, David. 1991. "Quantum Mechanics Near Closed Timelike Lines." *Physical Review.* D44, no. 10. 3197–3217.

2. *Primer* 2004. THINKFilm, 2004; Elton, Ben. 2014. *Time and Time Again*. Black Swan.

3. An alternative approach instead explains Jennifer's change in appearance. If Doc Brown's 1885 demise affected which sperm made it to which egg, then, in U_1-U_9, Jennifer could look like Claudia Wells while, in U_{10}-U_{19}, Jennifer instead looks like Elizabeth Shue. The first movie then has its starting viewpoint as U_1 (a universe where no time travel has occurred and Jennifer looks like Wells) while the second movie's starting viewpoint is U_{14} (a universe where time travel *has* taken place and Jennifer looks like Shue). Thanks to U-Wen Low for this insight.

4. Van Inwagen, Peter. 2010. "Changing the Past." *Oxford Studies in Metaphysics.* 5. 3–28; Goddu, G. 2003. "Time Travel and Changing the Past: (Or How to Kill Yourself and Live to Tell the Tale)." *Ratio.* 16, no. 1. 16–32; Effingham, Nikk. 2021. "Exterminous Hypertime." *Philosophies.* 6, no. 4. 85.

5. I have talked about mixed models elsewhere; see Effingham, Nikk. 2023. "The Metaphysical Possibility of Time Travel Fictions." *Erkenntnis.* 88, no. 3. 1309–1329. This essay is an extension of that work.

6. Effingham, Nikk. 2023. "The Close Possibility of Time Travel." *Philosophies.* 8, no. 6. 118.

Cinematic Determinism and the Grammar of Storytelling

Ryan Falcioni

In general, the *Back to the Future* movies demonstrate how changes made in the past have profound, often unpredictable effects on the future (cue any of Doc's speeches about the potentially disastrous consequences of disrupting the "space-time continuum"). This time-traveling plot device is, of course, at the very heart of the storytelling of the entire trilogy.

The original film only works as a story if we believe that Marty can causally undo the deleterious effects on his family's future existence that getting hit by his grandfather's car has introduced into the causal nexus of the universe. *Part II* only works as a story if Doc and Marty can stop Marty Jr. from committing the robbery with Griff and if they can also undo the new causal chain that is inadvertently introduced through elderly Biff's acquiring the sports almanac. *Part III* only works if Marty can go back to 1885 and stop Buford "Mad Dog" Tannen from killing Doc.

These core elements of the narratives from each film are all anchored in the reality and plausibility of a particular view of the science of time travel and the ability to initiate causal changes that determine new timelines. And although the *Back to the Future* movies are not exclusively science fiction films, they still lean heavily into the scientific mechanism(s) of time travel. Doc's scientific discoveries, musings, and on-the-fly innovations feature prominently in all three films. The point here is to highlight how central the "science" of *Back to the Future* is to the narrative storytelling of each film. In short, the science matters! More specifically, the plots depend on a type of causal determinism, where changes introduced by time traveling into the past have direct causal consequences for the future.

Great Scott! A Paradox of Determinisms?

Despite *Back to the Future*'s seeming reliance on determinism (of a sort), there are many instances in the franchise where substantial changes are made in the past via time-traveling intervention that would an undoubtedly significant impact on the future, and yet when there is a *return* to the future, no such changes have been realized. Think here of the reality that when Marty returns to 1985 in the first film, after altering the nature of his parents' first meeting and relationship, he wakes in the same middle-class home, with the same siblings. The McFly children are, of course, doing much better thanks to Marty's time-traveling shenanigans. However, they are still the same people.

Without getting too deep into the weeds (or Pines?) of the science of reproduction, the McFlys would have to engage in virtually all of the same acts of conception, on the same days, with many of the same environmental conditions (as they did before Marty's time-traveling) to conceive Dave, then Linda, and then Marty. However, given the dramatic differences in their life journeys and outcomes in this updated 1985, the probability of George and Lorraine having any one of the same children, let alone all three children, rapidly approaches zero.

And of course, this type of analysis could be applied to any number of outcomes and events in the updated 1985 timeline. For example, it doesn't make causal sense for Doc to still invent the time machine along the same timeline (including the epic showdown with "The Libyans!") in 1985, despite having seen and worked on a fully functional version some thirty years prior. In other cases, there seems to be a type of scientifically unnecessary double causation (e.g., Goldie Wilson getting the idea to run for mayor from a time-traveling Marty, when he was *already* mayor in 1985 which led Marty to *tell him* he's going to be mayor or Marty "inceptioning" rock and roll to Chuck Berry through his on-stage antics in 1955). These are all logically, scientifically, and arguably even ethically dubious occurrences. But even in such cases, they play a role in maintaining the continuity of the story or in advancing the plot.

I have come to see both the infinitely improbable sameness of the McFly family across numerous alternative timelines and the other instances that seemingly violate causal determinism as themselves embodying a rather different type of determinism. There is a logic to storytelling that involves a dimension of *narrative* or (in the case of film) *cinematic determinism*. The reasons for this phenomenon seem to be central to the art of storytelling itself; time-traveling heroics can change a lot, but certain things are off limits. Of course, there are no scientifically plausible reasons for the apparently selective nature of the changes that are allowed.

But they do make cinematic sense. Indeed, the arc of the narrative needs many of these anchoring realities for the story to work. The results of this occasional clashing of determinisms generate a rather curious philosophical paradox.

The core thesis of this essay is that throughout the *Back to the Future* trilogy, there are numerous instances of a paradoxical intersection between the dictates of causal (or even broadly scientific) determinism and what is logically required for the continuity of narrative or cinematic determinism. Furthermore, the *Back to the Future* films (in true storytelling fashion) generally sacrifice the science/philosophy of consistent causal determinism for the sake of the narrative. And although this might be problematic for some philosophically or scientifically inclined critics, the movies are generally better for this sacrifice. The decision to pursue the power of story over the dictates of science speaks to the power of storytelling and its internal logic.

What Is Narrative Determinism?

What exactly *is* narrative or cinematic determinism?[1] At the outset, I would like to make it explicit that I will not be using these terms in a very narrow or technical sense as seen in some areas of philosophy and literary theory. Rather, I am using these terms to capture a very general sense of the ways in which there is often a "just-so"-ness to many elements of a story. Certain places, events, plotlines, and outcomes simply must be in place for a story to work and for it to remain fundamentally the "same" story.

In many ways, all elements of all stories are determined by the storyteller. Once birthed, the story is fixed. That said, there is a profound logical difference between the sorts of things that can be changed in a given story (as it is told or even once it is told) and those that cannot. To change any of these details is fundamentally to tell a different story. On the other end of the continuum, there are elements of the story that are not essential in this way. If Marty's name were Arty, or if Doc were called Professor, it seems like the story could remain fundamentally intact. But if Marty/Arty was not a likable guy, or Doc/Professor was truly mad, the story would not work in the same way. Similarly, if Biff came across as a sympathetic character, the moral arc would dissolve. Professor Jonathan Gottschall and others have discussed the seeming necessity of "a moralistic trinary of heroes, villains, and victims."[2] Similarly, the basic elements of the plot of each film must not be altered, lest the story disappear like Marty's siblings from a photograph. So, although what is determined is relative to each act of narrative storytelling, it is clear that certain things must be determined. I am placing this notion of narrative determinism within the broader framework of the grammar of storytelling.

Homo Fictus *and the Grammar of Storytelling*

There are many rules for how stories can, and often must, be told. Some of these rules involve the necessity of certain components of the plot, and are thus narratively determined. So, in this way, the notion of cinematic determinism is a subset of the rules or "grammar" of storytelling itself. Gottschall is particularly helpful in elucidating some of these seemingly essential features of the human enterprise of storytelling. As referenced in the heading of this section, he sees the capacity (and even necessity) of storytelling as something essential to our species. He states that his work "is about the primate *Homo fictus* (fiction man), the great ape with the storytelling mind. You might not realize it, but you are a creature of an imaginative realm called Neverland. Neverland is your home, and before you die, you will spend decades there ... story is for a human as water is for a fish—all-encompassing and not quite palpable."[3]

Thus, the human capacity for storytelling has evolved to serve very essential roles in the human enterprises of making meaning, inculcating values, expressing emotions, etc. And in looking at storytelling in the myths, traditions, writings, and films in human history, he observes the emergence of certain rules or grammar involved in the art of effective storytelling. Referencing the work of Noam Chomsky, Gottschall and others have discussed the type of "universal grammar" involved in storytelling.[4] This is similar to what philosopher Ludwig Wittgenstein addresses in his notion of the grammatical rules for any/all linguistic practices. In order to be understood correctly in a particular context, one must abide by the grammar of that particular endeavor. In this Wittgensteinian sense, each act of storytelling reveals a particular grammar for how language is (and is to be) used in such contexts.

Scientist turned filmmaker, Randy Olson, articulates an "And, But, Therefore" template for storytelling.[5] He and others point to the power of storytelling in human history and how there are evolutionary origins to the nature and reception of this "And, But, Therefore" framework.[6] Gottschall also speaks of two "major components" of this universal grammar of storytelling: there should be "characters solving predicaments" and also "a deep moral dimension."[7] Depending on the nature, genre, or medium of the story, there might be many additional or different grammatical rules. For example, in many myths aimed at conveying ethical truths, there are implied rules about how the lesson is to be understood. And again, this involves knowing what kinds of questions to ask and also what kinds of questions should *not* be asked. The/a meaning of the flood myth in Genesis involves the importance of obedience to God, God's faithfulness in providing for those who obey ... and, most powerfully, the disastrous consequences of failing to obey. The story is about as profound a moral lesson as one can convey: obey God and all will be fine. Disobey, and you will die a horrible death. The story works because of the narrative force of the simple black and white, Manichean framework.

Of course, one may want to ask, "But why/how could God be the architect of global genocide?" Or "What about the children, the adorable bunnies, or even the beautiful ecosystems ... did they deserve to be destroyed?" And to be sure, such questions are asked by philosophers, ethicists, and theologians. But for the storytellers and their audience, these questions are not to be asked. To ask them is to ruin the myth. Other biblical stories like Job, The Fall, Adam and Eve, Abraham and Isaac, and even the Incarnation, can invite meaning-unraveling questioning. But again, such questions are not invited by the grammar of mythological storytelling itself.[8]

As with any meaning-making activity, there are various levels and dimensions to narrative storytelling. Both Olson and Gottschall articulate some of these seemingly essential grammatical elements for storytelling. Beyond these general grammatical remarks, each genre, subgenre, or even each medium of storytelling come with additional rules or guidelines. And of course, these rules and the lines between them can get very blurry. But if boundaries between science fiction and fantasy, or between comedy and drama, or horror and romance, mean anything, there are rules, often unspoken, about how such stories are to be told. This issue of boundaries in storytelling genres is part of a broader issue in the philosophy of language. Getting clear on what *anything* means is often a difficult enterprise. Wittgenstein offers the analogy of a language game to show how varied our uses of language can be. And although Wittgenstein is not primarily focused on storytelling, his comments on the varied uses of language in religion and in aesthetics more broadly are very instructive, here.

In many ways, this issue with the intersection between narrative and causal determinism is itself part of a larger issue with the science of science fiction. It is part of the grammar of many traditional sci-fi stories that the science has to be at least plausible. In other storytelling genres, the science does not matter that much, or even at all. There still has to be a certain bit of narrative arc and continuity. The *Back to the Future* franchise occupies an intriguing space along this sci-fi continuum. While not primarily a standard sci-fi series, there are still great efforts to get buy-in from the viewers about the legitimacy of many of the scientific elements. But in fantasy, for example, there can be any number of things that simply defy human reason, nature, and even scientific possibility.

So again, the grammar of storytelling is very much unique to each genre, often each storyteller, and even the exchange between storyteller and reader. The rules for what might make sense in the curious uptick in fairy-related fantasy might be altogether very different than those in sci-fi or in historical fiction. At times, and for some readers, the history of historical fiction is very important. For others, it is enough to have certain characters, events, or actions anchor the plot. In other stories, all of these genre-defining grammatical rules might be up for grabs. The mashup subgenre books, *Pride and Prejudice and Zombies* and *Abraham Lincoln: Vampire Hunter*, show how infinitely malleable these genres can be and then how unique the grammatical rules for each of these new creations can be. To be honest, I am not quite sure about why novels like *Abraham Lincoln: Vampire Hunter* are so appealing. But I find myself intrigued because of the ways that they push back on the accepted canons and associated rules for history, fantasy, and the supernatural. Other subgenres like fanfiction and even porn parodies raise questions about the nature and limits of the grammar of storytelling. The only point that needs to be made here is that stories have grammars. And as we see in the *Back to the Future* series, these grammars can sometimes conflict in paradoxical ways.

The Great Disappearing Act: Photos, Headlines, and Gravestones

Although arguably not fundamentally necessitated by the dictates of narrative determinism, the *Back to the Future* franchise commits to some visually appealing devices to illustrate the ongoing effects of causal interventions through time. To the time travelers and thus, the viewers, the (often) immediate effects on both the past and future are illustrated through disappearing and reappearing images and texts. And although the laws of causal determinism arguably make such visual devices impossible, they work wonderfully well to advance the narrative storytelling.

Watching poor Dave begin to disappear from the sibling family photo is heart wrenching for Marty and for us. A life without big brother Dave would indeed be very different. And when Linda begins to disappear, the narrative arc of showing the time-sensitive necessity of getting his parents to kiss at the dance becomes graphically and viscerally apparent. And of course, in the dramatic zenith of this scene, we see the slow disappearing that is happening in the photo is also happening to Marty while on stage. "Earth Angel" does not quite sound the same when the guitarist is playing one handed. Similarly, in *Part III*, the viewers share Marty's shock when he discovers the tombstone with Doc's 1885 death inscribed. The newspaper pictures and headlines in *Part II*, illustrating the financial ascendancy of Biff enhance the build up to his morally satisfying comeuppance, which is at the core of the plot. Similarly, the headlines about Doc's going from "Emmett Brown Committed" to "Emmett Brown Commended" anchor the plot and give us a narrative method to track with the changes that our time-traveling heroes cause.

All of these make for compelling cinema, but they are arguably impossible scientifically. If the causal laws of the universe are still in place, once a given timeline changed, all siblings would disappear … similarly with the newspaper headlines, gravestones, etc. The slowly dissolving (and conveniently reappearing) images just do not make sense. And although not necessarily impossible, it is also quite improbable that in each case, our protagonists happen to be looking at the headlines or pictures at precisely the moment when they change back. Given that these changes would happen in an immediate, non-temporal moment once the timeline changed, the odds of any one of these being witnessed in real time are very slim. But again, we, the viewers, are not invited to ask such questions. The fact that they violate the causal laws of the universe (or at best are incredibly improbable) is irrelevant. They make storytelling sense.

And really, this whole way of having slowly disappearing things reflects a way in which the storytelling needs a longer causal window to really allow for Marty to complete his work and to generate a narrative suspense for the audience. If Marty and his siblings simply vanished instantly (as causal determinism would necessitate) once new causal factors were inserted, the story would just end! A Marty who disappears once he has been hit by his grandfather's car would no longer be the protagonist in this film. In short, there would be no *Back to the Future* stories to be told, so the laws of causation must admit of a window of indeterminism … just enough for Marty to get his parents to kiss at the Enchantment Under the Sea dance before more than just his guitar-playing hands disappeared forever. So again, a privileging of the power of narrative (over and against causal) determinism is in play here. In such situations, the violations of the causal nexus in the universe are ultimately essential to these key moments in the advancement of the plot.

The Core: *A Case Study in Pseudoscience Fiction*

To flesh out this paradox of determinisms in storytelling a bit more, it is helpful to see what can happen when the violations of the laws of science go a bit off the deep end. With any storytelling, there's always a potential for narrative determinism that requires a suspension of logic, reason, or even ethics. A good story shows us what to focus on and, often more importantly, shows us what should not be focused on. But in most effective works of science fiction, the science must at least be plausible. If not, it can actually get in the way of the narrative storytelling altogether.

With science fiction and related literary genres, there must be some degree of believability regarding the science, especially when the science is actually integral to the plot. It's not that we must have all of our intellectual curiosities satisfied. But there has to be an aura of believability (or at least a reasonable suspension of disbelief) and an acceptance of the experts or scientists in the films and their qualifications and abilities. If the science is too farcical or just plain false, the entire plot can unravel. Think here of the disaster of a sci-fi disaster film, *The Core*. In virtually every scene involving the "science," the viewer is plunged into pseudoscience, stupidity, and even culpable scientific illiteracy. The utter balderdash that serves as a surrogate for real geological and nuclear science functions as an impediment to advancing the story. I, as well as many other viewers, cannot get beyond the "scientific" bastardization of all that is true in these scenes. It is hard to know where to begin (or end) a list of the scientific absurdities, but a few doozies should suffice: confusion of "electromagnetic" with magnetic, "terranauts" burrowing into the center of the earth to find open space (apparently without any pressure) and beautiful gigantic gems, pigeons losing their sense of navigation, certain pacemakers (and other electronic devices) failing, restarting the rotation of the earth's core with nukes, unobtainium, selective lighting strikes on the Colosseum, and painfully dumb science-adjacent monologues.

Reading the commentaries and articles chock full of offense and disgust from actual scientists is arguably much more entertaining than watching the movie itself. The outcry was so brutal that this film is often credited with generating a major movement (and the creation of the Science and Entertainment Exchange), demanding better science in science fiction films and other media. For many, the pseudoscience became a distraction to the storytelling. For such viewers (but not for all), it was an affront to their intelligence and an impediment to their being able to suspend disbelief in order to just enjoy the story.

An interesting exception occurs, however, when exploring the subgenre of campy sci-fi disaster films. Our ability to enjoy movies like *Sharknado*, *Lavalantula* (yes, this is the one about lava-breathing Tarantulas that terrorize Los Angeles), and my favorite spin-off, *Stonados* (which involves exploding stones dispersed by tornados), raise some interesting questions about the relationship between scientific believability and storytelling. Such movies are a testament to how, when pushed to absurdity, we can again enjoy a hackneyed plot not just in spite of, but because of, the shoddiness of the science. We're all in on the joke of just how impossible this all is: the flying sharks, the exploding stones, the arachnids born of lava ... and the weaponry, don't forget the weaponry. Arguably, the most glee-inspiring scenes in these movies involved the most pseudoscientifically ludicrous battles with the sharks and tarantulas, and even tornados, getting blown to bits. Like a first-person-shooter video game, the power is in the gratuitousness and absurdity of the killing itself. But again, the grammar for such disaster films is just rather different than straightforward sci-fi stories. The narrative determinism is not challenged by the implausibility of the science.

And this, of course, is not the case with the *Back to the Future* franchise. It does seem difficult to know exactly where to place it on the continuum between hardcore science fiction (where the science is front and center) and absurd pseudoscience sci-fi camp like *Sharknado*. But it does seem clear that the science matters here. I think of many of the scenes where Doc goes to great lengths to explain the details of the flux capacitor or of the plutonium, or of the 1.21 gigawatts. Furthermore, his repeated claims about messing up or ripping a hole or forever altering the space-time continuum are important to recognizing the gravity of the rules of scientific causation.

The goal here, of course, is not to get bogged down in the details of each sci-fi sub-genre and their attending grammars. It is merely to point out that films in general, genres and subgenres, and even individual films, invariably reveal particular conventions, rules, or grammars of storytelling. For example, while it might make sense for a fantasy film involving time travel to simply have a portal or even TARDIS, this would just not work for the type of sci-fi films that *Back to the Future* movies are. To be clear, similar films could have been written that combine these elements of fantasy and sci-fi. But *Back to the Future* does not go this route. And in not going this route, a grammar has emerged. For although there are corny jokes about time travel, and even less-than-scientific dimensions to elements of the time travel apparatus and theory, the plot depends on the scientific and philosophical legitimacy of the mechanisms of time travel itself.

And this again is where we see the rather unique paradox of determinism in the *Back to the Future* films. There are many places in the films where cinematic determinism takes priority over scientific legitimacy and even causal determinism itself. Ultimately, in most cases, I am in agreement with this move of the writers and filmmakers. The story must be told. And occasionally, this means bending the rules of the very science that undergirds the plot.

"Density" Over Determinism

So, in the end, what do (or should) we make of this paradox of determinisms? What if it is impossible to reconcile these often-competing grammars? Should such a conflict ruin the legitimacy of the *Back to the Future* films? My answer, which I believe to be the answer of nearly all *Back to the Future* fans, is a resounding "No!" Although there is no way to conclusively prove this contention, I hold that the grammar of storytelling should ultimately prevail here. And in general, narrative determinism is just a more important reality than any scientific or causal determinism in most stories and films. Of course, there are films like *The Core*, whose blatant scientific transgressions can make it impossible for some viewers to even engage with the power of storytelling. But the *Back to the Future* films are not *The Core*, nor are they sci-fi camp like the aforementioned disaster films.

The *Back to the Future* stories work because of the power of good storytelling. We identify with, and rally our emotions behind, the likable protagonist Marty and his efforts to save his family across the space-time continuum. We root against the Tannens, cheering with delight each time a truckload of manure spills over them. We share an appreciation for the eccentric Doc and his commitment to both the ones he loves and his science. And speaking of science, it just has to be plausible enough for the narrative to work its magic on us. It doesn't have to be perfect or even ultimately consistent. It is just one narrative tool to advance the great moral tale that is at the heart of the *Back to the Future* series. Of course, one could focus on the violations of causal determinism, or other scientific inconsistencies, and let it ruin the experience. But we would all be worse off for doing so. As with all great acts of storytelling, willfully suspending our disbelief is an essential and even noble part of the process. It is this act that allows us to be transformed by the magic of story. We are, after all, *Homo fictus*!

Notes

1. For the purpose of this essay, I will often use these terms interchangeably. I see cinematic determinism as type or narrative determinism applying specifically to cinema. At times I address more general concerns about determinism in narrative storytelling that have application beyond films and filmmaking.
2. Gottschall, Jonathan. 2021. "Our Fondness for Narratives Is Driving Us Mad We Seem to Be in a Golden Age of Storytelling. Is It Inhibiting Rather Than Creating Empathy?" *The Boston Globe*.
3. Gottschall, Jonathan. 2013. *The Storytelling Animal: How Stories Make Us Human*. Mariner Books, xiv.
4. For a detailed discussion of this "universal grammar," see Gottschall, Jonathan, 2021.

The Story Paradox: How Our Love of Storytelling Builds Societies and Tears Them Down. Basic Books, Hachette Book Group, Chapter 4.

    5. For a more thorough treatment of this "And, But Therefore" system and its role in film, politics, religion and beyond, see any number of Olson's public talks or his books: Olson, Randy. 2015. *Houston, We Have a Narrative*. University of Chicago Press; Olson, Randy. 2019. *Narrative is Everything: The ABT Framework and Narrative Evolution*. Independently Published.

    6. For an engaging look at the neuroscience of storytelling, see Vaccaro, Anthony G., et al. 2021. "Functional Brain Connectivity During Narrative Processing Relates to Transportation and Story Influence." *Frontiers in Human Neuroscience*, vol. 15.

    7. *Ibid.*, Gottschall, 2021, *The Story Paradox*, 100.

    8. Interestingly, there are some religious traditions that engage with ethical and even narrative questions involving biblical interpretation. Jewish Midrash often engaged with such complexities. Not surprisingly, this often is done through the vehicle of new storytelling.

McFly Meets McTaggart

John M. DePoe

What happens when Doc Brown's DeLorean hits 88 mph? "Now, if my calculations are correct," says Doc, "when this baby hits 88 miles an hour, you're gonna see some serious shit." Metaphysically speaking, Doc is right. The enthrallment of time travel is perhaps only exceeded by its paradox-inducing theories that attempt to provide coherence about what's happening in time travel. In fact, many philosophers are inclined to think time travel is impossible, and among those who dare attempt to argue that it *is* possible, there is widespread disagreement over what makes it possible. Let's use *Back to the Future* to explore the metaphysics of time, time travel, and universe-ending paradoxes.

McTaggart and McFly

So, what is time? Before there was Marty McFly, there was John McTaggart Ellis McTaggart (not a typo). Since McTaggart (1866–1925), philosophers have generally thought of time in two ways: the A-theory and the B-theory.[1] The A-theory describes time from the experiential perspective of the flow and passage of time. According to the A-theory, all time can be classified as either past (before now), present (now), or future (after now). Notice that this way of looking at time must refer to the present time or what's happening now. The other way to describe time is through the B-theory, which describes time by placing events in relation to one another as earlier than, simultaneous with, or later than other events. The death of John F. Kennedy comes after World War II, before the fall of the Berlin Wall, and is simultaneous with the death of C.S. Lewis. Everything in the last sentence is true no matter when it is uttered, because it makes no reference to the present time. However, statements that describe events from the perspective of the A-theory will only be true depending on the present moment when they are uttered. "The book *Back to the Future and Philosophy* does not exist" is true in the present time when I am writing this, but it will be false in the present time when you are reading it.

Movies actually provide a helpful way to think about the A-theory and B-theory of time. When you are watching a movie, it appears to have a present moment (what's happening now in the film when you are watching it). Typically, the movie presents a story where the audience watches the plot unfold through events that flow from a continuously rolling present moment. From the perspective of the A-theory, the only real time of the movie is what is on the screen right now. However, we can also think about movies from the perspective of the B-theory. From this perspective, the whole movie is complete. Imagine an old film reel with discrete cells for each moment of the movie that are placed in sequential order on the reel. Each moment (cell) of the movie is equally real, viewed from the B-theory, and it makes no sense to say that any moment is presently happening. They all exist at once in a sequential ordering that is fixed and unchanging. For this reason, some philosophers refer to the A-theory as the dynamic view of time and the B-theory as the static view of time.

Now, buckle up for the next step. McTaggart believed that both the A-theory and B-theory correctly describe time, even though he also thought that they created irresolvable paradoxes if they were both true. Let's start by looking at the B-theory. The B-theory cannot account for causation or change. McTaggart reached this conclusion because the B-theory describes events in time as stationary, fixed events. You can't get change from stationary, fixed events. But the A-theory is hopelessly contradictory, thought McTaggart. How to understand his argument for this is a matter of contentious dispute among professional philosophers. (Try to read McTaggart's "The Unreality of Time" and you'll see what I mean.) McTaggart claims that "being past," "being present," and "being future" are incompatible attributes (if an event has one of them, it cannot have the others). However, if the A-theory is correct, every event simultaneously has all three temporal attributes. Right now, it may *seem* like the moment you are reading these words is the present, but as I am writing this that is actually a future event. And when you are finished, it will become the past. But since it's contradictory to have all of these attributes, the A-theory can't be correct either. "That's heavy!" Indeed.

So McTaggart claimed that time must be understood as either the A-theory or the B-theory, but then he claims that they are both deeply flawed. What was his point? McTaggart's point was that time is unreal, that time is—in some sense—illusory. While few philosophers have agreed with McTaggart's views on time, his theories about time have served as the starting point for just about all philosophical discussions on time and time travel. Today, philosophers are still wrestling with his paradoxes about the A-theory and B-theory. And the perceptive viewer of the *Back to the Future* films will notice that they are playing off both the A-theory and B-theory of time.

Let me explain. The dynamic flow of time of the A-theory is portrayed not only by the viewer following the sequence of events from Marty's present perspective, but it is also evident by the way that the causal consequences are continuously related to what is happening in Marty's present moment. In the first film, if Marty fails to get Lorraine to fall in love with George, then the members of his family begin to fade from the picture. Near the end of the movie, Marty starts to fade away from reality up until the moment that George asserts himself to fight off one last bully on the dance floor and kiss Lorraine—then Marty is restored to his full existence along with the image of him and his siblings in the photograph. Clearly, *Back to the Future* takes the present moment from the viewer's (or Marty's?) perspective as the one that has a privileged reality, which is consistent with the A-theory. But it also relies on the B-theory of time. How so? The casual way the DeLorean can jump to different spots on the timeline implies that these moments are "out there." They exist as places that Marty can travel to. The implication is that these times are equally real with the present and that anyone with a time-traveling DeLorean can drive from one time location to another. If the past and the future are both immediately accessible from the present, the picture of reality presented in the movie is that they are all equally real in their ordered sequence, just as the B-theory says they should be.

Perhaps this is perfectly fine, but many philosophers of time have argued that you can't have it both ways. If the A-theory is correct, then you can't jump back and forth between different times as if they are fixed locations in reality. In other words, only the present time is real on standard views of the A-theory, which means you can't travel back-and-forth from the present to the past or the future because they don't exist. If the B-theory is correct, it makes time travel more plausible, but then you can't change anything. The fading photograph and its subsequent restoration don't make sense on the B-theory. If George gets together with Lorraine, it has always happened, and Marty's photograph, along with the people in it, have always been there. Before you think I'm being too hard on the film, consider this. Maybe Robert Zemeckis was a fan of McTaggart, and he was just trying to illustrate how the A-theory and B-theory of time both appear to be correct, but neither one can be correct. In other words, maybe the philosophical point of *Back to the Future* is the same as McTaggart's—that time is unreal.

We're Sending You Back to The Future

"Wait a minute. Wait a minute, Doc, are you telling me you built a *time machine* out of a *DeLorean?*" We go along with Doc and Marty, assuming that time travel is possible. Most of us didn't think the movie was utterly incoherent (at least when we first watched it). Even if the physics of time travel eludes us, I'm not sure what a flux capacitor does or why 1.21 gigawatts of electricity is the precise amount of energy needed to time travel—most people think that time travel is something that can be coherently imagined. It might be beyond our skill to create a real time machine, but most people don't think that time travel is absolutely impossible. Using *Back to the Future* as our test case, let's examine some of the best-known philosophical approaches to the coherence of time travel.

One of the most influential philosophers at the end of the 20th century, David Lewis, proposed what is probably the most popular view of time travel.[2] Lewis distinguished the personal time of the time traveler from the external or physical time of the timeline. If on October 26, 1985, Marty travels back to November 5, 1955, and then on November 12, 1955, he returns to October 26, 1985, Marty has actually experienced 10 more days of his personal time from his departure and return to October 26, 1985, even though no external time has passed on the calendar. In *Part II*, the film plays off this when Marty and Doc revisit the events of 1955 and Marty remarks, "Oh, this is *heavy*, Doc. I mean, it's just like I was just here *yesterday.*" To which Doc answers, "You were here yesterday, Marty, you *were!*" Marty was there the day before, according to an external measure of time (e.g., the calendar), but it has been longer for Marty's personal experience of time.

Most people who have a beef with time travel object to it because of the problematic paradoxes that it can cause. Most famously, if time travel is possible, then someone can go back in time and kill his own grandfather before grandpa has the opportunity to have any progeny with the time traveler's grandmother. Killing grandpa should ultimately lead to the time traveler not existing, and if he doesn't exist, then he can't kill his grandpa. Lewis's solution to this problem is to spell out two senses in which a time traveler can and cannot do paradoxical things like killing his own grandpa. In one sense, the time traveler will typically always have the ability to kill his grandpa in the sense that he is able to have hatred in his heart toward grandpa, he is able to put together a plan to kill grandpa, he is able to have the skills and tools necessary to kill grandpa, and so on. What he cannot do, according to Lewis, is ever succeed in changing anything from happening that has not already happened. Since the time traveler exists, it must follow that his grandpa succeeds in propagating his genetic material with the time traveler's grandma. Thus, no matter how hard he tries, the time traveler's efforts to kill his grandpa always fail. For instance, if he is about to shoot his grandfather, then his gun will jam as he pulls the trigger, or a bird will inauspiciously intercept the bullet before it strikes grandpa, or grandpa will bend over to tie his shoe at the right moment, or ... you get the idea. No matter what, the murderous intentions of the time traveler are always thwarted by something. It may sound contrived, but Lewis's point is that it isn't absolutely impossible.

Unfortunately for *Back to the Future*, it can't follow David Lewis's theory of time travel. According to Lewis, what has already happened in time is what has always happened, so there is no way to change anything in the past. In all three films, *Back to the Future* has Doc and Marty changing the past and creating new sequences of events. When Marty is hit by the car in the first film, it changes what happened (it was supposed to be his father who was hit by the car, which led Lorraine to fall in love with him). Old Biff giving young Biff the almanac in *Part II* changes what happened and results in a different 1985. When Doc accidentally tells Marty that acting on his temper will alter his life for the worse in the third film, it results in Marty (after he returns to 1985) declining to race Needles, which would have resulted in a serious accident and life-debilitating injury for Marty. These kinds of changes aren't possible in time travel, according to David Lewis. (*Bill and Ted's Excellent Adventure*, however, presents time travel in a way that is amenable to Lewis's theory.)

Other philosophers have proposed that time travel with changes to the past can occur because time travel involves visiting parallel universes.[3] These are other worlds that are very similar to our universe, inhabited by the same (or at least *very* similar) people as our world who do almost all the same things that they do in our world. The main difference is that in this parallel world, it has a time traveler interrupt the normal sequence of events (as defined by the "original" timeline). Time travel, on this view, means traveling to parallel universes where the past appears to change with respect to the way things went on the "original" timeline. This approach seems to cohere with the perspective of the time traveler. The people in his original timeline remember the past unfolding one way, while those on the new timeline have a different recollection of the past (they don't remember it as changing but as always being the "new" way). This is all easily explained by having multiple timelines with different sets of people with only the time traveler experiencing both universes. To the time traveler, it looks like there is one timeline that is changing, but to the other inhabitants of those worlds, their universe remains unchanged.

So does the multiple universes approach to time travel help us make sense of the *Back to the Future* films? As I see it, *Back to the Future* doesn't conform to this view of time travel either. One problem on the multiple universes interpretation of time travel is that once you change the past, you can't return to your own world.[4] So, while it seems like Marty is fixing his own world by burning the sports almanac before Biff can use it in the second film, he would only be traveling to a parallel world where Biff's plan is foiled. Unfortunately, this leaves the world where Biff takes over Hill Valley intact. Marty has saved the day only by traveling to a different world with a different timeline. The films, of course, portray Marty's actions as helping those who are on deviant timelines, so I don't see the parallel worlds interpretation of time travel as a compatible model for *Back to the Future*. (However, *Avengers Endgame* might be a more coherent example of this view of time travel.)

While the brief sketch of time travel given in this essay is nowhere close to an exhaustive summary of different philosophical theories on time travel, one thing is clear. It is difficult to give a coherent account of time travel for *Back to the Future*. To put it more charitably, *Back to the Future* appeals to many intuitively plausible beliefs about time that collectively are unintelligible. For instance, it seems broadly possible to time travel—at the very least, it's not contradictory on its face, like believing that one is equal to zero. Furthermore, most people find it very plausible to think that we have free will and that our free choices can change the future. The thought that events in time are permanently fixed in such a way that we can't do anything else other than what has already been scripted, well, most people find that hard to accept. But the belief in a fixed nature of a timeline that makes time travel possible contradicts the plausible belief in free will that is not predetermined by an immutable future. Ultimately, the philosophical analysis of time travel forces us to examine these initially plausible beliefs and to reassess them. Either find a way to make them all cohere with some theoretical explanation that "squares the circle" of time travel or reject some of these beliefs to form a credible and coherent set of beliefs.

The truth is that *Back to the Future* probably doesn't give a coherent picture of time travel. It is likely that they borrow bits and pieces of insights from different approaches and cobble them together in a way that may not ultimately make sense when you think about it carefully. My own view is that the time travel depicted in the films is incoherent, but that doesn't stop me from suspending my disbelief and enjoying the films for what they're worth. If nothing else, they provide the opportunity to tell my friends and family about the philosophy of time.

Notes

1. McTaggart, John M.E. 1908. "The Unreality of Time," *Mind* 17 (108): 457–73. See also McTaggart, John M.E. 1927. *The Nature of Existence*, vol. 2. Cambridge University Press.

McTaggart's work was also spread through the very influential Broad, C.D. 1933; 1938. *An Examination of McTaggart's Philosophy*, 2 vols. Cambridge University Press.

2. Lewis, David. 1976. "The Paradoxes of Time Travel," *American Philosophical Quarterly* 13: 145–52.

3. For example, see Deutsch, David; Lockwood, Michael. 1994. "The Quantum Physics of Time Travel," *Scientific American* 270, no. 3 50–56. A similar approach to time travel is given by Meiland, Jack. 1974. "A Two-Dimensional Passage Model for Time Travel," *Philosophical Studies* 26: 153–73.

4. As one philosopher argues, this would only involve avoiding the past, not changing it. See Smith, Nicholas. 1997. "Bananas Enough for Time Travel?" *British Journal for the Philosophy of Science* 48: 363–89.

Back to a New and Improved Future

Taylor W. Cyr *and* Grace Scott

It's after 1 in the morning in a barren parking lot where Doc Brown and Marty McFly mutter in front of a DeLorean, souped-up and kitted out to do what no car has ever done before. We don't know it yet, but this is the last moment of peace before the rubber really meets the road. A beaten-up Volkswagen careens into a streetlamp's sickly glow. A man is standing through the sunroof, unleashing a barrage of machine gun staccato. Doc lies dead while Marty—brave and impulsive—barrels into the front seat and floors the ignition. He shoots off in a tear, screaming down the asphalt. The odometer inches closer and closer and finally reaches 88 miles per hour. A crack of light and sound shakes the night, and the parking lot is empty once again.

Marty has jumped from 1985 to 1955 where he runs into his future parents (in a way that will potentially wipe him from existence) and eventually writes a letter to Doc to warn him about what will happen to him 30 years into the future. However, Doc doesn't want to know about the future, so he tears the letter to shreds before assisting Marty in harnessing the power of a lightning strike at the town square's clock tower to send Marty and the DeLorean back to 1985.

Marty arrives back in the future ten minutes before Doc's death. Dashing from the clock tower square, Marty arrives just in time to see his worst nightmare: Doc is shot. Again. However, a hopeful crescendo of string instruments heralds Doc shifting and groaning, miraculously alive in a bulletproof vest. Without speaking, Doc sticks a shaking hand into his lab coat's breast pocket and pulls out the letter, aged and taped together. The day is saved as Doc brushes off Marty's reminder about all of Doc's previously articulated worries about knowing too much about the future: "Well, I figured, what the hell!"

What's noteworthy about all of this—though audiences may have missed it, being swept up in the adventure—is that the story seems to contradict itself. How can Doc both be shot dead but *also* survive? This type of apparent contradiction is familiar to time travel stories in which a character seems both to be able and not to be able to do something past-altering, such as killing one's own grandfather before he has fathered any children.[1]

One way to try to resolve this issue—though it may only introduce additional problems—would be to suppose that time is multi-dimensional. It's normally assumed that time is linear, but in recent years, several philosophers have considered how giving up that assumption may resolve certain paradoxes of time travel, including the grandfather paradox.[2] In particular, by distinguishing between "time" and "hypertime," we can locate events such as Doc Brown's death and his survival at the very same "time" but at a different "hypertime." In this way, it is possible to model backward time travel that involves changing the past, and so, it seems to make sense of the plot of *Back to the Future*.

But even if hypertime helps to explain the plot of *Back to the Future*, some elements of the story may not be coherent—or may be coherent but wildly improbable. It is worth a closer look at *Back to the Future*'s fading photographs, on the one hand, as well as the movie's ending, when Marty returns to the future to find that he has the very same two siblings and no doppelganger, on the other hand.

How Doc Can Both Die and Not Die at the Very Same Time?

First, a visual metaphor is useful to ease into the abstract theory of hypertime. Imagine a group of generals at a meeting which concerns a war. The setting is vaguely medieval in the way that most fantasy epics adopt: chainmail, wall sconces, and grim, bearded faces. The war table is covered with an expansive map, useful for the planning of military actions. This map is a flat plane. It has two dimensions, length and width. Only by virtue of a third dimension, height, achieved by their vantage point over the map, can the advisors see both dimensions. They can identify the location of the tokens by reference to two separate data points—length and width. If a child who was only as tall as the table were to wander in, they might be able to stand on their tiptoes to put their line of sight right at the edge of the table. From the child's vantage point, only one dimension is visible. It seems like the tokens are lined up along a straight line. However, the child can only see one of two possible dimensions. Two tokens that are close to each other laterally and very far from each other vertically may seem close together from the child's point of view and very far apart to the advisors.

In this metaphor, we experience time from the child's point of view. One event happened. Another event happened after. We create timelines that reflect this view of time as a string, an arrow, a line. To add another dimension to time is to stand on a chair. When we add hypertime to our understanding of time, we enable more to be said about the precise location of specific moments. The relationship of length to width is distinct from the relationship between time and hyper time; however, it remains a useful analogy. It challenges us to expand our fundamental understanding of what information there is to be said about time.

A second way to understand the two dimensions of hyper time is explored by Jack Meiland in his aptly named paper, "A Two-Dimensional Passage Model of Time for Time Travel."[3] One dimension of time is time, represented as P_{1-7} in the figure below. Time—the dimension that most of us are intimately acquainted with—is represented as P_x, or as past$_x$, because the past is merely consecutive moments of time collected together. The other dimension of time is hypertime, represented as Pt_x, or the past *at* a certain time.

Each moment has a certain past associated with it. The past at t_1, also known as P_1, involves every moment up until t_1. At t_3, the past, also known as P_3, has grown to include the past as it was up to t_1, plus up to t_2 and t_3. When Meiland proposes that each moment has a different past associated with it, he is careful to define "different" in the manner of *qualitative*

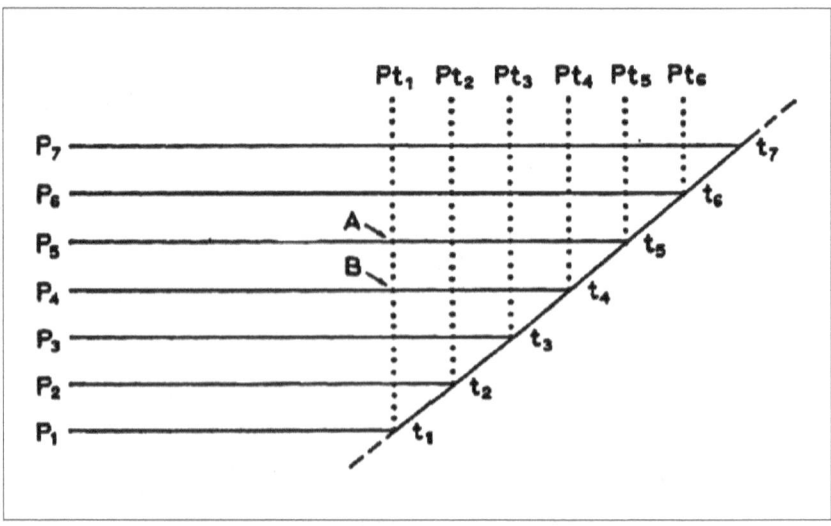

Meiland's two-dimensional mode of time.

differences vs quantitative differences. Meiland is not as interested in the implications of an infinite quantity of pasts. Rather, this model of time aims to describe time as a continuant, something that "exists at different times and therefore can be different at one time from what it is at another."[4] People are continuants. I exist in 2013 at 11 years old. I also exist in 2023 at 21 years old. In reference to two different times, I have different qualities but retain my selfhood. So too is the past able to exist differently at different times and retain its integrity as the past.

The third approach begins with visual metaphors and ends with graphical representation. The growing block theory, as described by Alex and Phyllis Eisenstein in their 1971 science fiction short story, "The Trouble with the Past," visualizes time as a never-ending chain with an infinite number of beads.[5] One bead is added for every moment that occurs. Others envision time as a block—hence the name—that grows by one slice per moment of time. Ryan Wasserman points out that these images of the growing block theory imply the question: What is the chain? Along what does the block expand? Predictably, the answer is hypertime. In other words, "the 'growth' of the block can ... be understood as temporal expansion along the hypertime dimension."[6]

The last method to describe hypertime is explored by G.C. Goddu, who considers the possibility that time might be two-dimensional, such that, in David Lewis's words, "an event might be momentary along one time dimension but divisible along the other."[7] Goddu is concerned with divisions of an instance, with temporal parts not yet explored. Typically, one considers a moment of time to lack temporal parts. It is the simplest unit of time. Goddu proposes that may be so along one dimension, but not the other (the other, of course, being hypertime). Consequently, "hypertimes" refers to the "temporal parts of temporal instances."[8] This particular phrasing of the notion of hypertime is quite useful for solving time travel's problem of the fixity of the past. An event that took place at t_1 with a hypertime of Ht_1 may have different qualities than an event that took place at t_1 with a hypertime of Ht_2. They hold different locations, making it perfectly coherent for the same event in time to have different qualities at different hypertimes. It is this feature that allows Doc to die and to live.

In other words, since the specific time that Doc is shot in 1985 exists at least twice—at two distinct *hyper*times—there is no contradiction in saying that he is shot dead but also not shot dead at that *time*. Just as there is no contradiction in your being hungry before breakfast and not hungry after breakfast (two distinct points in time), there is no contradiction in Doc's being dead at $<t_1, Ht_1>$ and alive at $<t_1, Ht_2>$ (two distinct points in hypertime). Marty turns out to be right when he says, "History is gonna change!"

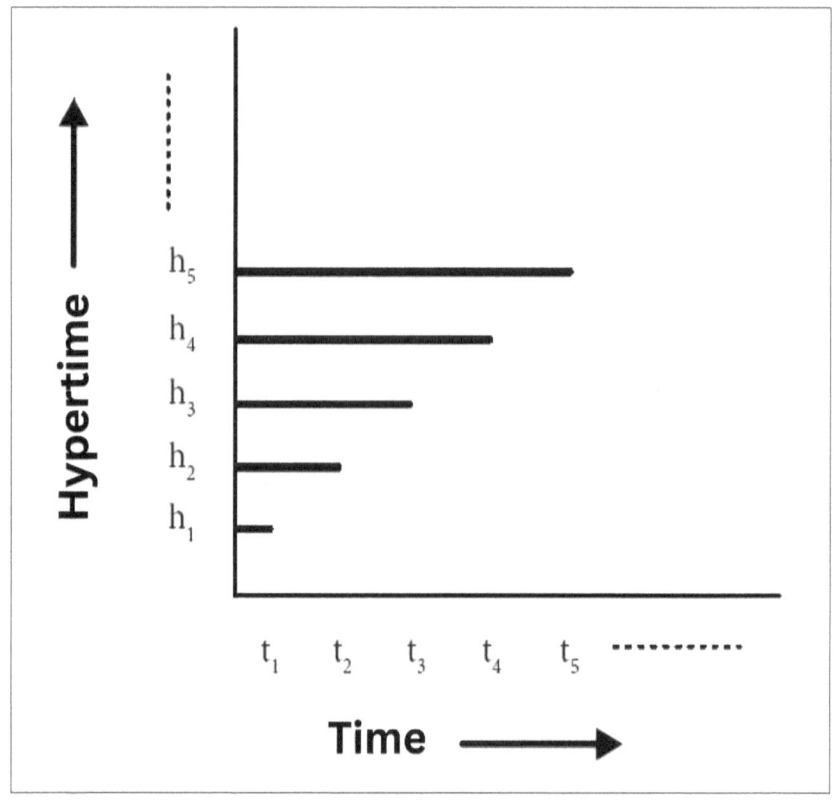

Wasserman's hypertime model.

A Problem That Does Not Fade Away

While the hypertime model can make sense of Doc's dying and not dying at the very same time, there is another element of the story of *Back to the Future* that remains a problem. While visiting the 1950s, Marty interacts with his parents who are teenagers and who have not yet become romantically involved. Marty's mother is smitten with him, and it is suggested that Marty is making it less likely that his parents will, in fact, get together, which Marty believes will erase him and his two siblings from existence. Now, even if he were to prevent his parents from getting together, this would not result in a contradiction, assuming the hypertime model of the story, as Marty would still have been conceived by his parents at a different hypertime.

But the writers of *Back to the Future* do not seem to have hypertime in mind, and they run into a problem that surfaces in two places in the story.

First, Marty is carrying a family photograph with him, and he periodically looks at it. As he spends more time in the past, his siblings begin to fade from the photograph—first his brother's head, then the rest of his brother, then his sister too. Later, when at the school dance, even Marty fades from the photograph. But whether we accept that time is linear or model the story with hypertime, such fading is incoherent. On the first option, as we have already seen, the past can't change, and so there wouldn't be any way to make sense of any of *Back to the Future*, let alone someone's disappearance from a photograph. Even on the hypertime model, though, the events at the earlier hypertime that caused the photograph to exist as it initially did are never erased, and so even if in this hyper-later timeline the photograph never comes to be (or somehow, mysteriously, comes to be in exactly the same way, minus Marty's brother's head), there is no basis for the photograph to change.

Second, still at the dance, Marty himself begins to fade out of existence, first forgetting how to play the guitar and then becoming wispier and more ghostly until his parents share their first kiss, at which time Marty unfades and can once again play the guitar. That there is a problem here has already been recognized. For example, in their introduction to metaphysics, *Riddles of Existence*, Earl Conee and Theodor Sider explain:

> That McFly begins to fade away into nothingness shows that the writers of *Back to the Future* were aware of the problem. But the fade-out solves nothing. Suppose McFly fades out completely after preventing his parents from meeting. He still existed before fading out (it was he, after all, who prevented his parents from meeting). Where then did he come from in the first place? Whatever its literary merits, as a work of philosophy *Back to the Future* fails miserably.[9]

Conee and Sider recognize that there is a problem with this element of the story, but they have misdiagnosed the problem. Where did Marty come from in the first place? From an earlier hypertime. On this model of time travel (which, as we've seen, the movie requires), there's no contradiction in supposing that Marty prevents his own existence, so long as that prevention takes place at a different hypertime than the one where he originated.

The real problem with Marty's fading away is that he is not affecting his own causal past, and so what he is doing in the past does not bear on whether he has come into existence. Even if it somehow did, moreover, there would be no way for Marty to "half-exist," not knowing how to play the guitar and looking like a ghost; if he really made it so that his parents never got together and this was a problem for Marty, then he shouldn't be there at all. As it happens, his parents *do* get together, and so there's no reason for him to have ever faded at all.

While seemingly incoherent, the fading element of the story is effective in communicating the idea that Marty's existence depends on his parents getting together, and audiences have never had a problem following the narrative of *Back to the Future*. (Perhaps this is why Conee and Sider are content to bracket the movie's literary merits.) What we have suggested, however, is that this idea is fundamentally confused. Even the move to the hypertime model, which solves some of the movie's metaphysical messes, can't resolve this issue.

The Not-Enough-Martys Problem

Let's set aside the fading problem. After all, we could subtract this fading element of the story without much change—the only substantial effects of the fading seem to be on Marty's anxieties and motivations for acting as he does in the past. Supposing we extract the fading and continue to use the hypertime model to avoid the Doc Brown contradiction problem, there is one lingering issue worth exploring, and it has to do with the movie's ending. While not impossible, Marty's changing the past in the ways that he does and still having the very same siblings that he does turns out to be particularly improbable.

To see why, consider how, even without time travel, some actions are identity-affecting. Who we have children with, and when, affects who will exist in the future. Supposing Doc's parents had waited a year longer to get pregnant than they in fact did, some other child, not Doc Brown, would have come into existence. More generally, one's identity depends on the timing of conception.

This point is taken for granted in the philosophical literature on the *non-identity problem*.[10] With this point in mind, consider the following case:

> Lorraine is considering having a fourth child, and her doctor tells her that she has developed a condition such that if she conceives now, any child she conceives will suffer from incurable blindness. However, her doctor also tells her that this result is not unavoidable. If Lorraine waits to conceive, and instead takes a pill every day for two months prior to conceiving, then she will conceive a child who is not afflicted with incurable blindness. Had Lorraine waited and taken the pill, she would have conceived and given birth to a perfectly sighted boy she would have named "George Junior" (after her husband, George). However, she decides not to take the pill in favor of conceiving immediately. As a result, she conceives and gives birth to an incurably blind baby boy. She names this child "Sam Junior" (after her father, Sam Baines).[11]

It seems to many that Lorraine has done something wrong. If she has wronged some*one*, it would have to be Sam Junior. But Lorraine does not make Sam Junior worse off than he otherwise would have been, and so it seems that she has not harmed Sam Junior. And yet, wronging someone seems to require harming them, and so it seems that Lorraine has not in fact wronged Sam Junior. How, then, does Lorraine act wrongly, if she does? This is the non-identity problem.

And this isn't a mere puzzle—many real-life situations give rise to the same problem. For example, in his influential statement of the problem, Derek Parfit considers a case in which a community must decide whether to conserve or deplete some natural resource.[12] It may seem that depleting the resource wrongs future generations (say all of the people in that community 200 years later), but if no future person in the *deplete* scenario would have existed had the resource been conserved, then it seems that no actual person was made worse off, and so no one was harmed, and so no one was wronged.

Now consider again the effects of Marty's antics in 1955. Almost certainly, the different set of experiences had by Marty's parents when Marty is there, not to mention the changes to his father's personality, will result in a slight difference in the set of events that occur immediately following the dance. These differences may balloon out into very different lives for Marty's parents, but even if we reject this "butterfly effect," the odds that Marty's parents would conceive children at slightly different times are incredibly high. Just think about what would be required for the very same conceptions to occur! It is wildly improbable that Marty would have the very same siblings in this altered timeline.

But even if we accept that the improbable has happened—that somehow Marty's parents have conceived the same children in this timeline as they did in the original—then we should expect them to conceive *Marty* in this timeline too! If this were to happen, then when Marty returns back to the future (but in a different hypertime), he would find another version of himself, conceived in this other hypertime. What happens at the end of the movie, however, is that Marty from the original timelines somehow "replaces" the new Marty who was conceived and grew up in this new hypertime. Perhaps a more fitting ending to the movie would have been a funeral.

Notes

1. Lewis, David. 1976. "The Paradoxes of Time Travel," *American Philosophical Quarterly* 13: 145–52.
2. See, for example; Meiland, Jack. 1974. "A Two-Dimensional Passage Model of Time for Time Travel," *Philosophical Studies* 26: 153–73; Goddu, G.C. 2003. "Time Travel and Changing the Past (or How to Kill Yourself and Live to Tell the Tale)," *Ratio* 16: 16–32; Van Inwagen, Peter. 2010. "Changing the Past," in *Oxford Studies in Metaphysics*, Zimmerman,

Dean (ed.). Oxford University Press: 3–28; Wasserman, Ryan. 2018. *Paradoxes of Time Travel*. Oxford University Press.

   3. *Ibid.*, Meiland.
   4. *Ibid.*, p. 160.
   5. Eisenstein, Alex; Eisenstein, Phyllis. 1971. "The Trouble with the Past," in *New Dimensions 1*, Robert Silverberg (ed.). Doubleday.
   6. *Ibid.*, Wasserman, p. 91.
   7. *Ibid.*, Lewis, p. 146; quoted by Goddu, p. 20.
   8. *Ibid.*, Goddu, p. 20.
   9. Conee, Earl; Sider, Theodore. 2005. *Riddles of Existence: A Guided Tour of Metaphysics*. Oxford University Press, p. 59.
   10. For a short introduction, see Purves, Duncan. 2014. "The Non-Identity Problem," *1000-Word Philosophy*, accessed June 3, 2024. For a book-length treatment of the problem, see Boonin, David. 2014. *The Non-Identity Problem and the Ethics of Future People*. Oxford University Press. For an illuminating discussion of time travel and the non-identity problem, see Bernstein, Sara. "Ethical Puzzles of Time Travel," unpublished manuscript: https://www3.nd.edu/~sbernste/EPTT.pdf, accessed June 3, 2024.
   11. This case is modified from one in Purves which is itself modified from a case in Boonin, pp. 127–128.
   12. Parfit, Derek. 1984. *Reasons and Persons*. Oxford University Press.

II
Knowledge and Belief in Hill Valley

Following Your Heart to the Future

Kate C.S. Schmidt

"Think, McFly! Think!" Biff angrily exclaims, knocking George on his head. Unhappy philosophers might agree with the sentiment, especially epistemologists who focus on understanding the best ways to acquire and use knowledge. The rest of us might say the same things to ourselves: "Think harder" or "Think carefully" when focused on something important. We might hope that by emphasizing cognition, we can, over time, become more successful at assessing the world around us and being successful by acting in accordance with that assessment. The central idea is that decisions will be more successful if you think with your "head" rather than thinking with your "heart." Perhaps decision-making ought to be a fully cognitive activity and not an emotional one. However, this distinction between head and heart is problematic, and the *Back to the Future* franchise clearly endorses the value of making choices with your heart.

"If you put your mind to it, you can accomplish anything"

One of the most appealing parts of time-travel stories is perhaps the idea that we could fix everything in our lives. Given enough time and careful planning, doesn't having a time machine mean that I can accomplish everything I want? Similarly, it seems that careful, cognitive, rational decision-making is the key to accomplishing most significant goals in life. Finding truth, doing the right thing, or succeeding at an everyday activity all seem to rely upon careful cognition. I just need to use my head!

When people talk about deciding with your "head" or your "heart" (as Doc and Marty do in *Part III*), the distinction is usually between more cognitive or more emotional styles of decision-making. Using your head implies carefully weighing reasons, consciously considering alternatives, and then staying cool and collected while choosing the best course of action. In contrast, using your heart means following your emotions. Traditionally, emotional decision-making is seen as less reliable and more biased. Additionally, emotional decision-making is often more subconscious, with people less able to articulate *why* they are making a decision. If you use your head, you can cite all the reasons you might have for a decision, but if you follow your heart, it could be harder to explain your choices.

The distinction between using your head or your heart seems appealing because emotional (heart-based) decisions frequently turn out poorly. Most of us have personal examples, but we also see throughout the *Back to the Future* trilogy how emotions can lead individuals astray. George McFly is too cautious to ask out his crush, too worried to stand up to Biff, and too uncertain to listen properly to Marty. Biff is clearly too power-hungry and impulsive to make good decisions, as illustrated by his impulse to reject the help of his older self in *Part II*. It would have been wiser to team up, but Biff is overly influenced by his own narcissism and high opinion of himself, refusing to acknowledge that he could receive help or advice from someone else. Throughout the series, both Biff and Marty struggle to behave rationally when directly challenged or mocked, predictably jumping into a fight.[1]

Marty turns around slowly, "*Nobody* calls me chicken!" he exclaims. We, the audience, can see that Biff is just taunting and manipulating Marty, and that Marty would be better off just walking away. In addition to the vice of anger, Marty also hesitates to share his music for fear it won't be liked. In the original film, he learns this is a fear he shares with his father, George, when George refuses to send off his writing for fear it won't be well received, "I just don't think I could take that kind of rejection." Marty and George both have a sense of pride or vanity, which causes them to fixate on the risk of rejection rather than acting as their authentic selves. In these cases, the emotions of anger and fear are both shown to be poor methods of decision-making; Marty's life could be going better if he resisted these urges.

The franchise shows over and over again that shame, anger, fear, overconfidence, and anxiety can all result in poor decisions that set up almost all of the problems within the plot. While Biff is an antagonist, it could be argued that the real source of all the problems in the first movie is the poor emotional decisions made by George, Doc, and Marty. This lends an initially compelling endorsement of the head vs heart distinction; it certainly seems that using your heart can cause problems.

Emotional Decisions as Rational Decisions

Philosophers thinking about decision-making often like to pay attention to "akratic actions," where "there is a conflict between the agent's better judgment and her motivation and intentional action."[2] These akratic actions can be conflicts between one's head and one's heart. For example, in the first movie, Marty writes Doc a letter, intending to slip it into Doc's pocket to save Doc's life in the future. Marty has clear reasons to think this is a bad idea: Doc has told Marty explicitly that there could be disastrous consequences and that Doc has no desire to learn any information about the future. Nevertheless, a worried Marty intentionally sits down and carefully writes the letter. It seems Marty's motivation conflicts with his judgment that the action is too risky, and Marty decides to take action anyway.

Examples like Marty's letter are interesting because sometimes when cognitions and emotions conflict, cognitive decisions are not the obvious best answer. Sometimes, using your heart is better than using your head. Marty's willingness to write the letter out of love for his friendship with Doc, despite the risks, ends up being a good thing. Philosopher Christine Tappolet argues that in some cases of akratic action, it is possible for an emotional decision to be "more rational" than using one's "better judgment"; this is possible because "emotions can inform us about our practical reasons."[3] Emotions can be reliable appraisals of the world and can point toward reasons for action. In some cases, emotions can be more accurate than carefully considered conscious assessments of the situation.

This seems to be the case with Doc and Marty: although Marty has concerns about the consequences of writing the letter, he ultimately trusts in his feelings of love and friendship that lead him to save Doc's life. Not only that, but Doc later makes a similar decision when he chooses to tape the letter back together so that he can read it (in Doc's future, Marty's past). In the face of uncertainty, both characters choose to trust their emotions and their relationship with one another. When Doc is asked by Marty about his decision to save and read the letter, Doc simply responds: "Well, I figured ... what the hell!"

Neither Doc nor Marty acts irrationally in this situation. While it's true that there are risks to writing and reading the letter, there are also possible benefits. Cognitive reasoning might lead to the conclusion that it is safest to avoid any possible action to change the timeline, but that reasoning fails to properly recognize that both Doc and Marty have good reasons to try and save Doc's life. As a viewer, I also find myself rooting for their friendship and the more emotional choice. Even in dangerous situations, both characters remain committed to each other, and that seems like the right thing to me.

In situations of uncertainty, it might be better to trust emotions rather than your "head." When you don't know what you don't know, that undermines cognitive assessment, but emotional assessment can still be a way to orient towards meaningful values. There are a variety of biases that apply to conscious cognitions: people overestimate their own capacities, ignore relevant evidence, and adjust reasoning processes based on the input received from other people. While it's true emotional decisions can go wrong, they can also go right! Especially when emotional habits are developed over time, they can be reliable ways to appraise the world around us.[4]

Repeatedly, Marty trusts Doc in a variety of uncomfortable situations, most notably standing in front of a speeding car in the first film. This is irrational (you can film from the side!), but it's a way of showing trust in Doc, and when the trust goes both ways (as in the train sequence at the end of the third movie), this trust helps to build their friendship. Not only that but Marty's trust is repeatedly rewarded. By reliably reacting to the same stimuli in the environment over time, emotions can be a reliable mechanism for understanding complex situations. Our emotions can help us when we get overwhelmed—even if we don't know what to think in the moment, our emotions can be a way to track important moral features of the world.

"I have to live my life according to what I believe is right in my heart"

As a piece of art, the *Back to the Future* trilogy consistently shows that it is committed to heart-based rather than head-based decision-making. The key reasons for the success of the protagonists, and major themes of the series, are heartfelt expressions of curiosity, courage, and friendship.

The characters in *Back to the Future*, both protagonists and villains, frequently make bad decisions. The films suggest that while errors happen to everyone, mistakes of the heart are more significant. In the films, having a healthy heart, or good emotional stability, is repeatedly shown to be more important than intellectual prowess. Having properly tuned emotions is portrayed as key to a good life: Marty learning the difference between false bravado and true self-confidence is a central conflict point in the movies. In *Part II*, old Biff is clever, but his selfish cleverness is portrayed as hollow when compared to the camaraderie, hope, and perseverance that result from the relationship between Doc and Marty.

Similarly, the conflict in the series is built around the emotional stagnation of Biff as the antagonist. Biff isn't portrayed as smart ("Who are you calling butthead, butthead?!"), but his cognitive skills (or lack thereof) don't explain why he is such an off-putting character. Rather, it is his aggression, brutality, and lack of ability to change that make him such a memorable villain. Biff shows what happens if one doesn't pursue healthy emotional habits—there's a risk of being trapped in an infantile emotional character forever.

Perhaps the hardest part of the series to watch is when everything falls apart in *Part II*. Doc and Marty are scared, overwhelmed, and don't know what to do. The landscape is as dark as Alan Silvestri's memorable, accompanying score. Marty has a moment of revelation, understanding that Biff has used the sports almanac to change the past: "It's all my fault," Marty exclaims, "this whole thing is my fault!" While Marty's decision to grab the sports almanac from the future might be understandable, it is the choice that triggers the series of events ruining his home and his past. Most notably, this bad decision is not a cognitive failure, but an emotional one. It is rational to try and get money to improve your life. But the movie portrays the choice as a moment of weakness, a point when simple greed, ambition, or selfishness overcomes our protagonist Marty, triggering all that follows. The low point of the series is initiated by an emotional failure, and the rest of the story is not only about how he fixes his mistakes, but how he can grow as a person because of them.

Overall, the success of the plot depends upon the heart, not the head. One way to look at the messages behind a piece of media is to look at what elements of the film end up making an impact on the plot of the story. On the whole, the *Back to the Future* franchise is largely uninterested in rational mechanisms of time travel and spends very little time on science (fictional or otherwise). That is because cognitive assessment is not what's important to the story. Marty is not motivated by his desire to understand the laws of the universe, to figure out the paradox of time travel, or to outsmart Biff. What ultimately fixes the problems of the characters are their brave and emotional actions. The highlight of the first movie, the very moment that resolves the most tension in the plot, is when George has the courage to stand up to Biff (and punches Biff in the face before dreamily walking into the dance with Lorraine).

"The future isn't written"

Understanding the *Back to the Future* trilogy this way (i.e., as a trio of movies deeply rooted in emotions and heartfelt decisions) can explain other central features about the series beyond just the plot progression. The series as a whole focuses on character arcs that emphasize emotional maturity: George learns to be brave, Marty learns to be authentic and brush off superficial challenges to prove himself, and, of course, Doc learns to fall in love. If the series has a moral, it's not a cognitive one—the overall impact of the story is not about the dangers of time travel, but about how to authentically follow your heart. The emotionality also makes the characters more lovable and relatable. Both Doc Brown and Marty McFly have appeared on a list of the top 100 movie characters of all time.[5] In contrast, the list of top movie characters did not include the protagonist of *The Time Machine* (2002), or any characters from *Jurassic Park* (1993), two other science fiction adventure films with much larger budgets. The emotionality of the *Back to the Future* series gives it a special quality, something encouraging and optimistic, that can help to explain why it remains popular after so many years.

A major theme in the story is the importance of finding joy and engagement in one's life, rather than merely pursuing superficial successes such as money or approval from authority. Marty is happy in part because he finds joy in music, regardless of any future success or what Principal Strickland says. The movies celebrate the way that Doc and Marty in particular dive headfirst into every interaction. At one point in the first movie, Marty is trying to coach George about how to boldly defend Lorraine (in the set-up scenario where Marty will suggest inappropriate behavior). George is unsure of what to say, and not sure if he should swear. "Yes, definitely goddamn it, George swear" is Marty's reply. This emotional engagement is also reflected in the soundtrack, cinematography, and script. The movies are very quotable, easily turned into gifs or memes, and are memorable because of the way we the viewers are fully invited into the character's emotions. The series is silly and joyful. This joy is the result of fully engaging in one's emotional life.

The theme of joy is also closely connected to the idea that relationships are key to flourishing—the series repeatedly re-focuses our attention not only on the friendship between Doc and Marty, but also the value of family. Huey Lewis's hit single, "The Power of Love," contributes significantly by setting the tone in the first movie. Healthy and successful characters are portrayed as being deeply grounded in joy, meaningful activity, and intentional relationships. Marty at the end of the first movie, and Doc at the end of the third, are seen as triumphing when they are standing with their families, smiling, off to pursue their next adventure.

Notes

1. This happens repeatedly in all three movies.
2. Tappolet, Christine. 2016. *Emotions, Values, and Agency*. Oxford University Press.
3. *Ibid.*
4. For example, see Kurth, Charlie. 2018. *The Anxious Mind: An Investigation Into the Varieties and Virtues of Anxiety*. MIT Press.
5. Empire. 2020. "The 100 Greatest Movie Characters." empireonline.com.

Time Travel and Knowledge of the Future

KRISTIE MILLER

In *Back to the Future Part II*, Doc incapacitates Jennifer soon after they arrive in 2015, in order to prevent her from having too much knowledge of her future. Doc clearly believes that having knowledge of the future, or at least, *too much* knowledge, is a bad thing. But if it is bad, *why* is it bad? This essay explores one reason why Doc might think knowing too much about one's future is bad: it undermines one's deliberative freedom. But why we might think this is so? As we'll see, there is reason to argue that if that *was* Doc's motivation, he need not have worried. Knowing about the future need not undermine deliberative freedom.

Deliberative Freedom

Here is one interesting difference between past and future events. If I ask you what you had for breakfast yesterday, you likely won't have any difficulty telling me. That's because there are lots of *records* of yesterday's breakfast: there are your memories or possibly even photos (if you Instagram your meals frequently enough). There might be diary entries that report what you had for breakfast or traces of your breakfast still in your stomach (if you digest slowly). On the basis of these records, you can relatively easily come to know what you had for breakfast yesterday.

By contrast, if I ask you what you *will have* for breakfast tomorrow, you won't be able to answer that question by looking at any records. You can't *remember* what you will have for breakfast tomorrow. There are no diary entries reporting what you will have, nor photos of tomorrow's breakfast, so you can't come to know what you will have for breakfast tomorrow by consulting records of what will happen.

Of course, you might still know what you will have for breakfast. Perhaps you always have the same thing for breakfast, and so you are able to *predict* what you will have. Perhaps you can consult your meal planner, which you always follow in regard to your meals. Or perhaps you know what you will have because you have already deliberated about what to have and have decided on that basis. If you decide to have oats, then (barring certain breakfast-related catastrophes), you will have oats. And if you decide to have oats, and intend to do so, then you can now know that you will have oats. That said, if you do know what you will have for breakfast tomorrow, the *way* you come to know that is different from the way you come to know what you had for breakfast yesterday.

Not only can we not know about tomorrow's breakfast by consulting records of what will happen, but equally, it looks as though we cannot know about yesterday's breakfast by deliberating about what to eat for breakfast yesterday. Why? It seems that we can only deliberate about taking some action if we take ourselves to have genuine options open to us with regard to that action. For instance, we can only deliberate about whether to catch the bus or to catch the train, if we take it to be open to us to do either of these things; that is, if we take both catching the train and catching the bus to be genuine options for us.

So, for instance, it seems right to say that Jennifer cannot deliberate about whether to move the sun two meters to the right or two meters to the left. This is because she believes herself to be incapable of moving the sun (and indeed she is correct about this), so she cannot think that moving the sun is a genuine option for her. Hence, she cannot deliberate about *whether* to move it, nor *where* to move it to. This means that even among actions each of us *can* perform, we are unable to deliberate about *whether* to perform those actions if we already know what it is that we are going to do.

Here is the idea. Suppose that on October 26, 1985, just prior to getting into the DeLorean, Jennifer is deliberating about whether she will have oats or toast for breakfast tomorrow. These are both the sorts of actions she can perform. Now, let's suppose that as Jennifer is deliberating (and contrary to what in fact happens in *Part II*) Marty arrives in an older DeLorean, having traveled into the future to 2015, and then back again to 1985, prior to Marty and Jennifer jointly traveling to 2015.

Suppose that one of the things that Marty did while in the future was look in on Jennifer in her kitchen tomorrow and watch what she has for breakfast. Now that Marty has arrived from the future, he tells Jennifer about her breakfast choices tomorrow: he tells her that she will have toast for breakfast. Jennifer believes Marty, and she is right to do so: after all, he's seen her having tomorrow's breakfast. Can Jennifer now deliberate about *what* to have, given that she *knows* what she will be having? It seems not. How can she genuinely deliberate about *what* to have for breakfast, given that she *knows* what she will have? After all, if she knows that she will choose oats, then, so it seems, she cannot take having toast to be an option that is genuinely open to her, so she can no longer deliberate about whether to have oats or toast.

Let's call the kind of freedom that we have when we can successfully deliberate about what to do, *deliberative freedom*. Deliberative freedom is important. It might not be all there is to our being free, but the fact that we can deliberate about whether to go to the cinema or the theater, whether to stay in our current job or move to another, and so on, is crucial to our being free. Bearing that in mind, we can hypothesize that the reason Doc was worried that Jennifer would learn *too much* about the future is that he believes that the more Jennifer learns about her future, the more her deliberative freedom is undermined. That is because the more Jennifer learns about her future *by being there in 2015*, the more she learns about what she does in the future. And the more she knows about what she does in the future, the fewer things she can deliberate about. In fact, if she were to come to learn about *everything* that she does at all times in the future, not merely in 2015, she would be unable to deliberate about *anything* at all, and as a result, she would have *no deliberative freedom whatsoever*. So, it would seem, Doc has good reason to want to limit how much Jennifer comes to know about how things are in 2015, since this is to limit the extent to which that knowledge impacts her deliberative freedom.

Despite it appearing as though Doc should be worried about Jennifer's deliberative freedom, however, in what follows, I argue that knowing about the future (even by traveling there) does not undermine our deliberative freedom. That is because knowing what we will do does not, after all, mean that we are unable to deliberate about what to do.

Freedom and Knowledge of the Future

Before considering deliberative freedom, it is worth thinking about freedom and knowledge of the future more generally. That's because you might think that Doc was wrong to worry about what Jennifer *knows*, or does not *know* about the future. That's because you might think that the mere fact that the future exists and is some particular way, already undermines Jennifer's freedom, whether she knows which way it is or not.

In what follows, I am going to assume that in the *Back to the Future* universe, past, present, and future all exist. They are all just different locations in spacetime, and consequently a time traveler can travel to any of those locations, so on this view the totality of the past and the future exists some *when*, although of course they are not located *here* and *now*. That is because other times are very much like other places. I am located in Sydney not Antarctica. Still, Antarctica exists even though I am not *there*. It's a perfectly real place, and in principle, I could travel there. Likewise, other times exist, it is just that they are not located *here* and *now*, and at least in principle I could travel to those past/future places.

If the future exists in spacetime, however, then it is already true, *here and now*, that the future is some particular way. For instance, it is already a fact that in, say, 2015, Jennifer will buy a red Chevy. If that is right, you might worry that whether or not Jennifer knows about the red Chevy purchase, if it's *already true* that she will buy the Chevy, and that *in itself* undermines her freedom with respect to Chevy-buying or not buying. That's because whether she knows it or not, Jennifer is going to buy the Chevy, and so it might seem that she is not free to *not* buy the Chevy. So it goes for everything else non-car related.

I think this reasoning is mistaken. What does it take for us to be free? I think we are free, if, roughly speaking, we make decisions on the basis of our reasons, and we are able to act on those decisions in an unfettered way. This characterization of free will is deliberately broad. It is consistent with a quite weak *compatibilist* conception of free will. According to that view, each of us is free if we are able to act in such a way as to satisfy our various desires. On that view, if in 1980 Marty buys a red Bentley, he does so freely if he desires a red Bentley rather than, say, a red car, and if he considers his various reasons for preferring the Bentley to the car, and these reasons inform his choice to get the Bentley, and no one is manipulating Marty by, say, putting electrodes in his brain, or forcing him to choose the Bentley by holding him at gun point or kidnapping his dog.

This compatibilist view of free will is consistent with the future being *determined*. The future is determined if there is only one possible way the future can unfold, given the way things are in the present and given the laws of nature. The characterization of free will I offered is also consistent with a stronger notion of free will, that is inconsistent with the future being determined. On that view, in order to count as deciding on the basis of your own reasons, there must be multiple ways the future could unfold, such that your reasons lead to your choices, which bring it about that the future unfolds one way rather than another. This is a *libertarian* view of free will. On either view, compatibilist or libertarian, what is crucial is that freedom is a function of acting on one's own reasons without manipulation or force.

So what of Jennifer and *her* car buying in the future? Let's suppose that future Jennifer deliberates about what kind of car to buy. She takes into consideration a range of factors; she thinks carefully, then she heads to the Chevy dealership and buys the car. It looks as though Jennifer's buying of the car is free in the same way that Marty's is. The mere fact that the event of her buying the Chevy exists in the future does not in itself mean that she does not act freely.

At this point, you might think that this is only so if we endorse a compatibilist view of free will. If we endorse a libertarian view, you might think that Jennifer cannot act on her own reasons, because in fact there are not multiple ways the future can unfold. There is only one way the future can unfold, which is the way in which Jennifer buys the Chevy. After all, that way is already out there in spacetime! But that is not true. There is an important difference between its being the case that the future *in fact* unfolds one way rather than another, and its being the case that there is only one way the future *can* unfold. In Jennifer's case, the future in fact unfolds in such a way that she ends up buying the Chevy. But that does not mean the future was determined: that there was only one way it *could have gone*. It just means that it did, in fact, go that particular way.

One way to see why this is, is to notice that the reason that the future event of Jennifer buying the Chevy exists, is that Jennifer deliberated about whether to get a car, what to get, and so on, and that she made the decision she did. Had Jennifer decided to get no car, or instead to get a Honda, or a Bentley, then the future would be different. The future is the way it is, in part *because* of Jennifer's reasons and deliberations. The reason it contains her buying a Chevy is that *this* is what she decided to do.

The moral of this is that there can be a fact of the matter about what Jennifer will do, vis-à-vis car buying, and yet it still be the case that she does that thing freely, and that's because what explains why in the future she buys the Chevy, is that she deliberates about which car to buy, and then buys what she decides she wants. So, regardless of whether you endorse a compatibilist view of free will or a libertarian one, there is no general problem for free will posed by the fact that the future exists. That is because the future exists as it does, *because* of the decisions we make.

Still, it does seem (once Jennifer *knows* what she is going to do in the future) that she cannot deliberate about what to do, and so she lacks *deliberative* freedom. Once Jennifer comes to know that she will buy the Chevy, she cannot deliberate about whether or not to buy it, because she cannot suppose that buying and not buying the Chevy are both genuine options open to her. And that *does* seem to undermine Jennifer's deliberative freedom.

I will argue, however, that the claim that we cannot deliberate about whether to P if we know that we will P is mistaken. I say that it must be mistaken, because there is a whole range of ordinary cases in which we do know that we will P, and we can make good sense of deliberating about whether to P. Given this, even if Jennifer were to learn what will happen in the future, it would not follow that she can no longer deliberate, and so it would not mean that she lacks deliberative freedom.

Deliberation and Knowledge of the Future

Suppose that when Marty appears in Jennifer's kitchen in 1985 after having traveled forward to the future, and then back again, he is able to tell Jennifer *everything* about what she is going to do for the next week. Let's suppose she learns, among other things, that she will buy a house in Hilldale on Tuesday. Let's suppose that learning this is quite surprising, because she never contemplated buying a house in Hilldale. Let's also suppose that having learned this, she does not deliberate about *whether* to buy the house. She knows she is going to, so when Tuesday rolls around, she just buys a house in Hilldale.

Something about this story should make you very uneasy. Jennifer's agency appears to be seriously impaired. Because she does not deliberate about whether to buy the house, she does not know *why* she bought the house. She cannot appeal to her various reasons for buying the house, since she has no such reasons. Not only can she not explain to others why she bought the house, she cannot explain it to herself. We all create narratives of our lives, which explain how who we are now is informed by what came previously, and how what will come later is informed by what is the case now. We try to make sense of our lives. We tie our various decisions and actions together within some broader context and narrative. Jennifer will be unable to do that with *any* of the things that she does in the next week, including buying the house. She will have no sense of *why* she does what she does, and there will be no coherent narrative within which she can fit those decisions. Her sense of who she is and why she does what she does will be almost entirely absent. This represents a significant way in which her agency will be impacted.

What this case tells us, I think, is that deliberation is required for a certain sort of freedom, namely deliberative freedom. And a lack of deliberation therefore results in a lack of this kind of freedom. So I accept that deliberation is necessary for deliberative freedom. And in this case, since there is no deliberation, there is no deliberative freedom. What I will argue, however, is that the fact that one knows what one will do, does not mean that one *cannot* deliberate about what to do. Hence, knowing the future *need not* undermine deliberative freedom, because we can still deliberate about what to do even when we know what we will do. Why think we can deliberate even if we know what we will do? I say we *can*, because we *do*.

We are all pretty good at predicting not just what *others* will do, but also what *we* will do. In order to figure out what other people will do, we take a *predictive stance*. We look at what they have done in the past under similar circumstances, what their motivations are, what they believe and desire, and so on, and then we predict their actions. Of course, sometimes we do a terrible job at this. But often we are very good at it. And we can, and do, take that same stance on ourselves.

Suppose that you have had oats for breakfast every day of the week for the last 20 years, and suppose you are generally a creature of habit. Suppose also that I ask you what you will have for breakfast tomorrow. You might answer that question by *deciding* what to have. Or you might answer it by taking the predictive stance on yourself. You might look at your totality of behavior, beliefs, and motivations, and use that information to predict that you will have oats for breakfast tomorrow. In either case, you might be extremely confident when you tell me that you will have oats tomorrow. In fact, in both cases, it looks as though what you say should count as *knowledge*. You will, in fact, have oats tomorrow. You believe that you will have oats tomorrow, and you are justified in believing that you will have oats tomorrow. So, in both cases, you know that you will have oats tomorrow. In one case, you have knowledge on the basis of forming an intention to eat oats, and in the other, you have it on the basis of predicting what you will do.

It is not unusual for people to take this predictive stance on themselves. Suppose you want to decide whether to go to the gym regularly. To make that decision, you might simply deliberate about the benefits of going, and then form an *intention* to go. Alternatively, you might shift to taking the predictive stance in order to predict whether you are *likely* to go to the gym each morning. You might look at your previous exercise routines and how successful they have been; how good you are at getting up early; how often you keep your commitments, and so on. You might then predict whether you will go to the gym.

This is a case in which there are two different stances we can take. We can take the deliberative stance, and deliberate about whether to go to the gym, and on that basis, we can form an *intention* to go to the gym, or we can take the predictive stance, and predict *whether we will in fact* go to the gym.

Not only can we take both stances, but we can shift between them pretty seamlessly. The alcoholic can deliberate about whether to stop drinking and can form the intention to stop. She can also shift perspective and make a prediction about whether she will stop drinking, given everything she knows about her own drinking patterns, about alcoholism in general, and so on. So it goes for many things. The fact that the alcoholic can take the predictive stance regarding her quitting drinking, and the potential gym-goer can take the predictive stance regarding gym attendance, does not undermine them *also* being able to take the deliberative stance in deliberating about whether to do those things.

The potential gym goer can predict that she is unlikely to manage gym attendance. On the basis of this prediction, the potential gym goer can come to *know* that she will not attend the gym. She can know this, because she can come to believe that she will not attend the gym (on the basis of her prediction) and that belief can be true (if she will in fact not attend the gym) and her belief can be justified on the basis of her reliability at such predictions. Yet, despite the fact that from within the predictive stance she knows she will not go to the gym regularly, this does not prevent her from entering the deliberative stance in which she deliberates about whether to go to the gym or not.

What we cannot do is *simultaneously* occupy two stances. We cannot both deliberate about whether to P, at the same time we hold fixed that we will P and hence take it that not P is not a genuine option. What we can do, however, is occupy different stances at different times. We can shift stances from the predictive stance to the deliberative stance and *vice versa*. We can occupy a predictive stance, in which we know that we will P, and later occupy a deliberative stance in which we deliberate about whether to P.

In the predictive stance, we can know that we will P (not go to the gym, not stop drinking) and yet when we enter the deliberative stance, we can deliberate about *whether* to P. That is because what it is to enter the deliberative stance is to take as genuine, the option of both P and not P. In the deliberative stance, the potential gym goer must take it that there is a genuine option of both going and not going to the gym, just as the alcoholic must take there to be a genuine option of both stopping and not stopping drinking.

So, suppose that when Marty returns from the future to 1985, he tells Jennifer that shortly, he and she will jointly travel to 2015. He knows this because he has *already seen both* of them in 2015. Now, it seems, Jennifer is no longer in a position to deliberate about whether to get into the time machine, since she already knows that she is going to get into the machine and travel forward to 2015. Marty's knowledge of her future seems to be getting in the way of her deliberative freedom. I've suggested that this knowledge need not undermine Jennifer's deliberative freedom. To be sure, when taking the predictive stance on herself, she can (and should) *predict* that she will get into the machine. That, however, does not prevent her from also taking the deliberative stance and *deliberating* about whether to get into the machine.

How so? How can Jennifer take the deliberative stance in which she takes it to be a genuine option *whether* to get into the time machine and travel to 2015, if she already knows, via the predictive stance, that she will get into the machine? Does she need to momentarily forget that she gets into the machine? Does she need to be irrational and cease to believe that she will get into the machine?

I think the best way to understand our ability to shift stances is to acknowledge that creatures like us have not entirely unified selves. We have various aspects of our mental functioning that function separately from one another. It is this disunity of self that allows us to shift perspectives. One aspect of self can take the deliberative stance, and another the predictive stance. One aspect of self can be predicating what the self will do, and another can be forming intentions about what it will do. Shifting between these stances is then shifting between which of these selves is active; which is in control; which is brought to conscious awareness. Therefore, to say that we cannot take both stances at the same time is to say that both aspects of self cannot be active, in control, and conscious at the same time.

This means that Jennifer can deliberate about whether to get into the time machine, because she can make it the case that the part of her that forms intentions is in control and brought to conscious awareness. When that part of her is at the forefront, she can deliberate about whether to travel to 2015.

Back to Jennifer

With all of this in mind, what does this tell us about Jennifer and Doc as they actually feature in *Part II*? Well, maybe Doc is right, and there is *some* reason to try and make sure that Jennifer does not learn too much about the future. If Jennifer were to learn a good deal about 2015 as part of her time travel exploits, her deliberative freedom *could* be undermined. It would be undermined if, upon learning about choices she makes in 2015, she became unable to shift stances and to move from the predictive stance to the deliberative stance. And of course, the more Jennifer learns, the more such shifting is required, and the greater the threat to her deliberative freedom. However, I have argued that the mere fact that Jennifer learns about her future choices need not undermine her deliberative freedom, because if Jennifer is like most of us, she *can* shift to the deliberative stance from the predictive stance, and so long as she can do that, her deliberative freedom is not undermined. As such, I say, Doc did not give Jennifer enough credit when he incapacitated her upon her arrival in 2015.

Was Marty Just Dreaming?

DAVID KYLE JOHNSON

At the end of *Back to the Future*, Marty wakes to his alarm clock playing "Back in Time" by Huey Lewis and the News. We are briefly led to consider the possibility that the entire adventure we just witnessed was a dream (or, as Marty puts it, "a nightmare"). And with its references to the '50s, playing guitar, and lightning never striking twice, Marty's mere familiarity with the song could've shaped his entire dream. It's worth noting, Marty comes to this sort of conclusion regularly. He suspects he's dreaming when he wakes up in his mother's bed in 1955, when he wakes on the 27th floor of Biff's casino/hotel in *Part II*, and when he wakes on the McFly farm in 1885 in *Part III*.

At the end of the first film, his subsequent experiences are supposed to make him (and us) conclude differently. For example, Marty seeing the differences in his family lead him to believe that he did actually travel through time, and Doc's arrival in the DeLorean seems to seal the deal. But, of course, he *could* still be dreaming. Maybe, like in the film *Inception*, he awoke from one dream into another. Might the idea that he is dreaming actually be a better interpretation of what he's experiencing? Might it even be a better interpretation of the movie? To answer these questions, we'll need to dig into some pretty "heavy" philosophical considerations that have nothing to do with Earth's gravitational pull.

Can You Prove That You're Not Dreaming?

The worry expressed in the title of this section was made most famous by the philosopher René Descartes (1596–1650). In his *Meditations*, he was seeking a foundation for knowledge—a kind of unshakable belief that could serve as the groundwork for his investigations into all matters, like the nature of the physical world. If he could find some belief that was indubitable (i.e., a belief that cannot be doubted), perhaps he could reason from that belief to others, and from *those* beliefs to others, until he ultimately could come to know what was true about the world through something like the scientific method.

He thus began to consider each of his beliefs to see if there was any room for doubt, any possible way that they could (even despite appearances) turn out to be false. He initially thinks that the fact that he is awake and experiencing the outside world is an indubitable belief. For Descartes, as he writes, he believes that he is sitting by his fireplace in his dressing gown, but then he remembers he's had dreams in which he was equally convinced that he was awake. "It certainly seems that I am awake," Descartes realized (I'm paraphrasing), "but since I have experienced that assured sensation while actually dreaming, the fact that it seems that I am awake is no guarantee that I *am* actually awake." And he can't prove he's awake simply by having someone pinch him, as Marty tries to do in a scene cut from the first film (the conservative woman he asks slaps Marty instead). Since one could dream the experience of being pinched but not waking up, it essentially proves nothing. But the fact that he cannot prove he is awake, Descartes reasons, threatens his ability to know anything at all. His belief that the world exists would seem to be the kind of foundational belief he is looking for; but if he can't even know *that* (because he can't prove he is not dreaming), what could he possibly know?

Unfortunately, in the eyes of some (e.g., scientists such as Neil deGrasse Tyson or [formerly] Billy Nye), considering these kinds of "can you really know the world is real" problems are all philosophy is[1]; one wonders what Doc Brown would have to say about the issue. Nevertheless, in making such statements, such people (a) are unaware of the history of philosophy, which served as the parent of every other academic discipline (especially science), (b) are not considering the myriad of other philosophical problems that philosophers deal with (like ethical problems, questions of religion, and the hard problem of consciousness), and (c) misunderstand the point of such "am I dreaming" arguments, both in their original context and how they are used by philosophers today.

For example, Descartes was not arguing that he was in fact dreaming; he didn't think that he was. He was simply worried that not being able to *prove* that he *wasn't* dreaming prevented him from having knowledge. Interestingly, he actually thought he could solve the problem; "I am, I exist" Descartes reasoned, "is not something I can doubt, because in the very act of doubting it, I prove that it is true." In other words, you can't doubt that you exist, unless you in fact exist. This, most philosophers agree, is right. The fact of our own existence is something that each of us can know for certain.

Granted, most philosophers are more skeptical of Descartes' attempt to reason from this little bit of knowledge to certainty about the outside world. Because Descartes thought he couldn't have invented the idea of God himself, Descartes thought that the fact that he had an idea of God entailed that God must exist. And since God wouldn't allow him to be the victim of a grand deception, Descartes concluded, the world must exist. The flaws in this argument include (among other things) (a) the fact that Descartes *could* have (like Doc Brown with the flux capacitor) just come up with the idea of God himself, and (b) the fact that Descartes' belief that God wouldn't deceive him is just an ungrounded assumption (or, more precisely, based in the ungrounded assumption that deception is always an imperfection).

That said, many philosophers today, including myself, use Descartes' dream problem in a different way. The lesson is not the realization that one *can* know for sure that one exists; the lesson is found in realizing the mistake Descartes made when he conceptualized what knowledge required. Descartes thought he couldn't know the world exists because he couldn't be *certain* that it did (because he couldn't be certain that he wasn't dreaming). But knowledge doesn't require *certainty*; if it did, we wouldn't know almost anything that we think (indeed, that we know) we do. In fact, the claim is nonsensical. Anyone who claimed to know that knowledge required certainty could never be certain that this was true and thus could not know it. Knowledge simply requires *justification*, and since a belief can be justified without being certain, we can know things without being certain. As one of my favorite philosophers, Ted Schick, puts it:

> If knowledge requires certainty ... there is little that we know, for precious few propositions are absolutely indubitable ... that you are reading a book right now ... [t]hat the Earth is inhabited, that cows produce milk, that water freezes at 32 degrees Fahrenheit, and so on are propositions we would ordinarily claim to know, yet none of them are absolutely certain. [But] if knowledge doesn't require certainty, how much evidence [justification] does it require? ... [E]nough to put it beyond any *reasonable* doubt.... To have knowledge, then, we must have adequate evidence, and our evidence is adequate when it puts the propositions in question beyond a reasonable doubt.[2]

Of course, the next question is obvious: when is something beyond a reasonable doubt? Schick's answer is equally obvious. "A proposition is beyond a reasonable doubt when it provides the best explanation of something ... it [need not] possess any particular degree of probability ... all that is required is that it explain the evidence and account for it better than any of its competitors."[3] Schick goes on to explain what it takes for a hypothesis to be better than others; that is the main point of his book from which I am pulling these quotes. He teaches us that the best explanation is the one that most adheres to the criteria of adequacy:

Testability: making observable predictions.
Fruitfulness: getting those predictions correct (and thus opening up new lines of research).
Scope (explanatory power): explaining much and not raising unanswerable questions.
Simplicity/parsimony: making fewer assumptions and requiring fewer (previously) unknown entities.
Conservatism: not contradicting that which is already well established.

And it is in this way that Schick and others like him solve Descartes' dream problem. Although none of us can be certain that we are not dreaming right now, that we *are* is not the best explanation for the evidence of our experience. That we are awake, and that the world generally is as it seems, is the better explanation. And thus, we can know this is true.

Why exactly is the hypothesis that I am awake the better explanation? Testability and fruitfulness will not help us here, because the vivid dream and awake hypotheses make essentially the same predictions about what I would observe: a sensory world and the feeling that I am awake. But the hypothesis that I am awake has a much wider scope. If the world is real, I have a pretty good understanding of how I experience it, and why I am experiencing what I am experiencing; but if I am just dreaming, I have no idea why I am experiencing what I am experiencing, or how I am experiencing it (especially for so long). The awake hypothesis also better aligns with our well-established beliefs, and is simpler in that it doesn't require the existence of a seemingly permanent dream.

In summary: knowledge doesn't require certainty; only justification. And I am justified in believing something when it is beyond a reasonable doubt. And it is beyond a reasonable doubt that I am awake right now because that is the better (more adequate) explanation for the evidence of my experience. It follows, therefore, that I can be justified in believing, and thus can know, that I am not dreaming right now—*ipso facto*, the dream problem is solved.

Should Marty Conclude He Is Dreaming?

At the end of the first film, is Marty justified in believing that he is awake and not still dreaming? The answer will depend on whether the waking hypothesis is the best explanation for his experiences. At first glance, it might seem that it is. Just like with us, the hypothesis that he is awake would seem to be the more adequate explanation for what he is experiencing. But a closer examination will reveal that this is not the case. The key to understanding why lies in understanding the criterion of conservatism and the logistics of time travel.

Recall that a hypothesis is conservative if it aligns with what we already have very good reason to believe; if it does conflict with well-established beliefs, a hypothesis is not conservative and is thus much less likely. And this is not a coincidence; by that I mean, the criteria of adequacy are not arbitrary; they were not chosen at random. They are what a good explanation must be and do, by definition; that is why they are the criteria by which one finds the best explanation. For example, of course a good explanation must have explanatory power; explaining things is the whole point of being an explanation. The simplest hypothesis is also most likely right, not only because in the past the simplest hypothesis has usually turned out to be right, but because the more assumptions a hypothesis makes, the more chances it has (and thus the more likely it is) to be wrong. And a hypothesis needs to be conservative—it needs to align with what is already well established—because, if it isn't, the preponderance of evidence for the well-established beliefs it conflicts with will be evidence against it; and if there is already a significant amount of evidence against a hypothesis, that makes it much less likely to be true.

Consider a vivid childhood memory of mine: a 1989 behind-the-scenes special, hosted by Leslie Nielsen, about *Part II* aired on NBC. At the end, the hoverboard scene is previewed, and director Robert Zemeckis describes the hoverboard as "a board that hovers on magnetic energy [that] works just like a skateboard except it doesn't have any wheels and you don't have to have any pavement to hover on it." He then goes on to claim that "they've been around for years; it's just that parents' groups have not let the toy manufacturers make them, and we got our hands on some and put them in the movie." My 12-year-old brain exploded. Indeed, my friends and I all believed him and eagerly awaited their inevitable release, given the popularity of the movie. But, if I had been a critical thinker back then, I would've realized that all of my experience was evidence that nothing, including magnets, floats unassisted over all surfaces; thus, the more likely conclusion was that he was joking. In other words, that hoverboards are real is not a conservative hypothesis, because it conflicts with a whole host of evidence that grounds my background beliefs and thus is most likely false.

When it comes to Marty, and whether he is dreaming (or even still dreaming at the end of the film), something similar is true. Yes, that he is dreaming raises some difficult questions, but it is not impossible. However, that he is awake (and thus that he traveled in time and changed the past) is impossible; in fact, it is logically impossible; it entails contradictions. And not only does Marty have good reason to believe that contradictions can't be true, he *knows* that they can't be true. The law of non-contradiction—which states that no proposition can be both true and false—is the groundwork of all logic, and logic is the groundwork of all knowledge. Therefore, all experience counts as evidence against it, and to believe that even a single contradiction is true, Marty would have to reject all other knowledge that he possesses. That is about as unconservative as a hypothesis can get.

Now, why is what Marty experienced logically impossible? The logic of time travel is covered elsewhere in this volume, but why the story of *Back to the Future* (whether it be just the first movie or the entire saga) is logically contradictory is straightforward: it invokes the grandfather paradox. The ability to travel in time and change the past would entail the ability to kill your grandfather (before he sired your father), thus preventing your own birth. But, of course, if you are not born, you can't prevent your birth, so you are born. But if you are born, you can travel in time and kill your grandfather, so you are not born. You are born, and you are not born. Paradox! Or to put it in the language of *Back to the Future*: if you can travel in time and change the past, you could keep your parents from meeting; but if so, you would never have existed; but if you never exist, you can't prevent them from meeting, so they will meet, and thus you will exist, so you will prevent them meeting, so you won't. If you can change the past, you can both exist and not exist. Paradox!

As I've pointed out elsewhere,[4] the only way to tell a logically consistent time travel story is by either (a) invoking parallel timelines where traveling to the past is actually just creating an alternative universe where things go differently (à la *Star Trek*'s [2009] "Kelvin" timeline) or (b) invoking what is known as "Lewisian" static time travel where, when someone travels to the past, they would find that no change was possible and that they were only able to cause what already happened; (à la *Indiana Jones and the Dial of Destiny*). Clearly, *Back to the Future* does not invoke the latter. If it did, it would have been a story in which Marty travels to the past and causes his parents to meet in exactly the same way that they always had; when he returns to 1985, he would realize nothing had changed. The movie would start with his parents telling a story about how a guy named Marty introduced them, and then we would later find out that "Marty" was him.

Back to the Future (especially *Part II* and *III*) tries to suggest that it is invoking the parallel timelines version of time travel, but clearly it does not. In "parallel" time travel, if someone goes back in time to kill their grandfather they can in no way endanger their own existence. Why? Because the person they are able to kill is not their grandfather; it is a copy (a doppelganger) of their grandfather in an alternate universe; their actual biological grandfather (the person responsible for their existence) is safe and sound in the past of their original timeline. By killing the copy of their grandfather in this timeline, they would prevent the birth of someone that looks like them in this new timeline; but they would not prevent their own birth (which occurred, and is safe and sound, in their original timeline). Thus, the whole detail of Marty and his siblings slowly fading out of existence (as his parents are less and less likely to get married) makes no sense on the parallel time travel view (or the Lewisian static view for that matter). So, as it is told, the story is logically contradictory; as such, it is logically impossible and cannot happen.

Of course, I'm not saying that any of this makes *Back to the Future* a bad movie; it doesn't (more on that in a moment). My point is simply this: at the end of the first movie, Marty has two choices: either (a) my adventure to the past was a dream, and I am still dreaming or (b) I was and am still awake. The former is not simple or wide scoping, but the latter entails that something logically impossible occurred. Since he not only believes, but knows, that logical impossibilities cannot occur, the better explanation for Marty to accept (by quite a large margin) is that he was and is still dreaming. And it will continue to be, regardless of how long the dream lasts.

Was Marty Really Dreaming?

But the fact that Marty would be most justified in concluding that he is dreaming doesn't mean that he was. If he were a real person, it would—because in the real world, logical contradictions can't be true. But we are dealing with a movie here. Whether, in the story, the character Marty is still dreaming has less to do with logic and more to do with how to interpret the film.

On the one hand, we might say that whether Marty is dreaming is just determined by the intentions of the film's creators, Bob Gale and Robert Zemeckis. And I think it's pretty clear that they did not make a movie which they intended to be thought of as one long dream. But this view, known as "authorial intentionalism," is fraught with problems. It makes the meaning of an artwork static, immune to context and cultural changes, and seems to violate the very nature of art (which is something that is presented by an artist to the public for interpretation). Ruth Tallman lays out the problems with this view nicely in the first chapter of my book *Inception and Philosophy*,[5] but I can sum them up pretty quickly: The fact that J.R.R. Tolkien didn't intend for *The Lord of the Rings* to have any deeper meaning doesn't entail that it doesn't have one.

On the other hand, we might say that we should use the principle of charity and interpret the movie in whatever way makes it a better movie. This is why Jason Southworth argued that all of the movie *Inception* (and not just the ending) is a dream.[6] If it's not, it's kind of a bad movie; all the characters are one-dimensional; they don't even have last names. But if it's all a dream, all the characters are one dimensional because they are elements of Cobb's subconscious, and that is kind of brilliant. But I don't think interpreting *Back to the Future* this way makes it a better movie. *Inception* is a rare exception; usually movies aren't that great if we find out "it was all just a dream" in the end.

I think that is true, even though, as told, the story of *Back to the Future* is logically contradictory. Don't get me wrong, I really like movies that have logically consistent time travel, like *Interstellar*, and I would like them less if they didn't. But a logically inconsistent time travel story can still be a *good story*.[7] So, while I think *Back to the Future* might have been better had it managed to be logically consistent, I still think a logically inconsistent *Back to the Future* is better than a *Back to the Future* that is just a dream (and thus doesn't contain any actual time travel at all). That's just not all that interesting.

Waking Up to Reality

So we can know that we are not dreaming; that we are awake provides the best explanation for our experience. The character of Marty McFly, however, should conclude that he is and was dreaming because the fact that he is awake (and thus that he actually, literally, experienced his time travel adventures) would entail that his time travel adventures occurred—and that is logically impossible. The story, as told, is logically inconsistent. But that doesn't mean that we must conclude that Marty is dreaming; not only do the film's creators not believe that is the case, but the better interpretation of the film is that he is not dreaming. Granted, if it contained logically consistent time travel, it would be a better film, but a *Back to the Future* film with logically inconsistent time travel is better than one with no time travel at all.

Notes

1. I was fortunate enough to actually help dissuade Bill Nye of this misunderstanding. After writing an open letter to him, I was lucky enough to meet him firsthand and discuss the issue. Later in an email exchange, after diving into my course (for the Great Courses) "Exploring Metaphysics," he said he had changed his mind. See Johnson, David Kyle. 2025. "A Friendly Open Letter to Bill Nye (About Philosophy)." *Psychology Today*."

2. Schick, Theodore; Vaughn, Lewis. 2024. *How to Think About Weird Things*, 9th Edition. McGraw Hill. 78–79.

3. *Ibid.*, 79.

4. Johnson, David Kyle. 2022. "The Time Travel in Avengers: Endgame" in William Irwin and David Kyle Johnson (eds.). *Introducing Philosophy Through Pop Culture*. 2nd Edition. Wiley-Blackwell. 136–144.

5. Tallman, Ruth. 2012. "Was It All a Dream? Why Nolan's Answer Doesn't Matter" in David Kyle Johnson (ed.). *Inception and Philosophy: Because It's Never Just a Dream*. Wiley-Blackwell. 17–30.

6. Southworth, Jason. 2012. "Let Me Put My Thoughts in You: It Was All Just a Dream" in David Kyle Johnson (ed.). *Inception and Philosophy: Because It's Never Just a Dream*. Wiley-Blackwell. 31–45.

7. Johnson, David Kyle. 2021. "Making Sense of Time Travel in The Orville" in David Kyle Johnson and Michael Berry (eds.). *Exploring* The Orville: *Essays on Seth MacFarlane's Space Adventure*. McFarland. 261–272.

III

Right and Wrong Across Time (and Space)

Quit Hitting Yourself!

Daniel Malloy

Time travel presents a range of possible unique experiences, including the possibility of ending your own existence before you're even born or meeting your past or future self. Marty McFly and Doc Brown are careful to avoid this, with more or less success. Biff, on the other hand, travels to the past precisely in order to meet himself, giving his younger self a copy of *Grays Sports Almanac,* which changes young Biff's future—possibly wiping out old Biff in the process.

There are many metaphysical problems posed by this, but time travel also represents an opportunity to explore an ethical problem. When old Biff travels back to 1955, he does more than give his younger self the sports almanac and instructions on how to use it. Biff, being Biff, also bullies his younger self, calling him a butthead and berating him for getting the "make like a tree" quip wrong.

This presents the opportunity to explore a confounding problem in ethics: the problem of duties to yourself. Simply put, this is the problem of figuring out whether you can have an obligation that you owe to yourself. Viewed from another angle, young Biff makes old Biff the implicit promise that he'll use the almanac as instructed. But since this is a promise he made to himself, he can release himself from it anytime he wants, so it would seem that his promise is not at all binding.

You Sound Like a Damn Fool!

Duties to yourself might seem like a no-brainer. For some time, the consensus was that of course you have duties to yourself. Taking care of yourself, striving to live the best life you can, isn't just good sense; it's a moral imperative. To do things that harm yourself isn't simply foolish or imprudent; it's morally wrong. Put it this way, when Marty is trying to get his parents together in 1955, he isn't just doing what was right for his parents and siblings but also for himself. If Marty's parents don't get together, he will be erased from existence, so failing in his mission would have been an odd sort of indirect suicide.

The agreement around duties to yourself fell apart a bit when the philosopher Marcus Singer pointed out that there's something strange about the idea. Singer noted that promises to one's self could never be binding. The problem—since called the paradox of self-release—is that when you make a promise, you give the promisee (the person you make the promise to) the ability to relieve you of the obligation by releasing you from the promise. If Marty promises Doc that he'll feed Einstein, Doc can simply erase Marty's obligation by telling him not to worry about it because he's made other arrangements. Note that Doc, as the promisee, has this ability. Marty can't release *himself* from the promise he's made. As the promiser, releasing himself would be no different than breaking the promise.

But when you promise *yourself* something, you're both the promiser *and* the promisee, so you have the ability to release yourself from your promise at will. If Marty promises himself that he'll practice the guitar an hour a day, and then one day he just doesn't feel motivated, he can simply release himself from his promise. Thus, a promise to yourself seems to have no real binding power, since there's no real difference between releasing yourself from the promise and just deciding not to fulfill it.

Similar reasoning relieves you of all supposed duties to yourself. If Marty only has a duty to pursue his best life if he *wants* to pursue his best life, then he has no such duty. Take Marty's dreams of being a musician. Jennifer might try to encourage him to pursue that dream by saying something like "You owe it to yourself." But, if that's true at all, it only holds as long as he wants to be a musician. If he changes his mind or finds a different dream, he no longer has any duty to pursue his music. Even if he still wants to be a musician, the worst he's done is show that he doesn't have resolve. That may not speak well of his character, but it's not the same as violating a duty.

The paradox of self-release is what makes Biff's case so interesting. If there are duties to yourself, young Biff and old Biff would have duties to one another that either could release them from at will. For example, when old Biff meets his younger self, he hits him with his cane. To strike another person is morally wrong, so old Biff has done something morally wrong. Except old Biff didn't strike another person; he struck his younger self. Therefore, old Biff must have given himself permission to strike his younger self, releasing himself from his duty to refrain from physical assault. He no more assaulted his younger self than I do when I slap myself on the forehead. There is a difference, of course. When I slap myself on the forehead, I feel it. When old Biff slaps his younger self, he presumably doesn't feel anything. At most, he *might* remember being slapped, but that leads us into grandfather paradox territory, so set it aside. Whether old Biff does or doesn't feel young Biff's pain is irrelevant if they're the same person. Provided that, old Biff can give himself permission to hit himself.

From the other side, consider Doc's decision to send Marty back from 1955 to 1885 in spite of the explicit instructions from *himself* that Marty is to return to 1985 and destroy the time machine. You could argue that Doc had a duty to respect his own wishes, but he knew something that his older self didn't: namely, that without Marty's help, his older self would be dead within a week of sending his telegram to Marty in 1955, shot in the back by Buford "Mad Dog" Tannen. In light of that information, he revised his desires and ignored his own instructions. Thus, he didn't wrong himself. In fact, if not for the paradox of self-release, you could argue that he'd lived up to a duty he owed himself by keeping himself alive.

"Who you calling butthead, butthead?!"

One attempt to solve the paradox of self-release is perfectly illustrated by Biff's meeting with himself. Called the second-person defense, this view derives partly from philosopher Stephen Darwall's book *The Second-Person Standpoint* and has been developed largely by Paul Schofield. It argues that you should treat your future self as though they were a different person. As such, you have an obligation to treat your future self the same way that you would treat any other person.

Before reconsidering the meeting of the Biffs, consider *George's* decisions and how they affect his future self. Think of how different his lives in 1985 are because of a single decision he made in 1955. In the original timeline, where George never stood up to Biff, he's stuck in an unfulfilling job, still being bullied by Biff. He's still doing Biff's work for him, groveling to Biff so much that when Biff crashes George's car while drinking, Biff blames George for it. And George takes it and apologizes to Biff for the fact that *Biff* crashed *his* car! Perhaps he even still writes stories that he's too afraid to show anyone, or maybe he's given up that dream altogether.

After Marty's adventure in 1955, George is a successful author, happy, fulfilled, and his one-time bully is now more of a lackey. George and Lorraine have gone from being a somewhat miserable couple to a pair of pitch-perfect Reaganite yuppies. Now imagine you had a single choice that you knew would improve someone else's life that dramatically at little or no cost to you or anyone else. With just one decision, you could take someone living a fairly miserable existence to having a happy and fulfilling life.

It's not hard to say that it would be wrong not to do that for anyone, let alone yourself.

The meeting between young and old Biff illustrates this idea nicely. Neither treats the other the way you should treat anyone. Young Biff is dismissive and curt, threatening to kill his older self if he dents his car. Old Biff is obnoxious and bullying, calling him a damn fool and slapping him on the head. According to the second-person defense, they are distinct people, and so they don't have the sort of automatic self-release that poses such a problem for the idea of duties to yourself. Therefore, in acting the way they do to each other, young Biff and old Biff wrong one another. The fact that they happen to be the same person at different points in time is an accidental consideration of no moral relevance.

How Could I Have Been So Stupid?!

While the second-person defense seems to solve the paradox of self-release, that doesn't mean it's problem-free. Oddly enough, the same thing that solves the paradox of self-release creates its main problem: what's known as the non-identity problem. Largely associated with philosopher Derek Parfit, the non-identity problem is about the identity of future people. The contention is, in essence, that you can't have any obligations to any future people because your actions now determine whether those exact people will exist at all.

This problem hits closer to home in regard to duties to yourself. The choices you make every day don't just decide what life you'll lead in the future. They decide what person you will be. You can't have duties to every possible version of your future self. Among other problems, that would lead to *conflicting* duties. For example, Marty's interference in 1955, and everything that happens as a result, means that the George McFly that Marty grew up with no longer exists. The "new" George is a happy and successful author. Marty in 1955 can either take actions that lead to his familiar, unfulfilled, bullied father, or he can take actions that lead to the "new" George. He can't do both.

Biff is the perfect example of this problem. Young Biff promises old Biff that he'll use the sports almanac to make himself rich. Because of that promise, and because he carries it out, that version of old Biff never comes into existence. In effect, that old Biff never exists, at least not in the same version of reality as the young Biff he gives the almanac to. But if old Biff has never existed and will never exist, then young Biff can't owe any sort of obligation to him. You can make all the promises you want to Santa Claus or the Man in the Moon, because you'll never have to live up to them. If young Biff has a duty to this one possible version of his older self, then he'd have similar duties to every possible version of himself—he'd be equally obligated to his mogul self and to his car-detailing self.

A proponent of the second-person defense might argue that the duties you owe to your future self aren't that specific. They're not duties to just any possible future self. Rather, the duties you owe to your future self are restricted to those you would owe to anyone at all, so young Biff doesn't owe it to old Biff to fulfill his promise. His duty to his older self is limited to making choices that will help him live well and be the sort of person he wants to be (or to at least make choices that won't interfere with those goals).

The trouble with this limitation is that it seems to eliminate the need to call these duties to yourself. To have a duty to yourself that obliges you to make the best choices you can for yourself is redundant. That's just being prudent. To be sure, prudence is a good thing, but it isn't obligatory.

Time Travel Is Too Dangerous!

But maybe there is a way to defend the notion of a duty to yourself by looking at duties you owe to everyone. That's one path taken by the philosopher Immanuel Kant. Kant's ethical theory has inspired the majority of attempts to solve the paradox of self-release. One of the ideas from Kant that is often used to defend duties to yourself is that of universalization. According to Kant, in order for an action to be right, it has to be universalizable. That is, if something is right for Doc or Marty to do, then it is also right for Biff or anyone else to do in similar circumstances. So, if it's right for Marty and Doc to travel through time to correct the timeline, then it's also right for Biff to do so.

Similarly, if it's wrong for Biff to bully George, then it would also be wrong for Marty to do it, and just as wrong when Needles bullies Marty. At its heart, the demand for universality is a demand for consistency. If, when you universalize an action, it becomes impossible to perform, then you shouldn't do that action. For example, suppose everyone, not just Doc and Marty, could time travel. Every human being could go to the past or the future and make whatever changes they wanted. In that case, the timeline would never be stable.

No one would have a "time" to call home. Instead of three versions of Hill Valley in 1985, there'd be as many of them as there were people who wanted to change it, or change anything that had anything to do with it. There would be 1985s where Hill Valley didn't exist at all, where it was the largest city in the world, where there were no McFlys or Tannens or Browns, and where it was populated *entirely* by McFlys or Tannens or

Browns. Time travel therefore contradicts itself, and thus (according to the idea that in order for an action to be morally right, it must be universalizable) no one should travel through time.

That seems to make sense, but can it be applied to how you treat yourself? The reasoning isn't hard to understand: if something is wrong for someone else to do to you, then it's wrong for you to do to yourself as well. If Biff shouldn't bully George, then it follows that Biff shouldn't bully himself either. So, when old Biff meets young Biff and bullies him into doing his bidding, he's wronging himself. Similarly, if it would be wrong of Marty to blow off his meeting with Doc at the Twin Pines Mall, it would be wrong of young Biff not to keep his promise to his older self and use the sports almanac to make himself rich.

Or consider another example. Marty repeatedly goes out of his way to save Doc's life. He gives him a letter in 1955 to warn him about the Libyan terrorists. On his second trip to 1955 (in *Part II* and *III*), he ignores Doc's instructions and goes back to 1885 to rescue him from Mad Dog Tannen. If these actions are both morally right, then it would follow that the times Marty takes actions to save his own life—traveling through time to escape the terrorists, getting his parents together, tricking Mad Dog with his makeshift bulletproof vest—are also morally right.

George Is a Peeping Tom

Unfortunately, the universalization approach doesn't quite solve the paradox of self-release. The reason is easy to see: there are some things that are wrong to do to others without their consent or permission, but perfectly okay to do to them *with* their consent. When Doc uses his alpha rhythm generator to knock out Jennifer and then Marty Jr. without their permission, he wrongs them both. But there'd presumably be nothing wrong with him using it on himself to get a good night's sleep.

Once again, with how you treat yourself, the presumption is always that you've given consent. Your consent may not be your wisest choice, and you may regret it afterward—or even as you're giving it, but it's still implicit in taking the action. So, at least for anything that is permissible if you have consent, the presumption is that you're not violating any duty to yourself by doing it.

So the question now becomes: are there actions that you can't morally give consent to performing on yourself, but can nevertheless take? Consider again the act of bullying. A case can be made that bullying is only bullying when the bullied person doesn't consent to it. George doesn't, so Biff's bullying him is wrong. But Biff may consent to his own bullying of himself. But if he consents to it, then it may not be bullying. Though it plainly is. So that raises the problem of why some actions may not be morally permissible, even when they're consented to. These actions would seem to be the ones where you could have a duty to yourself, without raising the paradox of self-release.

Nobody Calls Me Chicken!

There are things you shouldn't consent to. There are actually a wide variety of them, but they can all be lumped together as things that denigrate or degrade you. This defense once again refers back to Kant, but this time, looking at his notion of dignity. Dignity is a sort of value that some things have. Humans have dignity and therefore deserve respect. Actions that denigrate or degrade you are actions that violate your self-respect. Self-respect is the acknowledgment that you're deserving of respect. Marty displays self-respect by resisting Needles' taunting and not racing him, for example.

But the movies are rife with people who lack self-respect. George won't stand up for himself against Biff. Even when he slugs the bully, he's still not standing up for himself. He's defending Lorraine. Admirable all the same, but this is not the same as demanding acknowledgment of his own dignity.

Biff also utterly lacks self-respect in all of his various incarnations. This may seem strange, given Biff's selfishness and bravado. But young Biff is a high school bully who feels the need for the admiration of his gang of hangers-on and the fear of the people he bullies. The car detailing Biff of 1985 and his older self in 2015 likewise lack self-respect; they just display it by being sniveling toadies who secretly seethe with resentment of the McFly family. Even Biff the mogul from the dystopian 1985, for all his money, can't buy himself even a modicum of self-respect. He is still the same bully he was in high school, depending on other people to validate him, either through their cringing dependency or their fear.

All of these actions and attitudes degrade and denigrate the people who take them. Biff the mogul may not see it, but he's a clown and little more. Instead of valuing himself as a person, he values himself as a bank account and the power and influence over others that brings. He's living the best life of any of the versions of Biff, but he's still entirely dependent on others for what little sense of self-worth he has. Consider his relationship with Lorraine. The two are married, but there's plainly no love or devotion there. And yet, Biff can't stand the thought of her leaving him. Lorraine is a conquest, a trophy to him. For all he desired her in high school, he can't see her as any more than that, because he can't see anyone, including himself, as anything more than a conduit to satisfy his needs and desires. Because he lacks self-respect, Biff is little more than an animal.

Biff's Pleasure Palace

One of the recurring themes for Marty and George is their need for self-confidence. Father and son both have a crippling fear of rejection. Doc, on the other hand, is loaded with self-confidence. Considering where to go on his first time travel jaunt, the Doc chooses a "red letter day for science": the day he first conceived of the flux capacitor. Doc is a genius. Marty's a good guitar player. One version of George is a successful author. These are all good reasons for them to appreciate themselves and for others to esteem them. But they aren't necessary for them to respect themselves, or to demand the respect of others. The only thing necessary for that is for them to have dignity. People have dignity because they are rational beings, which means that they can rule themselves. Rational beings are autonomous beings. And because not everything is autonomous, that makes them special. It grants them the unique value of dignity.

In contrast, consider Doc's dog, Einstein. Doc loves Einstein, Marty loves Einstein, you and I love Einstein. Einstein has value. But Einstein doesn't have dignity. Einstein can't rule himself. Put food in front of Einstein, and Einstein eats. He doesn't weigh pros and cons or consider his ideal weight. If Einstein thought things through, he'd have hesitated at least a little bit before hopping into an untested, nuclear-powered DeLorean.

Biff, although he is a rational being and therefore has both autonomy and dignity, acts more like Einstein than he does like Doc or Marty. Biff isn't a creature of plans; he's a creature of impulses. When he sees the time machine and the sports almanac in 2015, he doesn't for a moment consider the possible ramifications of altering the timeline. He just thinks about what he wants. You might call him selfish, but I'm not even sure it rises to that level. By acting impulsively, Biff denies his own ability to think things through, and his own freedom to act on considered principles rather than just doing whatever seems best at the time. That's why the name of Biff's casino is so fitting: Biff's Pleasure Palace. That's all Biff can see, all he can really think about, is his own pleasure. With all his wealth in that timeline, he still gives little thought to anything beyond his own immediate wants and desires.

Don't Race an Asshole

Biff shouldn't bully people, including himself. When old Biff meets his younger self, he has no more right to strike him and call him names than he does when he treats George the same way. The fact that old Biff and young Biff are the same person at different points in time makes no difference. Biff owes himself, whether in the present, the past, or the future, the same basic respect and consideration that he owes to everyone.

It's because of old Biff's lack of respect for his younger self that young Biff has no obligation to do what his older self says. Young Biff may have at least implicitly promised to carry out old Biff's instructions, but he did so under duress. A promise elicited through coercion and bullying isn't a real promise, regardless of who did the bullying or the promising. Just as young George would be well within his rights to refuse to do Biff's homework, even if he promised to, young Biff would be well within his rights to burn the sports almanac, in spite of any promise.

The importance of self-respect and the ways that it guides and limits your actions, even toward yourself, is the ultimate lesson that Marty learns from his time-traveling adventures. He nearly dies, repeatedly, and nearly ruins his life, because of his inability to accept that he is in ultimate control of his actions. That he is the only person responsible for, or to, himself is the insight that leads him, finally, to brush off Mad Dog Tannen and Needles, to live his own life, his own way. Who knows? Maybe Marty will make it as a rock star in this timeline. Or maybe he'll follow in the footsteps of the series' only explicit advocate for self-respect, young Goldie Wilson, and become mayor of Hill Valley.

On Keeping People in the Dark About the Future

Don Fallis

Time travel can cause serious problems. For example, in Ray Bradbury's classic short story "A Sound of Thunder," a time traveler accidentally steps on a butterfly in the distant past, and as a result of this tiny alteration in the timeline, the present ends up becoming a dystopian fascist state.

However, even worse than simply bringing about seriously undesirable consequences, time travel can lead to paradoxes, the most familiar of which is the *grandfather paradox*. Suppose you travel back in time and kill your grandfather before he has any kids. Were you to do so, you would end up preventing your own birth. Since being born seems like a prerequisite for traveling back in time (or doing anything really), how could you go back in time and kill your grandfather? It's a paradox!

In *Back to the Future*, when Marty McFly travels back in time, he does not kill his grandfather. In fact, it's Marty who's nearly killed as he saves his father from being hit by his grandfather's car. But, with respect to generating a paradox, Marty does something just as bad; his presence in the past prevents his parents from getting together and having kids. But, if Marty were never born, how could he go back in time and prevent his parents from getting together?

Moreover, such time travel-induced problems do not require the *physical* presence of the time traveler in the past. When Marty goes back to 1955, he doesn't just bring a DeLorean and himself. He also brings *information* from the future, and this alone can be enough to generate paradoxes, such as the *bootstrap paradox*. For example, where did the idea for "Johnny B. Goode" actually come from if Marty got it from Chuck Berry, but Chuck Berry got it from Marty (via his cousin Marvin)?

Indeed, mere information from the future can generate the

grandfather paradox itself. Getting new information about the world often causes people to make choices they wouldn't have made otherwise. Thus, if you send information back in time, it might change the course of events so that you would not end up being there to send the information. As Doc warns Marty, "information about the future could be extremely dangerous; even if your intentions are *good*, it can backfire drastically." Thus, it is critical for Marty to *keep people in the dark* about the future.

Keeping Humans (and Aliens) in the Dark in Sci-Fi

Keeping certain people in the dark about certain things is a standard trope in science fiction. For example, the Men in Black use the neuralyzer to erase the memories of anyone who observes alien activities on Earth. And, in order to obey the Prime Directive in *Star Trek*, Starfleet officers have to keep "pre-warp civilizations" in the dark about advanced technologies, such as space travel and energy weapons.

While the stakes tend to be higher in these science fiction universes, the Men in Black and Starfleet keep people in the dark for essentially the same reason we keep people in the dark in real life. Namely, they want to avoid the negative consequences that might result from sensitive information being revealed. For example, as Agent K explains when Agent J asks in *Men in Black*, "Why the big secret? People are smart, they can handle it," there would be chaos if people realized that the earth is infested with aliens. Similarly, there could be anarchy if a primitive alien civilization got access to advanced technology before it could handle it. In a line that is reminiscent of Doc's warning to Marty, Captain Jean-Luc Picard tells Dr. Crusher that "history has proven again and again that whenever mankind interferes with a less developed civilization, no matter how well-intentioned that interference may be, the results are invariably disastrous" (*Star Trek: TNG*, "Symbiosis").

Yet, in addition to avoiding negative consequences, there is another reason why we keep people in the dark. Sometimes, our major concern is simply not being the *source* of the information. For example, someone might not want to be the bearer of bad news. And the Prime Directive arguably falls in this category as well. It does not require Starfleet to prevent primitive alien civilizations from acquiring advanced technology from other sources. For example, as Admiral Chekote tells Commander Ben Sisko, "the Cardassians may involve themselves in other people's civil wars, but we don't; the Prime Directive applies" (*Star Trek: DS9*, "The Circle"). The Prime Directive just requires that *Starfleet* itself not reveal information about advanced technologies.

Nevertheless, I want to argue that *time travelers* have reasons to keep people in the dark that go beyond what we face in real life—and even in science fiction that does not involve time travel. As Doc tells Marty, information from the future can "endanger his own existence" and potentially "screw up the spacetime continuum." But before we can fully explore why it is so critical for time travelers to keep people (in the past) in the dark, we should clarify what it means to keep someone in the dark.

Shedding Light on Keeping Others in the Dark

When it comes to messing with people's beliefs and knowledge, philosophers have tended to focus on lying and deception. For example, from at least as far back as the medieval philosopher, Saint Augustine to Roderick Chisholm (writing in the 20th century), philosophers have grappled with the question of what lying is.[1] Sometimes, however, and though we needn't necessarily lie to achieve this end, we do need (or at least want) to merely prevent certain people from arriving at true beliefs (i.e., as opposed to causing them to arrive at false beliefs). A few philosophers have recently analyzed what it means to *keep someone in the dark* or to *keep a secret from someone*.

In her book, *Secrets*, philosopher Sissela Bok argues that "to keep a secret from someone is to block information about it or evidence of it from reaching that person, and to do so intentionally: to prevent him from learning it."[2] In other words, to keep someone in the dark is to conceal information from them.

Several episodes in the *Back to the Future* trilogy clearly fall under Bok's definition. When Doc and Marty travel to 2015 in *Part II*, Doc uses a "sleep-inducing alpha-rhythm generator" to knock out Marty's girlfriend Jennifer and leaves her sleeping in an alley. That way, when she returns to 1985, she won't have learned anything about the future. Also, when Marty writes Doc a letter in 1955 to warn him about the terrorists who try to kill him in 1985 for stealing their plutonium, Doc rips it up in order to keep *himself* in the dark about the future.

Of course, concealing information is not the only way to keep people in the dark. You can also keep people in the dark just by keeping your mouth shut. In other words, it can be an act of *omission* as well as an act of commission. Indeed, this is actually what Doc emphasizes to Marty: "You must not see anybody or talk to *anybody*. Anything that you do could have serious repercussions on future events!"

In his book, *Lying and Deception*, philosopher Thomas Carson gives a definition of keeping people in the dark that captures such cases of withholding information, as well as cases of concealing information.[3] Not unlike Bok, he claims that "a person S keeps another person S1 in the dark about X if S actively and intentionally prevents S1 from learning about X." But in addition, he claims that "a person S keeps another person S1 in the dark about X if S fails to inform S1 about X."[4]

Strictly speaking, Carson's definition does not yet capture all cases of keeping people in the dark. For example, when the Men in Black use the neuralyzer on people, they are not concealing or withholding information. They are directly erasing beliefs that these people have already formed. In a similar vein, in the "Pen Pals" episode of *Star Trek: The Next Generation*, Captain Picard obeys the Prime Directive by ordering Dr. Pulaski to remove memories of interactions with the Enterprise and her crew from the brain of a young alien. Thus, Carson probably should add to his definition that "a person S keeps another person S1 in the dark about X if S intentionally erases S1's belief about X."

As a matter of fact, Carson sets aside cases of erasing beliefs and implanting new ones on the grounds that they only occur in science fiction. In 2010, he wrote that "at present, we cannot directly cause other people to have beliefs.... We should not use this case as a test for the adequacy of definitions." But only a few years later, I learned from the "Memory Hackers" episode of PBS's *Nova* that scientists are now able to do just that. Indeed, with Elon Musk's Neuralink opening for business, it may become commonplace.

Now that we have a better grip on what it means to keep someone in the dark, we can return to our question of why it is especially important for time travelers to keep people in the dark. It turns out that it depends on exactly what type of time travel we are talking about and that we have no shortage of possibilities in that regard.

Lewisian Time Travel

It's tempting to conclude from the grandfather paradox that time travel into the past is not even possible. Yet, several philosophers (most notably, David Lewis) have argued that it still is.[5] According to these philosophers, this is how time travel could work: there is only one timeline. And, at least as far as events in the past go, how events in this timeline proceed is completely fixed. Thus, while a time traveler can jump back into the past of this timeline, they cannot alter the past. Their presence and their actions in the past were always part of this timeline. So, in particular, since the time traveler's grandfather was not killed before he had kids, it is just not possible for the time traveler to kill him.

Now, if you can time travel into the past, it seems like you should be able to take a gun with you and kill your own grandfather. But a time traveler has to have been born in order to time travel, so they can't do anything in the past that would prevent their own birth. A time traveler might shoot and kill someone in the past. But it can't be their own grandfather. In a similar vein, a time traveler can't prevent their parents from getting together and having kids.

Since a time traveler cannot alter the past in *Lewisian time travel*, there is no grandfather paradox, so trying to avoid this paradox is not a reason to keep people in the dark about the future. In fact, there is no need at all for time travelers to be careful about keeping people in the dark. If they reveal any information about the future, that is just what was destined to happen.

But even in Lewisian time travel, there is still a reason for time travelers to *want* to keep people in the dark. For instance, even though the time traveler in *12 Monkeys* knows that he cannot change the past, he starts to worry that he was the one who gave a crazy terrorist the idea of causing a global pandemic. Even if the death of billions of people is inevitable, he still doesn't want to be part of the causal history such that "maybe I've wiped out the human race." But, as noted above, not wanting to be the source of certain information is a reason why we might want to keep people in the dark in real life.

In addition to *12 Monkeys*, several movies depict Lewisian time travel, such as *Star Trek IV: The Voyage Home*, *Bill & Ted's Excellent Adventure*, *Harry Potter and the Prisoner of Azkaban*, and *Arrival*. That said, this is not the sort of time travel that is depicted in *Back to the Future*. In *Back to the Future*, Marty *can* alter the past, so it still might be particularly important for *Marty* to keep people in the dark about the future.

Multiverse Time Travel

Marty grew up in a timeline where there hadn't been any Marty McFly activities in 1955. However, once he travels back in time, there ends up being a whole bunch of Marty McFly activities in 1955. As such, Marty does not travel to the past in the timeline in which he was born. Instead, he travels to the past of a timeline that is exactly like his original timeline up to the point that a Marty McFly arrives in a DeLorean. Or, as several philosophers (most notably, Michael Lockwood along with the physicist David Deutsch) might put it, Marty travels to a different universe in the infinite collection of possible universes known as the *multiverse*.[6]

Here's another way to see that *Back to the Future* depicts *multiverse time travel* rather than Lewisian time travel: When Marty gets back to 1985, it is clearly not the same timeline that he left. In the original timeline, Marty's parents get together because George is hit by a car and Lorraine tends to him. Yet, in the new timeline, George has to stand up to Biff at the school dance in order to win Lorraine. As a result, Marty's parents are now cool in 1985 rather than boring. Also, the incident with the terrorists takes place at the Lone Pine Mall (rather than the Two Pines Mall) since Marty has run over one of the trees with the DeLorean in the new timeline.

If time travel into the past is really just travel to another timeline, there is no grandfather paradox. You can travel back in time and kill someone who is indistinguishable from your grandfather. But you don't kill your *own* grandfather in your original timeline. You just kill someone exactly like him in a new timeline. As a result, someone exactly like you is not going to be born in the future of this new timeline.[7] But that doesn't affect your existence since you were born in a different timeline.

Since there is no grandfather paradox in straightforward multiverse time travel, trying to avoid this paradox is not a reason to keep people in the dark about the future. But there can still be a reason for time travelers to keep people in the dark. Namely, they want to avoid the bad consequences that might result in the future—of the timeline that they are now in—from sensitive information being revealed. For example, this is why the time travelers in *Primer* hide away in a hotel room and keep their cellphones turned off while they are in the past. Also, in *Part II*, Biff uses Doc's time machine to take an almanac from the 21st century to his younger self in 1955. The young Biff then uses the information in the almanac to amass a great fortune, which he puts to various nefarious purposes. Thus, it would be much better if the young Biff were kept in the dark about future sports scores, which is precisely what Doc and Marty aim to do by burning the almanac in 1955. Still, as noted above, avoiding bad future consequences is the same reason that we typically have for keeping other people in the dark in real life.

In addition to *Primer*, several movies depict straightforward multiverse time travel, such as J.J. Abrams's recent series of *Star Trek* movies. But this is still not exactly the sort of multiverse time travel that *Back to the Future* depicts. In *Back to the Future*, Marty *is* going to cease to exist if he is not born in the future of the new timeline.[8] Thus, it might yet be critical for *Marty* to keep people in the dark about the future.

Back to the Future *Time Travel*

The sort of multiverse time travel that is depicted in *Back to the Future* regularly shows up in science fiction. For example, in *Looper*, a time traveler (and/or pieces of that time traveler) disappears if a younger version of that time traveler in the new timeline dies (or loses those pieces). And in the "The City on the Edge of Forever" episode of *Star Trek*, the entire Federation winks out of existence when Dr. McCoy saves Edith Keeler from dying in a traffic accident in 1930. But I have to admit that I'm at a loss as to exactly how this sort of time travel works. Maybe other essays in this volume can straighten it out.[9]

Nevertheless, what is clear is that it *really* is critical for Marty to keep people in the dark about the future. When Marty's parents don't get together as a result of his time traveling, the universe does not "promptly disappear in a puff of logic" like God does in *The Hitchhiker's Guide to the Galaxy*. The time-traveling Marty just slowly fades away since he is not going to be born in the new timeline. Yet, this is still pretty bad at least as far as Marty is concerned.

In the *Back to the Future* series, this sort of existential catastrophe will occur unless the events in the new timeline are sufficiently similar to the events in the original timeline. Most notably, Marty's parents need to get together so that he can be born in the new timeline. But, since new information often leads people to make different decisions (e.g., about whom to marry), information about the future can easily cause the new timeline to diverge drastically from the original timeline.

In order to escape existential catastrophe, time travelers like Marty clearly need to avoid *doing* things—like pushing people out of the paths of automobiles or stepping on butterflies—that significantly change the course of events, and they also have to, on occasion, keep people in the dark about the future.[10]

Notes

1. Augustine. 395. *De Mendacio*; Chisholm, Roderick M., and Thomas D. Feehan. 1977. "The Intent to Deceive." *Journal of Philosophy* 74(3):143–59.
2. Bok, Sissela. 1983. *Secrets*. Random House.
3. Carson, Thomas L. 2010. *Lying and Deception*. Oxford University Press.
4. Carson places some restrictions on this; he recognizes that "not every case of failing to correct another person's beliefs or remove his ignorance about something one knows counts as 'keeping someone in the dark.'"
5. Lewis, David. 1976. "The Paradoxes of Time Travel." *American Philosophical Quarterly* 13(2):145–52.
6. Deutsch, David, and Michael Lockwood. 1994. "The Quantum Physics of Time Travel." *Scientific American* 270(3):68–74.
7. In similar vein, Marty does not prevent his own birth in his original timeline. He just prevents the birth of a Marty McFly in the new timeline.
8. In straightforward multiverse time travel, the opposite problem can arise. There might end up being *too many* versions of the same person in the same timeline. As in *Primer*, time travelers might have to start drugging other versions of themselves and hiding them in the attic.

9. But what if it is just not possible to straighten out this sort of time travel? In other words, what if *Back to the Future* depicts an impossible state of affairs? In that case, while there may be a special reason for Marty to keep people in the dark in the fiction, there may be no special reason for time travelers in the (presumably self-consistent) actual world to do so.

10. Strictly speaking, it is consistent with the events in *Back to the Future* that there is only a single timeline. But it would have to be a timeline that is *malleable*. (It doesn't change *over time*, of course, but it does change when people travel in time.) However, this does not affect my argument about the importance of keeping people in the dark. If anything, the existential catastrophe is even worse if Marty no longer exists in any timeline. Finally, I would like to thank Peter Lewis, Kay Mathiesen, Anncy Thresher, and Dan Zelinski for several helpful discussions about how time travel works.

Back to Morality

Xuanpu Zhuang

In *Back to the Future*, Marty McFly travels from 1985 to 1955 in Doc Brown's time-traveling DeLorean. Marty's journey changes the fortunes of his whole family—his meek father, George, becomes successful and confident, and his alcoholic mother, Lorraine, becomes healthy and vibrant. At the same time, George's tyrannical supervisor, Biff, is relegated to a subservient role to the McFlys.

In a reversal of time-traveling fortune, in *Part II*, Biff steals the time machine in 2015 and gives a sports almanac to his younger self in 1955, which the young Biff takes advantage of, creating a timeline in which he is rich and powerful, while the McFlys are downtrodden (to put it nicely). However, in the end, Marty succeeds in nullifying the changes made by Biff, saving the McFlys and the rest of Hill Valley in the process. Biff is a bad guy, for sure; he bullies George, steals the DeLorean, and turns Hill Valley into a chaotic dystopia. And it seems morally wrong for him to take advantage of time travel to benefit himself and sacrifice others in the way that he does. However, Marty, the trilogy's protagonist, does essentially the same thing (or at least, something very similar); he creates a timeline that favors his family and puts Biff in a much less desirable position. Is Marty morally wrong in doing so? Is he no better than Biff?

We've heard plenty of warnings about the dangers of time travel, and indeed, the consequences of altering the past could be disastrous. To be sure, the uncertainties of traveling through time can be a problem, but changing the timeline itself can also pose *moral* problems. A number of actions done while (or specific to) time-travelling can be morally problematic, such as a great deal of what Biff does in *Part II*. Marty's case, however, is arguably much more complicated. Of course, it's only natural to daydream about what *we* would do if we could travel through time. However, insofar as time travel could put us in morally sticky situations, perhaps we should think through some potential issues, should we be put in

Marty or Biff's shoes and our time-traveling dreams come true. Of course, at least part of the reason to do so is that, as we'll see, it seems as if the ethical dilemmas surrounding time travel might be just as complex as time travel itself.

Do No Harm

A familiar moral norm is "do no harm." When an action harms a victim, it means that the victim leads a worse life than the life they would have led had the action not been taken.[1] For example, when Biff bullies George, George is worse off in a variety of ways (e.g., he is belittled, his feelings are hurt, he's coerced into doing things he doesn't want to do, etc.). George's life would be better without Biff's bullying, so we can say that Biff's bullying *harms* George. It is wrong to do harm, and thus Biff does something morally wrong by bullying George.

A slightly more specific norm follows in regard to harm as it relates to time travel: it is wrong to harm others *by traveling through time*. Now, recall the start of the first film; Biff seems to lead a relatively good and comfortable life as George's supervisor. However, Marty's time-traveling adventure creates a new timeline in which Biff is worse off as he's timid and subservient to the McFlys in his role as a car detailer. It seems inarguable that Biff would be much better off had Marty not traveled back in time (or if Marty had not significantly altered the timeline on his trip). So, bearing in mind the "do no harm by traveling through time" norm, we should conclude that Marty's time-travel harms Biff and is therefore morally wrong (just as we would conclude that Biff's time-travel is morally wrong for similar reasons).

However, this account may be a bit too simple. For example, suppose that a 14-year-old girl chooses to have a child.[2] As the girl is so young, her child will likely have a challenging, potentially pitiful start in life. One might try to persuade the girl, "It will be better for the child if you wait and have him later." However, the problem with making such an argument is that if the girl waits, the particular child (whom she conceived at 14) would have never existed. The child she *would* have at some point in the future will not be *the same* child as the one she is considering to have at 14. It's no easy task to compare a child's difficult life with a world where the child doesn't exist at all, but it is arguable that even with a bad start, the child's life is still worth living. So, although the child has a bad early life, if the girl decides to have the child, we cannot appropriately call it "harming" given the definition above. In this case, the action which *seems* to harm the child also results in the child's existence. Call this the *non-identity* problem. In the non-identity problem, the victim has a bad or undesirable existence, while the only alternative is to nullify the victim's existence or bring a different person (i.e., a *non-identical* person) into existence. As a bad life seems still worth living, neither choice looks satisfying.

With all of the changing timelines in *Back to the Future*, it's easy to imagine some non-identity cases resulting from time travel. For example, in *Part II*, Biff creates a timeline in which he is rich and powerful, turning Hill Valley into (as Marty puts it) a nightmare. Suppose however that in this timeline, Biff fathers a child with Lorraine: Biff Jr. Also suppose that Biff Jr. has a bad life (with a father like Biff, that's not difficult to imagine). When Marty travels back to 1955 and nullifies all the changes made by Biff, this will of course mean that Biff Jr. will no longer exist. Biff seems to treat Marty's family badly, but without the changes made by Biff, Biff Jr. would never have been born. Does Biff harm Biff Jr. (simply by conceiving him) because he forces Biff Jr. to have a bad life? Perhaps. If Biff Jr. has a bad life but one that is still worth living, does Marty harm Biff Jr. because he nullifies his existence? This is no doubt a puzzling issue. It is hard to compare the levels of well-being between timelines with and without Biff Jr. Perhaps "do no harm" can be a good moral norm in ordinary life, but it seems difficult to apply when it comes to adventurous time travel.³

Be the Master of One's Life

Another idea worth considering in regard to the morality of time travel is familiar in pop-psychology: you are the master of your life. What is typically meant by this is that we have control over ourselves—we decide what we want, and what we do, and we ought to live in alignment with our "true selves." It also implies that no one else can (or should) control or interfere with our life. For instance, if we decide to stay home and watch the *Back to the Future* trilogy all weekend, it would be wrong for someone to hide our DVDs and demand that we go to work. We own those DVDs, and more importantly, we *own* our lives. We own not only our private weekend plans but also our life projects. Others are morally forbidden to interfere in our lives in such a way.

If it is wrong to interfere with one's personal choices or plans, it seems *seriously* wrong to interfere with one's *timeline*—a larger picture of one's life, including one's family, fortune, events, and so on. Thus, it seems morally wrong to interfere with one's timeline through time travel. This sounds plausible if we reflect on the important goods in our timeline. For example, Doc and Marty seem to be good friends even before their adventures in the movies. Suppose that someone (perhaps another antagonist for Marty, Needles) takes the DeLorean back in time and interferes with Marty meeting Doc. Without meeting, Marty and Doc never become friends. Both of them may still do well in life; Doc still invents the time machine, and Marty pursues his music career. But the friendship between Marty and Doc is destroyed by Needles, even though no one will ever come to realize this.

However, as fans of the trilogy, we know what their friendship means for both Marty and Doc, and Needles' action therefore seems morally problematic. Friendship is a crucial part of a well-lived life. Try to imagine a world in which you'd never met your best friend; it would be a potentially devastating loss. The same reasoning works just as well for other goods in our lives, such as our relationships with family, lovers, our educational opportunities, jobs, and so on. If we own our timeline and reject changes to it, then any changes made in time travel take the risk of changing one's whole life. If so, Doc's words are now morally weighty: the consequences could be disastrous, as changing one's life is morally wrong. With that said, Marty and Biff both succeed in changing the timelines and each other's lives in the story. As such, it seems that both of them do wrong.

Of course, it's worth pointing out that Doc doesn't even heed his own warnings. And the motto "Be the master of your life" may be an exaggerated. There are plenty of things that fall outside of our control, and some of those things can be significant. Suppose Marty's sister Linda has graduated and is seeking a job. She's received an offer for a position in Los Angeles, but she prefers a position closer to home in Hill Valley. Whether she gets her desired job, however, is determined by a hiring manager. As we can imagine, living in Los Angeles and living in Hill Valley would lead to two extremely different lives for Linda, so the manager's decision will have a huge influence on her life. She would have different friends, lovers, children, communities, etc., depending upon the choosing of someone other than Linda. Nevertheless, it would be absurd to complain that the manager interferes with Linda's life or her timeline. The job choice can certainly be influential, but the manager's decision seems to be part of her life. We interact with one another and have an influence on one another's lives all the time. Every word and every act can change the life of another person. Some changes are slight, while others are monumental, but it would be counterintuitive (if not bizarre) to claim that literally every change we make in the lives of others is morally wrong.

Nevertheless, one might argue that the point is not about changing one's life but one's *timeline*. The manager's decision is part of Linda's life, but no matter which decision the manager makes, that is part of Linda's timeline, and no one is allowed to change it. However, it is also misleading to say that anyone *owns* their own timeline. After all, different timelines are no more than different possible worlds where we *may* live, and the real timeline is the one where we *do* live.

One's timeline is a larger picture of one's life, including one's family, fortune, events, and so on. Nevertheless, one's family, fortune, or events cannot be owned in the manner suggested. Living in Los Angeles does not make Linda own Los Angeles. Living in a timeline does not make one person own the timeline either. Without ownership over one's timeline, it is hard to see why one has no right to forbid others' influence on it. It is morally wrong for another person to steal your DVDs, but if the potential thief instead travels to the past and buys the DVDs before you have a chance to buy them, then you never owned the DVDs in this timeline and have little standing to complain about not being in possession of them. It simply seems difficult to see why you have the right to reject others' influence on your life or even timeline. In sum, the motto "Be the master of your life" is inspirational, but it seems doubtful whether we can own our timeline and forbid others from changing it.

Great Power and Great Responsibility

It is difficult to evaluate the moral significance of the harm done by time travel. And it is unrealistic to claim ownership over one's timeline in a way that is morally informative. But is there *nothing* we can say about the morality of time travel? Here is one additional ethical lesson which might help us navigate the issue.

The idea in question comes from another popular movie franchise: "With great power comes great responsibility." Uncle Ben famously gives Peter Parker this advice, which is particularly relevant for him as it applies importantly to Peter's alter-ego, Spider-Man. As such, Peter's choices will have outsized consequences beyond those of ordinary people. Spider-Man seems to have a moral obligation to catch the bad guys and do good for humankind rather than to just enjoy himself. Similarly, suppose Doc builds a nuclear bomb (as he was conscripted to do by the Libyans). The weapon is so powerful that it could easily destroy a country; the existence of such a weapon will be a huge risk to the world. The weapon could support coercive power that threatens our free and equal moral status as individuals in modern society (e.g., by coercing individuals to obey the demand). To protect basic human values, we have good standing to control the powerful weapon in a reasonable way.

If weapons like Doc's nuclear bomb are too dangerous for private ownership or control, it seems like we might want to make similar prohibitions on the ownership and operation of time machines. First, the consequences of changing the future are hard to predict. As the butterfly effect reveals, a minor change in circumstances can cause a large change in outcome. In *Part II*, all Old Biff does with time travel is give a sports almanac to his younger self in 1955, but this turns Hill Valley into a chaotic dystopia. The power of time travel is huge, and could be used to create different timelines for the whole world rather than just two families or a medium-sized town in California. What would stop someone, for example, from traveling back in time and (inadvertently or purposefully) changing the outcome of World War II? Again, the consequences of time travel could *really be* disastrous. It follows that we cannot use the time machine arbitrarily, which perhaps also means we should not allow private control over such technology.

Second, time travel comes with a kind of coercive power. If one travels back to the past to change the timeline, we have no way to find the original timeline without the time machine. If one travels forward to the future to see what is coming up and then comes back to prepare for it, it is a strength that we cannot counteract. The use of coercive power would need to be justified and regulated by certain rules.[4] If so, although the time machine was invented by Doc, we have good reason to establish certain rules for time travel (that even Doc must obey). For example, private use of the time machine should probably be forbidden, given the risks. Perhaps we can only permit the official use of time machines for the public good within strictly minimal boundaries, when the risks are acceptable. The private use of the time machine simply seems hard to justify. After all, Biff travels back only for his own benefit (just as Marty plans to do for himself before Doc intercedes). It seems that both Biff and Marty are wrong in (their plans for) changing the timelines for personal purposes.

A related reason for regulating the use of time travel is general fairness. We care about fairness which is sometimes seen as the core of justice. As a kind of coercive power, the private use of the time machine itself produces extremely unfair results. If you can travel back to the past and forward to the future while I cannot, then it seems there is an unequal distribution of crucial resources between us. With the time machine, you can also grasp more information about the future and have chances to change your own timeline whenever you want. When facing the power of the time machine, one's efforts, diligence, and other virtues seem meaningless, as any results could be changed by others. People without a time machine will also be in an inferior position and vulnerable to those who do own a time machine. To avoid extreme unfairness, it seems that the use of time travel has to be regulated by reasonable rules.

It may be argued that in ordinary life, our actions can be influential and sometimes risky. It's true. That is why some materials and weapons are regulated by the official agents while ordinary citizens are denied access to them. As we've seen, the reason for being careful is not only that time travel can bring huge risks but that the time machine itself comes with an immeasurable power. The power is coercive for ordinary people, and thus we have reason to control and regulate it. But here is one additional, final concern: can official agents such as the government do better than private individuals? Indeed, similar to the regulation of weapons, the regulation of time travel will not be perfect. But the government could at least attempt to keep time travel under control and avoid the chaos of private use. We know that Doc and Marty are good people, and it seems as if they don't cause a moral disaster by the end of the trilogy. Most stories of time travel have happy endings like this. But we cannot expect real life to have the same equally pleasant resolutions, so think twice before you decide to travel through time.

Notes

1. For example, see Parfit, Derek. 1987. *Reasons and Persons*. Oxford University Press.
2. *Ibid.*
3. For a discussion on different theories of harming, see Gardner, Molly. 2021. "What Is Harming?" In *Principles and Persons: The Legacy of Derek Parfit*. McMahan, J.; Campbell, T.; Goodrich, J.; and Ramakrishnan, K. (eds.). Oxford University Press.
4. For example, see Dworkin, Ronald. 1986. *Law's Empire*. Harvard University Press.

Betting on the Past

Zack Garrett

In *Back to the Future Part II*, Doc, Marty, and Jennifer travel from 1985 to 2015, where Marty notices a book displayed in the window of an antique store: *Grays Sports Almanac: Complete Sports Statistics, 1950–2000*. He comes to realize its great value (particularly to a time traveler such as him). When he returns to 1985, he reasons, he'll be able to use the information from the almanac to place bets on competitions until the year 2000 which would almost effortlessly make him a wealthy man.

Unfortunately (?) for Marty, Doc finds the almanac and forces him to throw it away as Doc argues that using time travel to make money would cheapen the achievement. Time travel, Doc claims, should be used for science, not financial gain. Thus, Marty never ends up using the information from the almanac to place even a single bet. However, Biff Tannen, the ever-present antagonist of the McFlys, overhears Doc and Marty's conversation and proceeds to grab the almanac, steal the time-traveling DeLorean, and deliver the almanac to his younger self (along with instructions of how to use it) in 1955. When Marty and Doc then return to 1985, they find it substantially altered. The idyllic American life that Marty's family had achieved by the end of the first film is gone. Biff is almost unfathomably wealthy, and Hill Valley is dwarfed by Biff's absurd monstrosity of a casino.

With all of this in mind, it's worth examining the ethical questions that are raised using time-travel to place bets on sports. Of course, Biff's use of his winnings to transform the town into a dystopian fiefdom involves a variety of ethical wrongs, but the question we'll consider here is the morality of the bets themselves, not how someone *uses* their winnings. So, did Biff do something wrong when he placed those bets? As I'll argue, the morality of time-travel betting hinges on how the bets in question are placed. Smaller bets placed with competent bookies can be morally acceptable, even when made using time-travel. Larger bets placed with incompetent bookies or bets with friends are morally wrong.

How Sports Betting Works

Most of us are likely familiar with gambling on blackjack or poker, but sports betting works somewhat differently from typical casino or card games. Sports betting takes place either between friends or through a bookie (i.e., a bookmaker). In the former case, one friend might offer a wager to another (e.g., "I'll bet you $100 that the Cubbies will beat Miami") that the friend can either accept or reject. Call this first kind of betting "friend-betting." A similarly common form of betting happens through bookies—individuals or corporations that offer wagers with varying payouts. Most bookies now are located in casinos or through websites like DraftKings and FanDuel. Call this second kind of betting "bookie-betting."

Friend-betting is often very simple. Two individuals come to a *friendly*, straightforward agreement about the payouts for winning. When the results of the bet are determined, the loser pays the winner the agreed-upon amount. In the context of sports betting, these kinds of bets often turn simply on which team wins, not the margin of victory.

In contrast, three common forms of sports betting can be found with just about any bookie: spread, moneyline, and over/under. Betting on the spread means that you bet that the favorite team (the one people think is more likely to win) will win by a set amount or that they will fail to win by that set amount. For example, suppose the Sacramento Kings are playing the Golden State Warriors. Golden State is the favorite, and the spread is set at +8 for Sacramento and -8 for Golden State. If you bet on Sacramento, you are betting that Sacramento will either win the game outright or lose the game by fewer than eight points. If you bet on Golden State, you are betting that Golden State will win by more than eight points.

Moneyline betting is closer to the way friend-betting typically works. You may bet for either team, but you are only betting that that team will win; the margin of victory doesn't really come into play. That said, who is thought to be more likely to win does affect the payout; betting on the moneyline doesn't pay the same for each team. Consider again the Sacramento-Golden State game. Suppose the moneyline for the game is +275 for Sacramento and -340 for Golden State. If you bet $100 on Sacramento and they win, you will profit $275. If, on the other hand, you bet $100 on Golden State and they win, then you'll only earn $29.41. This substantial difference in payouts is because Golden State is very likely to win the game.

Over/under betting isn't about betting on either team in a competition. Instead, the bet is on the sum of the scores of both teams. For example, an over/under for the game between Sacramento and Golden State might be set at 242. One can bet that the final scores of the teams will add up to over 242 or under. If the final score is 132 to 116 (totaling 248), then if a gambler bet that the score would be *over* 242, they'll win the bet.

This might have you wondering, how exactly does a bookie make a profit? To do so, the bookie must make sure that there is the same amount of money on both sides of a wager. So, if $1,000 has been bet on Golden State beating the spread, then the bookie will also want $1,000 to be bet that Golden State will *not* beat the spread. That way, regardless of what happens, the amount of money the bookie has to pay out to winners will be equal to the amount that they receive from losers. Of course, this would not result in a profit, so bookies also change the payouts so that they pay-out less to winners than they take from losers. Winning a bet on the spread usually pays around 90 percent of the bet, so a winning spread bet of $100 would net $90 in profit. Suppose ten people each bet $100 on Golden State to beat the spread, and another ten people each bet $100 that Golden State will *not* beat the spread. If Golden State then fails to beat the spread, the bookie loses $900 to the winners but gains $1,000 from the losers for a profit of $100. The task for the bookie is to set the spread number, the over/under number, and the payouts so that bettors are equally likely to bet on either side. As bets trickle in, the spread can change to entice bettors to swap sides. In a sense, bookies do not gamble; they skim profits off the top of the gambling of *other* people.

Harm to Bystanders

Entering into a wager with either a friend or a bookie involves entering into an agreement or a contract with that friend/bookie. These agreements state the conditions for who will pay whom, given the outcome of a sporting event. Many of the ethically relevant details of time-travel gambling and gambling in general will relate directly to the ethics of contracts. Many of these details are complicated. As such, before delving into them, it's worth considering the bystanders to those contracts. When making a bet through a bookie, one is only entering such a contract with the bookie; any other gamblers who use the same bookie are bystanders who may be affected by one's bet but have their own separate agreements with the bookie.

Suppose Biff places a substantial moneyline bet on the 49ers in the 1982 Super Bowl (in which the 49ers beat the Bengals by five points). Recall how bookies set their spreads and payouts; they want a balance of bets between both sides of a wager. When Biff sets a massive bet on the 49ers, this changes the moneyline for other gamblers. Let's say that the bookie changes the moneyline for the 49ers from -110 to -150 and for the Bengals from -105 to 120. In other words, anyone who places a bet on the 49ers after Biff will stand to win less money, and anyone who places a bet on the Bengals will stand to gain more (were the Bengals to win). Two scenarios might unfold.

Suppose Marty's brother Dave wanted to place a bet on the 49ers at the -110 moneyline. If Biff had not placed his bet, then Dave would have won some money, but with the -150 moneyline after Biff's bet, Dave is unwilling to place the bet. Suppose instead that Dave wasn't planning on betting on the game, but after Biff's bet changed the payout for the Bengals, he was enticed to bet on them. As a result, he places a bet on the Bengals and loses his money.

If Biff places a massive bet on the 49ers and the moneyline changes as a result, each of the above scenarios will play out repeatedly. Gamblers who stood to win by betting on the 49ers will be less likely to place their bets, and gamblers who wouldn't have lost anything will be more likely to place losing bets on the Bengals. Of course, these scenarios play out any time the spread and payouts change, and it would be misguided to say that any bet that leads to a bookie changing these values is morally wrong.

The issue for Biff in such a case is that he knows that his bet is guaranteed to lead to more people losing their money or failing to gain money. If Biff were merely confident, instead of certain (that the 49ers will beat the spread), then it would still be an open possibility in his mind that he could lose the bet. Biff could justify the bet on the grounds that were he to lose the massive bet on the 49ers, then the change in the moneyline would have actually benefited the other gamblers. In such a situation, those who were enticed by the better payout and bet on the Bengals would win money, and those who decided not to bet on the 49ers would have saved their money. Of course, Biff is certain about the result of the game, and so he can be certain that placing a massive bet will harm many people.

One of the most important criteria for judging the morality of an action is the harm that the action inflicts. Regardless of which ethical theory one accepts, harming others is frowned upon, especially *knowingly* harming others. That said, ethics cannot be reduced to just questions of harm. That an action harms someone does not *necessarily* make the action morally impermissible. If this weren't the case, then pretty much every action would be wrong. After all, almost every action we take will harm *someone* to *some* degree. Driving a car, for example, increases traffic and slows down other commuters. So, to judge Biff's bet, we're obliged to consider its positive effects as well.

Utilitarianism is the view that we ought to take the action that promotes the most happiness in the world and limits the most sadness. As the

19th-century philosopher John Stuart Mill (utilitarianism's most important defender) describes it: "The doctrine that the basis of morals is utility, or the greatest happiness principle, holds that actions are right in proportion as they tend to promote happiness, wrong in proportion as they tend to produce the reverse of happiness."[1]

To apply utilitarianism to Biff's bet, we weigh the happiness that Biff gets from his winnings against the harm done to the other gamblers. Importantly, because of utilitarianism's strict prioritization of the production of happiness, Biff's prior (potentially "unfair") knowledge of the outcomes of games is largely irrelevant to the question of the morality of his betting. Still, I take it that it should be relatively uncontroversial that Biff's happiness will easily be outweighed by the sadness of the other gamblers. There are, however, ways that the harm to other gamblers might be mitigated.

How much money is needed to shift the spread or payouts of a bookie? For a small-scale bookie, even $100 could have an effect, but what about the casino sportsbooks or modern apps like DraftKings and FanDuel? Information from these sources will, of course, be limited. But we have a sense of how much money is being wagered on these websites. FanDuel, for example, had $29.12 billion wagered in 2022.[2] With this amount of money going into bets on the app, it would take a particularly large bet to single-handedly alter the spread or payout in a single competition. Even placing a bet of this size may be impossible because the bookies will often limit the maximum bet a gambler can make. Bookies do not want to take bets so large that they are not confident that they can even out the other side. So, if Biff places a bet so large that it affects the spread or payouts, he may harm other gamblers, but it is unlikely that he'll be able to do this. If he places a bet that does not affect the spread or payouts, then he has not harmed the other gamblers.

Contracts with Friends

Regardless of the utilitarian assessment of Biff's bets, many philosophers disagree with John Stuart Mill and think that ethics is not just about happiness.[3] It is possible to wrong someone without making them worse off. For example, lying to your friend may spare their feelings and make them happier. Many philosophers, however, think that dishonesty is morally wrong, even when it makes others happier. For example, Immanuel Kant famously defends a moral prohibition on lying by imagining a world where *everyone* lied to get out of trouble, like by telling hard truths to friends. Since one would not be able to lie in such a world (because every time someone would try to successfully tell a lie, everyone would immediately know they are lying!), a moral principle allowing lies would be irrational.[4]

For the remainder of this essay, we'll consider the ethical implications of Biff's bets for those with whom he makes them. That is, we will evaluate the contracts and agreements Biff enters into with friends and bookies. Contracts and agreements give us rights, and if rights matter for ethics, then violations of them count as moral wrongs. After all, violating a contract is a lot like breaking a promise or lying to get out of a difficult situation—actions that Kant argues are unequivocally wrong.

Suppose Marty, during his visit to Biff's casino in *Part II*, drops by a craps table. Biff, ever the dishonest fellow, has his employees using loaded dice. They have a higher chance of coming up 12—a value that is generally bad for the players. The players are not informed of the nature of the dice, and so they assume that the dice are fair. Does Biff morally wrong Marty and the other players by using loaded dice without telling them? Of course, he does. They go in thinking that the game will be fair when it is not. But what if Marty was informed of the nature of the dice? If the gamblers know that the dice are loaded and still agree to play the game, then the moral problems go away. Sure, their decision to keep playing would be ill-advised, but it would be made willingly with full information.

The ethical principle at play here is *informed consent*. For a contract to be enforceable, both parties must consent to it and be properly informed of the details of the contract—they need to exhibit informed consent. In Biff's rigged game of craps, the participants do not give informed consent—since they lack important information—and so it is morally wrong.

There is one very important distinction between gambling on dice rolls and gambling on sports that plays a role in the discussion of informed consent. In dice rolling, the probabilities are public information; players need only know that the dice are fair and how many sides are on them to provide informed consent in such wagers. In sports wagering, on the other hand, the probabilities of various outcomes are unclear, and gamblers must determine them on their own through research on the teams and players. Friend-betting is effectively a competition in regard to one's ability to analyze information about sports teams, so unequal information alone is not enough to undermine informed consent in sports wagers.

Suppose that in early January 1982, Biff says to Dave McFly, "I'll bet you $100 that the 49ers will beat the Bengals." Dave takes him up on the bet and loses his $100. Has Biff wronged Dave? Of course, he has, though this is nothing new in the relationship between Biff and Dave. But what is the source of this wrongness? Unequal information isn't enough to undermine informed consent in sports wagering, but it feels like Dave has been tricked, and so hasn't given informed consent. The issue isn't that Biff has information (acquired through time travel!) that Dave lacks. Instead, the moral wrongness comes from the perceived difference in their information levels.

If Biff gambles with Dave while using the almanac, he is like a pool hustler in a bar or a chess hustler in a park in New York City. He pretends to be bad or equal in skill to his competition when he is actually especially skilled. When someone enters into a wager on a game of pool with a hustler, they have been wronged since they were led to believe that the hustler's skills were comparable to their own, so they were not informed of the true nature of the challenge. If Dave takes up Biff's bet, he puts himself into a similar situation. Biff's skill in the competition of predicting the outcomes of sporting events is immeasurably higher than he lets on. As such, Dave does not give informed consent to such a wager.

Friend-betting with time-travel acquired information will almost invariably be morally wrong for the reasons just explained. Of course, if the party is informed of the existence of the sports almanac, they could give informed consent, but there would be no reason for them to make a bet against the holder of the almanac.

Contracts with Bookies

What about the bookies when Biff makes a bookie-bet? Do they give informed consent to the agreement? In some respects, a bookie like FanDuel or DraftKings effectively gives tacit consent to anyone who falls within their terms of use. They recognize that gamblers of all skill levels will use their apps to place bets, and so they do not treat differences in knowledge among gamblers as problematic. Of course, as was mentioned in the section on Harm to Bystanders, bookies like this will set limits on how much gamblers can wager on any one competition. Remember that bookies are not gamblers themselves. Their business model is designed to turn a profit regardless of who is betting on their site.

Bookies will not have time-travel as a consideration in their terms of use. So, to determine whether the level of information contained in the sports almanac would violate their terms and conditions, we will have to read between the lines a bit. The following terms appear in FanDuel's Sportsbook Terms and Conditions:

> 9.1 Suspicious betting shall include, but not be limited to:
> 9.1.3 Where the integrity of an event (or events) has been called into question, including, for example, but not limited to where one (or more) of the participants in an event displays exceptional form which we reasonably believe

was known to you or someone connected to you at the time of Bet placement but was concealed from the public generally in order to gain an unfair advantage in any bets placed on that event (or those events).[5]

9.1.3 makes it hard to justify a bet placed by Biff using the sports almanac. Of course, not every match will involve players displaying "exceptional form," but the spirit of the rule seems to indicate that exceptional knowledge on the part of a gambler that is not known to the public—like knowledge of the final score of the game—would count as suspicious betting. Since Biff would have to agree to the terms and conditions of FanDuel to place bets with them, the use of the sports almanac would likely violate the contract he entered with FanDuel. As such, it would be a moral wrong. FanDuel does not consent to wagers with individuals who have the kind of knowledge about sports that Biff (when making use of the sports almanac) has.

Perhaps a different reading of rule 9.1.3 is available that would allow for Biff to place bets using the sports almanac. Alternatively, one could accept an ethical theory like utilitarianism and ignore the contract. FanDuel is an exceedingly profitable company that will not even notice a few hundred dollars lost here and there. So, if Biff makes small enough bets that no individual in FanDuel becomes aware of the losses and no bystander gamblers are affected, then the happiness Biff gets from winning could outweigh any harm he does. Who reads the terms and conditions for apps anyway?

The Payoff

There are situations where Biff could ethically place bets using the sports almanac, but these situations are few and far between. A time-traveler can almost never ethically make friend-bets. As for bookie-bets, these will only be permissible when the bookie does not have restrictions like FanDuel's 9.1.3. That is, rules that invalidate bets made by those with knowledge that is not accessible to the public. If the time-traveler can find a bookie like that, then they can only make bets that are small enough that they do not change the payouts and spread for other gamblers. If they do make a large bet with a bookie, then they run the risk of harming the other gamblers who use the same bookie.

Of course, the movies never show us how Biff places his bets. If, however, we imagine how Biff might go about using the almanac, then he surely did not use it in an ethically permissible way. And with just a passing glance at Biff's "Pleasure Paradise" and the dystopian nightmare version of Hill Valley that surrounds it, it also goes without saying that Biff uses his winnings in unethical ways as well.

Notes

1. Mill, John Stuart 2017. *Utilitarianism*. Cambridge: Hackett.
2. https://www.businessofapps.com/data/fanduel-statistics/.
3. In recent decades, T.M. Scanlon and Phillipa Foot have provided powerful arguments against utilitarianism. They both claim that utilitarianism has a strong appeal, but that we should not be bewitched by the theory. Scanlon, T.M. 1982. "Contractualism and Utilitarianism." *Ethical Theory: An Anthology*, 593–607. Foot, Philippa. 1985. "Utilitarianism and the Virtues." *Mind* 94, no. 374: 196–209.
4. See Chapter 1 of Kant, Immanuel. *Groundwork for the Metaphysics of Morals*.
5. https://sportsbook.fanduel.com/terms.

IV

Matters of Value

Nostalgia and Mimesis

S. Evan Kreider

What is the attraction of nostalgia? *Back to the Future* offers a narrative that respects nostalgia while simultaneously subverting it. Especially interesting is how the film's initial release spoke to two generations of viewers: the Baby Boomers who actually lived through the 1950s and Generation X who experienced the '50s aesthetic through the stories of their parents. Philosophically speaking, the film aims to arouse and critique certain emotional responses through an '80s representation (known as "mimesis" in philosophical theory) of the '50s, both by imitating but also pointing out a certain falsification of typical portrayals of the era. Philosophers such as Francis Hutcheson, Plato, and Susanne Langer wrote extensively on the intersection of mimesis and emotion, and their ideas shed light on this aspect of the movie.

Hutcheson and the Beauty of Representation

The 18th-century British philosopher Francis Hutcheson is counted among the earliest of philosophers to treat aesthetics in a genuinely modern way, as a branch of philosophy in its own right rather than a collection of loosely related questions that fall under the other branches of philosophy such as metaphysics, epistemology, or ethics. According to Hutcheson, human beings have a dedicated aesthetic sense, independent of other psychological faculties such as reason or everyday desires. This sense is responsible for our experience of beauty, a sense of pleasure we experience in response to objects that give rise to a specific aesthetic idea that Hutcheson called "uniformity amidst variety."

Hutcheson further differentiates between absolute beauty and relative beauty. In both cases, uniformity amidst variety refers to the formal qualities of the aesthetic objects that stimulate our sense of beauty. In the case of absolute beauty, "uniformity" means order, while "variety" means complexity. According to Hutcheson, objects with these qualities are pleasurable to experience, and the more of each quality, the better: the more orderly and the more complex things are, the more pleasure we experience from them. Relative beauty, on the other hand, involves mimesis, the aesthetic notion of imitation or representation, and in this case, "uniformity" means similarity, while "variety" means difference (or so we can infer, though Hutcheson never defines "variety" explicitly). Unlike absolute beauty's uniformity and variety, which are independent features, relative beauty's uniformity and variety seem inversely proportional: insofar as things are more similar, they are less different, and vice versa. Unfortunately, Hutcheson never specifies the ideal ratio of these two things, but it seems that both are necessary to some degree.

Thus far, we might think that Hutcheson intended to apply these two types of beauty to two different classes of objects. It seems easy enough to apply the idea of absolute beauty to natural objects such as a sunset or the Grand Canyon, which have formal features that could be described as orderly and complex. So too it seems that relative beauty applies to works of art such as paintings which can be straightforwardly representational, as in the case of a portrait of a person, and therefore displaying a certain degree of similarity to and difference from the object represented. However, this is not the avenue that Hutcheson pursues. Rather, he thinks that all aesthetic objects, natural or artificial, can display both absolute and relative beauty. In the case of art, this is not difficult to believe since a painting also displays formal qualities such as order and complexity. In the case of natural beauty, Hutcheson surprisingly says that it too is a source of both absolute and relative beauty. This is puzzling, since few would claim that the Grand Canyon represents anything. It turns out that Hutcheson's deism is the root of this claim: God apparently creates natural beauty to represent something. Luckily, it's not necessary for us to address Hutcheson's metaphysics here, since we are focusing on a cinematic work of art rather than an object of natural beauty, and we are primarily concerned with its common-sense (mimetic) qualities.

Back to the Future makes great use of representation to evoke a sense of aesthetic pleasure in the audience. In the case of its contemporary young Gen X viewers, it goes to great lengths to create an authentic '80s atmosphere, especially as experienced by teenagers. Right off the bat, we are treated to scenes of a typical day in the life of Marty McFly. This includes definitive '80s culture, such as Marty skateboarding, which was both a common activity among teens as well as a means of transportation to school. And of course, Marty's route takes him past an aerobics studio, a form of exercise that came to prominence at that time. A bit later in the film, Marty meets Doc at a shopping mall, where all important things happened in the '80s, of course. Marty's wardrobe also evokes common '80s fashion, including a puffy orange coat vest. The soundtrack is also very '80s, including songs by Huey Lewis (who has a brief cameo in the movie) and Lindsey Buckingham of Fleetwood Mac (who had moved into a largely solo career in the '80s). Late in the movie, after Marty returns to his own time, he's able to immediately see that he's back in the '80s from the more modern and worn Hill Valley scenery, which includes a movie theater advertising pornographic films (something we're presumably to believe didn't exist in the '50s, at least not in idealized suburbia). Overall, the film presents an '80s vibe that spoke to contemporaneous Gen Xers in a pleasing way.

For viewers from the Baby Boom generation, the pleasure rose from the nostalgic portrayal of their own teenage American culture. As soon as Marty arrives in 1955, he is confronted with the '50s aesthetic, or at least a romanticized version of it. As soon as Marty makes it to town, he's treated to an ideal picture of suburban American life. The town sign proclaims, "Hill Valley: A Nice Place to Live." A full-service gas station boasts multiple attendants per vehicle to fill the gas tank, check the tire pressure, and wash the windshield. In contrast to the '80s stylings of Huey Lewis, the soundtrack shifts to the well-known pop song "Mister Sandman" with all the sweetness and innocence of a supposedly simpler time.

The film's aesthetic is designed to appeal to two generations, but especially to the Boomer generation by way of the nostalgic portrayal of America in the '50s. However, there is a dark side to nostalgia, in that it can falsify our memories and whitewash the past. In order to see the dangers of nostalgia, we have to move past Hutcheson's simple view of aesthetic pleasure and examine the epistemological risks of the arts.

Plato and the Dangers of Mimesis

In contrast to Hutcheson, Plato's views on aesthetics are decidedly pre-modern, and thus much more intertwined with his theories in other branches of philosophy, such as metaphysics, epistemology, and ethics. Of all his ideas, he is historically best-known for his metaphysical theory of Forms. Plato subscribes to a version of transcendent dualism, in which there are two distinct realms: the immanent material world and a transcendent immaterial world. The material world is the ordinary, everyday world of empirically observable physical objects around us. The immaterial world is the realm of the Forms: transcendent ideal objects undetectable through observation by the five senses but knowable through reason itself. On Plato's view, the Forms are the truest form of reality, constituting perfect ideals of the Good and the Beautiful. On the other hand, the world around us is a mere reflection or copy (mimesis) of the ideal Forms; thus, a person might be more or less good or beautiful, but never perfectly the Good or the Beautiful itself. Although it might seem counterintuitive, that means the material world is less real than the immaterial world. This also means that we can only have real knowledge of the perfect Forms, while any knowledge gained from the imperfect physical world would be imperfect knowledge, or more correctly, mere belief rather than actual knowledge.

When it comes to the arts, things are even worse. On Plato's view, art is mimetic as well, simply a copy of physical objects in the world around us. Since those physical objects are also copies, then art is a copy of a copy, less real than the physical objects it represents, and even more removed from the true reality of the Forms that the physical objects themselves represent. Furthermore, our understanding is similarly diluted. We can have actual knowledge only of the Forms. From physical objects in the world, we might still acquire some true beliefs, but not real knowledge. From art, we cannot even form true beliefs, but merely engage our imagination, which is even more divorced from knowledge and reality. Thus, the arts are not only metaphysically inferior to everything else material or immaterial, but epistemologically inferior as well.

For Plato, this is no mere abstract concern. In fact, it has very real ethical and political consequences. Our individual actions and the laws of our society should be guided by knowledge of the good, specifically the Form of the Good. Such knowledge is, of course, only attainable to philosophers, which is why (as Plato argues) society should be ruled by philosopher-kings. Implausible government leadership aside, Plato's point is that the Good is the most real source of moral knowledge, and we should be guided by such. For those of us without that knowledge, we can still form some correct beliefs about right and wrong by following the example of good people, themselves with knowledge of the Good. We may not fully grasp why our actions are good, but at least our actions will still be functionally correct. It is much worse, however, if we follow the artificial representations of good people, such as those found in arts such as literature, theater, and film. By basing our lives on representations of representations, twice removed from reality and knowledge, we are far more likely to go wrong.

Back to the Future explicitly critiques some of the nostalgia that it portrays in a manner of which Plato would have approved, demonstrating how nostalgia can falsify our memory and knowledge of the past. When we meet Marty's family in the '80s, we find them wallowing in mediocrity.

Neither his parents nor his siblings display any signs of success or ambition. His parents in particular engage in nostalgic "things were better when we were young" talk. His mother claims to have been a paragon of virtue as a teenager, especially in regard to dating and sex (or the lack thereof). She recites (presumably for the umpteenth time) the story of how she met their father, a fairy-tale-like recounting of their first date at the Enchantment Under the Sea dance at the high school. She tells it with an obvious sense of romance and an equally obvious sense of disappointment about how her marriage and life in general have turned out.

However, Marty's trip to the past falsifies many elements of her story. It turns out that his mother was actually quite interested in boys: perhaps not sexually promiscuous, but definitely not as pure as she pretended. She pursues Marty (whom she does not know is her son from the future, of course) very aggressively and even admits to him that she has "parked" with boys before. She also drinks, smokes, and wears revealing clothing (at least for the time) on her date with Marty. She eventually kisses Marty (without his consent) before finally realizing that there is something not quite right about it, admitting that it was like she imagines kissing her brother would be.

Marty's mother is the most obvious example of the disconnect between the '50s as they actually occurred versus how they are spoken about three decades later, but there are certainly other examples. Marty's father is revealed to have been peeping on his mother, which ultimately led to their first meeting, despite Lorraine never learning of it. Marty's father's classmates are also revealed to be less than squeaky clean, especially the school bully Biff and his friends, who exemplify the type of troublemaker gangs that early American teen culture gave rise to at the time and eventually prompted youth curfews in many places (as well as the famous "Do you know where your children are?" public service announcements). Teen events such as the high school dance were also seedier than Marty's adult folks would admit, not simply for the aforementioned "parking," drinking, and smoking, but as occasions for other troublesome aspects of teen culture, such as new and rebellious music, noting that the band is shown doing drugs outside the school during their breaks.

Clearly, nostalgia is not what it used to be. Since *Back to the Future* not merely indulges nostalgia but also critiques it, one might wonder what the point is of displaying it in the first place. One might even be tempted to take the position that it would be better to simply avoid it altogether, as Plato might have suggested. Contrary to Plato, however, there may still be value in demonstrating nostalgia, even if it runs the risk of falsifying the past. To see this, we should consider a philosopher with a more positive view of the arts than Plato.

Langer and Virtual Feeling

After considering Francis Hutcheson as an important early modern philosopher of art and beauty, we went back to his philosophical past and looked at a classical source of aesthetics from Plato. Now we can go back to the future—that is, Hutcheson's future—and consider a much more recent philosopher, Susanne Langer, one of the more important figures of the 20th century to discuss aesthetics. As with Hutcheson and Plato, mimesis plays an important role in Langer's theory of the nature and function of the arts. According to Langer, all art forms use mimesis to represent or create something virtual, a kind of sensory illusion. Though any particular form of art can create more than one type of illusion, each form of art has an illusion that is primarily associated with it. For example, a two-dimensional painting can create the illusion of three-dimensional space, whereas the primary illusion of music is that of the virtual passage of time through tempo and rhythm, the rise and fall of melody and harmonic progressions, and so forth.

In the case of films such as *Back to the Future*, a virtual sense of the present moment is created, much in the manner of a dream. As in a dream, the audience of a movie is always in the middle of events, experiencing them up close and personal, moving with any shifts from place to place or time to time—perhaps even through time travel! Moreover, the movie presents the virtual qualities of the events that make them seem real to the audience, taking us from our theater seats and drawing us into the cinematic world. Though a film, like a dream, is an illusion, our experiences while viewing it have an authentic quality.

However, the purpose of art is not just to represent virtual situations for their own sake. Rather, mimesis is a means to expressive ends. Specifically, art serves the function of expressing emotions. On Langer's view, art acts as an incomplete symbol. Unlike complete symbols, such as language used for straightforward literal purposes to communicate specific, determinate ideas and meaning, art captures the qualitative form of feelings so that the audience can experience it for themselves, rather than simply have it explained in an abstract manner. To that end, art needs to mimic some features of reality, but needn't be a perfect imitation; in other words, art can be similar to but also different from whatever it represents, much as Hutcheson would have said. Thus, art's metaphysical or epistemological accuracy is not an issue for Langer, as it was for Plato, as long as it expresses feelings to the audience. This could be for the purpose of contemplating the feelings in a more philosophical manner than one can when experiencing emotions more directly from real life. For example, it is difficult to be philosophical about grief when attending the funeral of a loved one, but easier to do so when watching a movie that involves a funeral scene.

The portrayal of the '50s in *Back to the Future* does precisely this, expressing feelings of nostalgia while also allowing the audience to contemplate it in a distanced way by pointing out its flaws, and (intentionally or otherwise) suggesting additional issues for the audience to consider. One of the more obvious issues is that of race in America. The idealized version of '50s America presented is also an exceedingly white society. The film clearly calls attention to this fact through the scene in Lou's Cafe when a young Goldie Wilson is shown employed in a menial position as a busboy and cleaner, despite having greater ambitions. Marty recognizes Goldie as the African American town mayor from his own time, even blurting out this fact, which (in appropriate time-travel fashion) serves as the inspiration for Goldie to set his sights on just that goal. Interestingly, the film does not seem to recognize that Marty's influence could be seen as an example of the "white savior" trope, but the occasion provides for the audience the chance to contemplate the problematic nature of the scene, authorial intent aside.

Similarly, Marty inspires the birth of rock and roll by fronting the Starlighters—the band composed entirely of African American musicians playing traditional pop and classic rhythm 'n' blues—after their leader and guitar player, Marvin, injures his hand. When Marvin suggests that they play something that "really cooks," Marty's song of choice is "Johnny B. Goode," written by rock and roll pioneer Chuck Berry. The joke, of course, is that Marvin is Marvin *Berry*, Chuck's cousin, who calls Chuck to have him listen to something for that "new sound" he's been looking for. In actual history, many white musicians such as Elvis Presley made a great deal of money from songs originally written and recorded by African American artists, and to suggest that it was a white boy from the '80s who actually inspired them all along is, if amusing, highly problematic. Again, this is clearly meant as a bit of a time-travel gag, but unintentionally, the film's creators have suggested and perhaps even exacerbated the issue of cultural appropriation, but in doing so, they have again given the audience the occasion to consider the issue in a more distanced and contemplative manner.

Conclusions, Nostalgic or Otherwise

Back to the Future is a classic film that both represents the archetypical '80s Gen X aesthetic and the nostalgia that middle-aged Boomers felt for the '50s of their youth. By imitating and representing these eras, it gave the occasion for an audience composed of two generations to experience the pleasure of their respective ages. However, instead of merely indulging these pleasures, it also provided an opportunity to think critically about the phenomenon of nostalgia, and perhaps come to understand that nostalgia isn't always what it's cracked up to be.

The Punch That Changes Everything

John Garcia

It's easy to forget the life and family Marty McFly leaves behind in 1985 when he hops in Doc Brown's DeLorean and winds up back in 1955. However, it's helpful to remember the state of the McFlys when we first meet them. Marty's dad, George, is depicted as weak and placating as we see him cowing to Biff, who we soon learn has been bullying George since high school. Meanwhile, Marty's mom, Lorraine, is drinking heavily and is clearly unhappy. And Marty's brother and sister seem to be aimless (at best).

This picture becomes important when we contrast it with the portrayal of this same family after Marty returns to 1985. There, we see a confident George, no longer Biff's lackey, along with the entire family happy and apparently thriving. So, what changed? After all, before Marty's intervention, George and Lorraine meet and fall in love all on their own. However, when Marty prevents George from being hit by a car driven by Lorraine's father, he interrupts the sequence of events that were to have led to his parents meeting and falling in love. Having done this, Marty risks being "erased from existence" (along with his siblings). As such, in order to ensure his very survival, he sets out to ensure that George and Lorraine still meet and fall in love. In the end, of course, Marty *does* succeed, saving himself and his siblings. So, what explains the transformation of the McFlys that Marty discovers upon his return to 1985? The answer rests in the fact that, while his parents meet and fall in love, both with Marty's intervention and without it, the *reasons* Lorraine falls in love with George are entirely different.

Originally, Lorraine is moved by a sense of pity and compassion, as George is nursed back to health in her home after having been hit by her father's car. But through Marty's intervention, her reasons for falling in love with George are instead that he protects her by standing up to and knocking out Biff. This act—the punch—makes all the difference in the life of Marty's entire family. This essay is an attempt to examine just that punch and why it is so important. I will argue that George's punch of Biff is a key turning point for him, because it is where he begins the process of developing the virtue of courage. With this in mind, by looking at Aristotle's analysis of the connection between virtue and a well-lived life, we'll be able to see why George's transformation of character also changes everything else in his life as well as the life of his family.

A Note About Punching People

When I told a friend about the idea for this essay, he jokingly replied, "Oh, what a good message ... punching people is *good*." And indeed, it is important to pause and confront the idea that a defense of George's punch is a defense of violence generally or that it is yet another way of perpetuating the idea that what makes males "real men" is physical aggression. To be sure, too often we see depictions of men "winning the affections" of a love interest by taking on a male rival and physically defeating him. Those examples are (at a minimum) pretty tired and worn out. Worse than that, they risk teaching the ideas that violent behavior is an attractive quality and that women are a prize to be won in a contest.

However, George's punch of Biff is different. George does not challenge Biff to a fight (nor does Biff challenge George). Instead, George winds up confronting Biff without ever having meant to. Marty and George had hatched a plan in which Marty would pretend to get sexually aggressive with Lorraine, only to have George intercede. But the plan goes sideways, and when George finds Lorraine, he encounters not Marty but Biff, with Biff in the process of *actually* attempting to sexually assault Lorraine. His reaction and punch of Biff is thus a spontaneous action caused by his affection for Lorraine and his desire to protect her from genuine harm. The punch is not an attempt to establish dominance to win a prize; it is actually an act born of concern for someone else and one that was arguably necessary in that particular situation, so don't worry. We don't have to feel bad for rooting for George when he knocks Biff out.

"What does your mother ever see in that kid?"

It's important to understand that before Marty travels back to 1955, the "love" between George and Lorraine was born out of a sense of pity that Lorraine felt for George, rather than any admirable qualities George possessed. When we first get a glimpse of the McFlys, Lorraine recalls the story of how she and George first met and "fell in love." Lorraine reminisces: "He seemed so helpless, like a little lost puppy, and my heart just went out to him." Marty's sister then interrupts, saying, "I know, Mom, you felt sorry for him." It also becomes clear right away that the somewhat pathetic "lost puppy" that Lorraine first "felt sorry for" is still very much a feature of George's character in the present. We see this when we first meet Biff, who has taken George's car and crashed it but blames George for the accident. He also makes George do his reports for him. George is spineless, and Lorraine's drinking can be seen as a sign of her unhappiness at being married to such a person. When pushed by Marty about why he doesn't stand up to Biff, George meekly replies, "I'm just not good at confrontations." When we again encounter George in 1955, it isn't difficult to see how he has come to think this way.

Soon after Marty arrives in 1955, he stumbles into Lou's Cafe (bewildered by the realization that he's traveled back in time) to try to find a phone to contact the young Doc Brown. There, he encounters George, with Biff bullying him into doing his homework, in a manner nearly identical to the older Biff demanding that George write his reports for work. In response to having witnessed George's unwillingness to confront Biff, Goldie Wilson, the cafe's employee who will go on to become Mayor, interjects. "Have some respect for yourself … don't you know if you let people walk all over you now, they'll be walkin' over you for the rest of your life?" This point is made even more powerful by the fact that Goldie is a black man saying this in 1955, at a time when such a person standing up for himself could potentially invite very real, life-threatening danger, so it paints George's unwillingness to stand up for himself in an even more pitiful light.

We also see that George's lack of courage involves more than a fear of physical confrontation. When Marty learns that George writes science fiction stories and asks to read one, George replies, "I never let anybody read my stories…. What if they didn't like them? What if they told me I was no good?" In the same conversation, Marty also pushes George to ask Lorraine to the dance; George replies, "What if she said no? I don't know if I could take that kind of rejection." George is clearly someone who, at this point in his life, finds himself unable to take risks of any kind.

George's cowardice is more than just a small character flaw. As we see him first as an adult and then as a teenager, it is clear that his cowardice is connected to a larger sense of him being a rather pathetic person. We see this most clearly when Marty and Doc go to the high school and witness George literally being kicked around. Seeing George being repeatedly kicked (with a literal "Kick me" sign pinned to his back), Doc can't help but ask Marty, "What does your mother ever see in that kid?" to which Marty replies, "I don't know, Doc, I guess she felt sorry for him." In this moment, Marty is again reminded of the potentially disastrous consequences of having interfered with the course of events in history by preventing his eventual father, George, from getting hit by the car of Lorraine's father. However, when all things are said and done, it winds up being a rather *good* thing that Marty prevents his parents' relationship from being built on pity. Doc astutely observes that Lorraine's "love" for George was originally born out of no more than "the Florence Nightingale effect," where nurses fall in love with their patients. When Lorraine's "love" for George was simply based on pity, it could not serve as a solid foundation for a real relationship, so it should be no surprise that the family built on that foundation ends up floundering. Again, as we will see, the fact that Lorraine's love for George after Marty's intervention will come from admiring a quality in him, the virtue of courage; this will change everything for the McFlys. Indeed, George's ability to begin to acquire the virtue of courage is going to translate into his living a "successful life" more generally.

Aristotle and the Connection Between Virtue and "Living Well"

The simple fact that someone like George transforms from a person utterly lacking in courage to one who has learned to be courageous would not, by itself, be all that interesting. What is far more significant is that George's journey toward courage brings with it a larger transformation. We see this at the end of the original movie when not just George's life, but the lives of all of the McFlys are radically changed. However, in order to understand the connection between developing courage and having a successful life, it will help for us to briefly consider how the ancient philosopher Aristotle connects these two things in his work, *Nicomachean Ethics*.[1]

The fascinating thing about Aristotle's discussion of virtues like courage is that his focus isn't virtue but "happiness." Aristotle begins *Nicomachean Ethics* by arguing, some would say unnecessarily, that the ultimate goal in life is happiness and that we do everything else for the sake of being happy.[2] The claim that we do everything else for the sake of happiness should immediately signal to us that Aristotle means something very different by the word (that gets translated into English as "happiness") than the way we often use the word today. We are used to hearing the word happiness to describe a feeling. Understood this way, Aristotle would mean that we do everything we do because it makes us *feel* happy. So why do homework? Why work at all? Do we do these things because the actions make us feel happy? That would be great, but often, we don't do them for any pleasure they bring immediately but because we think they are necessary as part of a larger journey that we think of as a "good life." We work or do homework because they help us achieve larger goals, and these larger goals are all part of a happy or successful life. Aristotle makes this clear when he says that happiness is the same as "living well and faring well."[3]

It is easier for us to understand what Aristotle means if we imagine someone looking back at life and wondering, "How did I do? Did I crush it?" If we do this, we can easily imagine what some of the ingredients seem to be for a life that was "crushed." It seems to include having friendships, and love, and a bit of "good fortune" and even "sufficient external goods" (e.g., enough money to have a bit of comfort and freedom from suffering). Yet, we can also see that this idea of having "crushed it" seems to also include something else—the sense of being able to be proud of the kind of person one is.

It is hard to imagine someone like George (who is constantly being abused by others), who lacks any kind of self-confidence, sitting back at the end of life, being proud of how well-lived his life was, regardless of whether or not he has a loving family and "sufficient external goods." The goal is to live excellently, and it's not hard to see how closely related the ideas "living excellently" and "being excellent" are. Put simply, an awesome life includes having qualities that we think are an important part of being an awesome person.[4] And of course, one such quality is the virtue of courage. When we first meet him, it is this virtue that George completely lacks but eventually develops by the end of the first movie. And, in developing this virtue, it's not merely George's character that changes but his *life* itself.

Let's Dance, Biff

Marty's goal of finding a way to cause Lorraine to fall in love with George rests on a plan that culminates at the Enchantment Under the Sea dance. The plan is to have George encounter Marty and Lorraine in the car, with Marty pretending to be "out of line" with Lorraine. In this plan, George will pretend to stand up to Marty, saving Lorraine. It is crucial for the McFlys' eventual flourishing that this plan fails; if it had succeeded, George would have never been required to possess any real courage. His "courage" would have been entirely manufactured. Instead, when George finds Lorraine in the car, she's not with Marty but Biff, and she's in all too real danger. Lorraine pleads for his help: "George, help me, please!"

It is only then that George finds it within himself to finally stand up to Biff, saying, "No, Biff. You leave her alone." Biff then man-handles George, twisting his arm behind his back. When Biff then turns away, pushes Lorraine down, and lets out a maniacal cackle, George finds it within himself to deck him. And it is this act that is the beginning (but not the end!) of George's journey to finding courage within himself.

Importantly, it is not directly after being rescued from Biff that Lorraine kisses George. Instead, sometime after they head into the dance, Lorraine impatiently asks George, "Aren't you going to kiss me?" George hesitates, revealing that it is still uncertain whether the punch was an isolated incident, an act totally unconnected to a larger change to his character, perhaps made possible only by the extreme risk to Lorraine back in the car with Biff. It is then that yet another bully (albeit one much less intimidating the Biff Tannen) cuts in on George. "Scram, McFly," Lorraine calls out for George, eventually summoning him back. George swiftly deals with the lesser bully and finally kisses Lorraine. Only *then* does everything change. Lorraine and George fall in love at that moment and (unbeknownst to the happy couple on the dance floor) Marty and their other future children are saved. This second act is incredibly important because it shows that George's punch of Biff wasn't a fluke. On the contrary, it shows that George is slowly building the capacity to stand up for himself and for those he cares about (which will serve the McFlys well into the future).

Back in "the Future"

Again, when Marty arrives back in "the future," the situation for the whole family has radically changed. Marty's older brother, Dave, who had previously worked the night shift at Burger King, is now someone who always wears a suit to the office. Marty's sister, Linda, formerly lacked any sort of social confidence, but now has numerous suitors calling her. And of course, we also see a much more agreeable and subservient Biff waxing George's car.

It's all too easy to equate success with having material possessions, but that's not what Aristotle means by success. As we have seen, Aristotle's idea of "living well" or being successful is about much more than one's social status or wealth, so it could be argued (as Crispin Glover himself did) that emphasizing the McFlys' *financial* success is a disappointing, shallow way of communicating the idea that George's newly acquired virtues (especially the virtue of courage) has made him *truly* successful. But the connection between the success of developing one's character and outward rewards as a result of that development becomes clear when we see the source of the McFlys' finances. George is simply a more all-around, confident and courageous person. In fact, he's even recently published his first science fiction novel. This is an important detail as it shows that his courage was not just limited to protecting the woman he loves with physical violence. He has also clearly developed the courage to show others his writing, and his courage has paid off.

This last detail is extremely important as it connects to Aristotle's way of thinking about virtue. For Aristotle, simply performing a courageous act does not mean that one is yet a courageous *person*. George would not truly become a courageous person unless he has made a habit of acting courageously.[5] This is why it is important that, back in 1955, George stands up for himself not just in the parking lot with Biff, but again later at the dance with the subsequent, lesser bully. But even then, had we not seen George back "in the future," we would only be able to *hope* that he had gone on to make a habit out of acting courageously. The fact that he went on to publish a book of his science fiction (and to hold Biff accountable for putting on a second coat of wax to his car) shows that he has.

Aristotle's point—that virtuous character is the product of habit—is important for George, *and* for us. It is tempting to often believe that our characters are simply a product of our natures, that they are something fixed and unchangeable. George certainly has this view at the beginning of the movie. When Marty asks him why he doesn't stand up to Biff, he replies that he's "just not good at confrontations." However, Aristotle makes a point of reminding us that "none of the moral virtues arise in us by nature; for nothing that exists by nature can form a habit contrary to nature."[6] We see that George (after Marty's return to 1985) has clearly learned to appreciate this point, as he reminds Marty, handing him a copy of his new book, "It's like I've always told you, if you put your mind to it, you can accomplish *anything*."

Moral Exemplars, Past and Present

The line, "if you put your mind to it, you can accomplish anything," echoes throughout the movie, and it shows us another important part of the journey toward virtue—the role of moral exemplars. It's easy to think of Marty and George as opposites, with Marty in a daring skateboard chase just days after George was getting his literally butt kicked between classes at school. Yet, things are a bit more complicated. George's lack of courage has echoes in Marty himself, at least *before* Marty goes back to 1955. When we first meet Marty, his girlfriend, Jennifer, encourages him to send his demo tape to a record company, to which Marty replies, "What if I send in the tape and they don't like it? I mean, what if they say I'm no good? ... I mean, I just don't think I can take that kind of rejection. Jesus, I'm starting to sound like my old man!" In response, Jennifer tells Marty, "Remember what Doc's always saying..." to which Marty interjects, "Yeah, I know, I know, 'if you put your mind to it, you can accomplish anything.'" In this moment, we get a glimpse of the fact that Doc has served as a mentor to Marty, someone who possesses a virtue and can be a model for others. This is the idea of the moral exemplar—someone we can use as a light to guide us as we try to develop in virtue. Back in 1955, Marty takes on Doc's role for George, repeating the line to George as they plan out the ruse for George to "save" Lorraine from Marty at the dance. Things then come full circle when, back in the future, it is George who repeats the same advice to Marty.

There is an important difference between a moral exemplar and someone who simply offers advice. Moral exemplars do more than simply talk about how to act; they also show the ability to do so themselves. Doc has dared to create many inventions, so his words carry more weight than if they were just advice from an eccentric old man Marty happens to know. Marty also demonstrates that he is more than just talk, first when he prevents George from getting hit by Lorraine's father's car, and later when he stands up to Biff. Finally, it is only when we see that George's success has come from having the courage to pursue his writing that we hear him repeat the line back to Marty.

The Importance of Courage

I'm always surprised to hear resistance to the idea that some ways of being are better or more admirable than others. I do understand the tendency; it seems smug to say that one way of living is better than another, as if we are looking down on certain people. Yet, it is easy to see that the life George is living when we meet him in high school, where he is literally being kicked around, is no kind of life. Someone who lets people walk all over them is not the sort of person we would call successful, nor is such a person someone we would want to be. George is a rather obvious depiction of someone desperately in need of courage, and his form of standing up for himself and for someone he cares about, is a pretty "Hollywood" version of courage, where he literally knocks the bad guy out, kisses the girl, and lives happily ever after, so it is easy to see courage as simply standing up to bullies. When we watch George, we hopefully do not see very much of ourselves in him. If we are not facing a bully in our own lives, we may not feel any reason to think any more about how important the virtue of courage might be in our own lives.

Remember that George found the courage not just to stand up to a bully, but to share his writing. That example is likely much more relevant to many of us. So often, we are held back from what we truly wish to do through fear of some kind—of being judged, or of failing. Perhaps more significantly, we are shaken from our beliefs and our values all too easily by someone who dismisses them as foolish or misguided. The virtue of courage applies to all of these areas. I would suggest that it is no accident that, in the various places in the *Nicomachean Ethics* that Aristotle discusses the various moral virtues, he invariably lists courage first. The need to stand up for what is right is at least as common as the need to stand up to bullies, and so the lessons we can draw from Aristotle, and yes, from George and his punch, are relevant to all of us.

Notes

1. All references to Aristotle are from Aristotle. 1998. *Nicomachean Ethics*, translated by David Ross, revised by J.L. Ackrill and J.O. Urmson, Oxford University Press.
2. *Ibid.*, I.1.
3. *Ibid.*, I.4.
4. Aristotle actually makes it easier to see the connection between virtue, or human excellence, and happiness, or a well-lived life, by connecting these two ideas through a third idea. Aristotle says that we can better understanding of what he means by happiness by looking at the human "function" (I.7). To avoid distracting the reader, I didn't include that in the essay, but the concept is easy enough to understand. If happiness means "living well," it should occur to us that what it means for a mushroom or a snail to live well is different than what it means for a human to live well. So, we should look at what makes a human being *human*, in order to see what it would look like to live a *human life* well. Once we see that, we can see that someone who is living a human life well (or excellently) is doing an excellent job at being human—or, simply, they are an excellent human being, with a set of qualities that we think make people excellent. These qualities of character, or human excellences, are what gets called virtues.
5. Aristotle makes it clear that virtue is produced by habit, and, while it takes more than two actions to form a habit, it is important for us to see that George's first act of bravery is followed by a second, and we have to then imagine that this is the start of a change in his pattern of behavior, II.1.
6. *Ibid.*, II.1.

The Flux-Series of Time

Dennis M. Weiss

Are you a time-travel snob? Will you only tolerate logically rigorous time-travel narratives? Do you prefer *Interstellar* over *Bill and Ted's Excellent Adventure*? *Primer* rather than *The Adam Project*? I have a feeling that philosopher Theodore Sider is just such a snob. Sider has written extensively about the nature of time and when it comes to time travel and philosophy, he suggests that *Back to the Future* just doesn't cut it. "Whatever its literary merits," he notes, "as a work of philosophy *Back to the Future* fails miserably."

Sider is more a fan of *The Terminator*: "Let's not be too hard on careless screenwriters and authors. (We can't all be philosophers.) Though it's not easy, paradox-free time travel stories can be told. The movie Terminator is an excellent example."[1] It's worth noting, however, Sider immediately qualifies this: "*Terminator 1*, that is. *Terminator 2* appears to be incoherent." Those careless screenwriters should've paid closer attention when they were undergraduates slogging through Philosophy 101. In the entry on "Time Travel" in *The Stanford Encyclopedia*, Nicholas Smith would seem to agree, observing that "in the popular imagination, backwards time travel would allow one to change the past: to right the wrongs of history, to prevent one's younger self from doing things that would later be regretted, and so on. In a model with a single past, however, *this idea is incoherent*: the very description of the case involves a contradiction...."[2] We might conclude that despite its cultural success and impact, as philosophy, *Back to the Future* is incoherent and fails miserably. And yet...

Might those "careless screenwriters" school our philosophers on a thing or two? Don't get me wrong; I'm a fan of logically rigorous time-travel stories. Films like *Interstellar*, *Primer*, *12 Monkeys*, or its progenitor *La Jette* are fascinating films worthy of philosophical analysis. They remain paradox-free and so, in Sider's terms, don't "fail miserably." The *Back to the Future* franchise *does* seem to be in a different class of time-travel films, one less geared toward logical rigor but more broadly entertaining. For instance, in *Part II*, Marty's encounter with his future self creates a temporal paradox that defies strict logical rules, yet it serves as a compelling narrative device to explore the complexities of self-identity and agency. Are we right to suggest that, at least philosophically, such films fail miserably? Are they, as Smith suggests, incoherent? I'll suggest not.

Back to the Future embraces a more experiential understanding of time and a playful subversion of stringent temporal logic to foster an alternative interpretation of time—what I'll call the "Flux-Series" model of temporal narrative, symbolized by the narrative's central device, the flux capacitor. The Flux-Series portrays a cinematic articulation of time that captures both the calculable progression of events and the personal, affective journey of the film's characters. By inviting viewers to empathize with the characters' struggles navigating the complexities of time travel, *Back to the Future* encourages reflection on the philosophical and existential implications of temporal displacement. Far from failing miserably as a work of philosophy, the trilogy is a philosophically engaging work which employs a distinctive take on time and time travel narratives to engage with questions of identity, agency, and the possibility of transformation—themes that resonate deeply within the shared human experience and are explored through the imaginative possibilities of science fiction.

The Inexorability of Clock Time

What drives Sider's philosophical condemnation of *Back to the Future*? To answer this question and to get a handle on some difficult philosophical ideas, let's turn to the film itself—I mean the actual film *stock* (not that many movies are filmed on actual film stock these days). Imagine the film spread out before us across a series of frames on a film reel. Each frame represents the movie at a specific moment, and when you play the reel quickly, you see the movie as a continuous story. In this movie, Marty McFly's adventures through time can be likened to navigating the "film reel" of the universe. Each moment in time is like a single frame on this reel. Normally, we move through these frames in order—one after the other—just as a movie plays from start to finish. However, with a time machine, Marty can skip back and forth to different "frames" in the movie of reality.

Sider's view of time, what philosophers call four-dimensionalism, posits that objects and persons are thought of as being "spread out" over time, much like scenes in a movie. This idea connects closely to what's known as (following John McTaggart's influential account of time)[3] the

B-series of time, where events are ordered not by what's happening now, but by their relations of "earlier than" or "later than" each other. In the context of four-dimensionalism, Marty, the time machine, and everything else in the universe extend not just through space but also through this B-series timeline. This means that all moments, whether past, present, or future, are equally real, allowing for the conceptual possibility of moving between different points on this timeline, much like skipping scenes in a movie.

But of course, each frame in that reel of film is "fixed." As Marty skips from one frame of the film to another, he is not free to change what happened in earlier frames of the film. This immutability of the frames underscores an important element of four-dimensionalism: all moments in time—past, present, and future—are predetermined and unchangeable within the spacetime continuum. However, this notion of immutability seems to clash with Marty's experiences in the film, where his actions in the past appear to alter the present and future, creating alternate timelines and realities. Marty's actions, perceived as changes from his perspective, must already be accounted for in the "film." The "film" of the universe, with all its frames, is a complete entity where every scene and sequence, including Marty's time-traveling interventions, are fixed and were always meant to be part of the story.

This view of time, as encapsulated by four-dimensionalism, would likely resonate deeply with Doc Brown. Consider the film's opening scene, which meticulously showcases his house adorned with an array of clocks, each one ticking in perfect harmony, symbolizing the objective and unalterable nature of clock time. This imagery, combined with the portraits of great minds like Newton, Einstein, Edison, and Franklin adorning his mantle, underscores Doc's reverence for the principles of science and the immutable laws of the universe. Initially, Doc warns Marty of the severe risks associated with altering the timeline, reflecting his understanding that the fabric of time is delicately interwoven and not to be tampered with lightly. And yet...

The Flux-Series of Time

In those first few frames of the film, we are reminded both aurally and visibly of the inexorable passage of time. We hear the incessant ticking of the clock and we see dozens of clocks marking the objective passage of time. But soon things go sideways. The toast is burnt. The dog food ends up on the floor. And finally, Doc informs Marty that time is off by 25 minutes (which means Marty is late for school). And courtesy of Principal

Strickland, we learn that Doc Brown is a real nutcase. "You hang around with him, you're gonna end up in big trouble." Time goes awry, and *Back to the Future* signals a resistance to the straitjacket of four-dimensionalism and the logical rigors of time travel.

It's not like Doc and the films aren't aware of the challenges in addressing philosophically rigorous time travel. As Doc ominously warns Marty early into his trip back to 1955, "You must not leave this house! You must not see anybody or talk to *anybody*. Anything you do could have serious repercussions on future events. *Do you understand*?" One oft-cited time travel challenge is the Grandfather Paradox—Marty can no more go back in time and kill his grandfather than he can travel to an earlier frame of the film and make script changes. *Back to the Future* embraces a kind of Grandfather Paradox. Marty's grandfather, rather than running over George, runs over Marty, resulting in a different kind of paradox, as it leads to Lorraine crushing on Calvin (er ... Marty). Putting aside dark visions of parricide or Lorraine's potential Jocasta complex, the trilogy embraces instead a light-hearted approach to the complexities of time travel, weaving humor and heart into the fabric of its narrative. By sidestepping the dire implications of the Grandfather Paradox, *Back to the Future* cleverly navigates through the potential pitfalls of altering the past. Instead of focusing on the impossible task of changing a "script" which has already been written in the continuum of time, the film plays with the idea that our interactions can lead to unforeseen consequences.

It's that playful approach which is at the heart of Doc's invention of the flux capacitor that powers his souped-up DeLorean. Doc's time travel revelation comes as he's standing on the edge of his toilet.

> That was the day I invented time travel. I remember it vividly. I was standing on the edge of my toilet hanging a clock, the porcelain was wet, I slipped, hit my head on the edge of the sink. And when I came to, I had a revelation! A vision! A picture in my head! A picture of *this* [Doc points to an electric gizmo in the back of the DeLorean]: this is what makes time travel possible. The flux capacitor.

The introduction of the flux capacitor represents a pivotal moment in the film's departure from the constraints of four-dimensionalism. Unlike the fixed and predetermined nature of time in that philosophical framework, the flux capacitor symbolizes the fluidity and malleability of time, paving the way for the Flux-Series. It's the flux capacitor that ultimately serves to sideline Sider and introduce a different conception of time, a Flux-Series of time that challenges the logical rigors of four-dimensionalism.

The Flux-Series places the lived experience of time at the forefront, rather than just its logical progression—highlighted by the trilogy's focus on the personal growth and development of the characters as they journey through time. What's more important is this transformative power of time and personal growth, rather than the rigid logic of an unbending temporal structure. The Flux-Series emphasizes a dynamic, experiential view where events aren't fixed, but fluid, and can be influenced by the characters' actions, reflecting a less deterministic conception of time where the potential for change is ever-present.

Central to this portrayal is the notion of narrative time, distinct from objective, clock-based measurements. The Flux-Series embraces time as a mutable continuum shaped through storytelling, causal flexibility, and the intersection of personal timelines. At its heart is the idea of time as dynamic and transformative, allowing for the possibility of change and alternate realities. The series underscores the interconnectedness of individual experiences, stressing how human connections collectively shape temporal realities. This relational, subjective understanding of time stands as a counterpoint to Sider's demand for paradox-free, logical rigor. *Back to the Future* suggests that exploring the human condition through time travel narratives need not adhere strictly to traditional temporal logic but should appreciate the complexity and subjectivity of temporal experience.

Sidelining Sider: It's Science Fiction, Not Science Fact

While Doc might have a pantheon of inventor scientists decorating his fireplace mantle, that doesn't stop him from taking a more playful stance toward science fact. When Marty tries to warn Doc about his future death, Doc will have none of it. "No! Marty, we've already agreed that having information about the future could be extremely dangerous. Even if your intentions are *good*, they could backfire drastically. Whatever you've got to tell me, I'll find out through the natural course of time." But Marty later discovers that Doc has taped back together the letter Marty had earlier written, warning him about his fate, and invested in a bulletproof vest.

> MARTY: What about all that talk about screwing up future events, the space time continuum?
> Doc: Well, I figured, *what the hell.*

When confronted with the inexorability of the space-time continuum, maybe the best reply is indeed, "what the hell." Rather than abiding by the rigors of four-dimensional time travel and staying true to science, *Back to the Future* features a canine named Einstein as the world's first time traveler. This humorous and imaginative choice not only sets a playful tone but also signals the film's willingness to prioritize creative storytelling over strict adherence to scientific principles, allowing for a more expansive exploration of the human experience of time.

Back to the Future repeatedly signals that it's more interested in science fiction than science fact, and it's science fiction that allows us to imaginatively explore the human experience of time. The film's constant nod to science fiction tropes and its self-aware handling of time travel conventions illustrates its playful engagement with the genre. By posing time travel paradoxes and conventions, only to then sideline or subvert them, *Back to the Future* invites the audience to engage with the narrative on a level that transcends literal interpretations of temporal mechanics.

This is most clearly seen in Marty's budding relationship with his future father. Marty is surprised to discover that George is something of a creative writer, spending his days scribbling sci-fi narratives into his notebook. Scribbles he shows no one, for the same reason Marty doesn't share his music:

> Alright, okay, Jennifer. What if I send in the tape, and they don't like it? I mean, what if they say I'm no good? What if they say, "Get outta here, kid, you got no future." I mean, I just don't think I can take that kind of rejection. [sighs] Jesus, I'm beginning to sound like my old man.

But it's the power of science fiction that ultimately drives the narrative forward. When arriving in the past, Marty is shot at, because he's thought to be a space invader, just like the cover of Sherman's pulp science fiction magazine. George suggests he can't take Lorraine to the school dance, because he'll miss his favorite television program, *Science Fiction Theater*. And later, when Marty shows up in George's bedroom in his Devo-inspired radiation shoot, he ominously claims to be "Darth Vader," an extra-terrestrial from the planet Vulcan. It's that scene that ultimately leads to one of future George's successes, his first novel, *A Match Made in Space*, featuring a cover similar to George's experience with Marty.

Science fiction as a genre celebrates the power of human imagination to envision alternative realities and futures. *Back to the Future*'s playful and creative handling of time travel, exemplified by its subversion of tropes and its prioritization of imaginative storytelling over strict temporal logic, underscores the philosophical possibilities of the Flux-Series model. By embracing the imaginative possibilities of science fiction, the film reflects the genre's broader capacity to inspire wonder, caution, and reflection about the human condition across different temporal and spatial dimensions. Rather than fail miserably as a work of philosophy, we might say instead that *Back to the Future* sidelines Sider and four-dimensionalism and embraces a Flux-Series of time more concerned with its characters' journeys than paradox-free time travel. In doing so, the film suggests that exploring the richness of human experience through time travel narratives need not adhere strictly to traditional temporal logic but can instead appreciate the complexity and subjectivity of temporal experience through the lens of creative storytelling.

The Power of Rock and Roll and the Erasure of History

That *Back to the Future* is more interested in the Flux-Series of time than the B-series of four-dimensionalism is underscored by its emphasis on "the power of love" rather than the power of time. Huey Lewis's "The Power of Love," beyond being the film's main theme, metaphorically underscores the idea that love and human connections transcend temporal boundaries. Through Marty and Jennifer's relationship, along with George and Lorraine's evolving romance, *Back to the Future* illustrates how personal connections can defy and redefine temporal constraints, emphasizing love's transformative power. The song complements the Flux-Series by highlighting emotional continuity across time, suggesting that relationships and emotions are as influential in shaping the course of events as any physical action.

The *Back to the Future* franchise regularly flirted with the power of rock and roll, from its featured cameos by Lewis, ZZ Top, and Flea of the Red Hot Chili Peppers, to Marty's strategic use of "Edward Van Halen" to awaken George from his sci-fi slumbers. Rock and roll, with its history of cultural disruption and innovation, parallels the film's portrayal of time as dynamic and subject to change, reinforcing the Flux-Series' emphasis on temporal fluidity, personal agency, and the impact of individual actions on the broader tapestry of history. Despite all those time-travel curmudgeons who dismiss the film, its philosophical and thematic richness doesn't lie in the power of time but in the power of rock and roll and love, which are more flexible and fluid than time. But while the film's exploration of these themes through the Flux-Series model is commendable, it's equally important to acknowledge the potential pitfalls and narrative responsibilities that arise when reimagining history and cultural realities.

It's here that the film does flirt with philosophical problems—not the problem of changing history but the problem of erasing history. The problems of the Flux-Series of time are less about incoherence and more about anachronistic and culturally problematic interventions into history. While the Flux-Series explores the dynamic and mutable nature of time, these particular narrative choices reflect a lack of sensitivity to the real-world historical and cultural contexts, especially regarding race and cultural contributions. Marty observes that "history is gonna change," and that seems central to the Flux-Series. But as the film imagines history changing, it does so in racially insensitive ways.

The scene in which Marty performs "Johnny B. Goode" at the Fish Under the Sea dance, leading to the implication that he, rather than Chuck Berry, originated rock and roll, has been critiqued for cultural appropriation.[4] Rock and roll has deep roots in African American culture, and crediting its creation to a white teenager from the 1980s overlooks the genre's true origins and the contributions of Black artists.

Similarly, the scene where Marty inspires Goldie Wilson, a Black diner worker in 1955, to become mayor of Hill Valley, touches on issues of revisionist history. While ostensibly positive, this interaction suggests that individual inspiration from a white character is necessary for a Black character to aspire to or achieve political success, which can overshadow the realities of systemic racism and the self-determined civil rights movements led by Black communities. This narrative choice, while well-intentioned, could be seen as an oversimplification of the complex social and political struggles faced by marginalized communities, further emphasizing the need for thoughtful and nuanced representation in time travel stories.

This critique highlights a broader issue of narrative responsibility, especially in science fiction and time travel stories. While these genres offer unique opportunities to reimagine history and explore alternative temporalities, they also bear the responsibility of handling historical and cultural realities with sensitivity and awareness, avoiding the perpetuation of stereotypes or the diminishment of historical figures and movements.

To fully realize the philosophical potential of the Flux-Series and the film's playful temporal manipulation, our "careless screenwriters and authors" need to engage with these complex issues a bit more thoughtfully. Marty observes that "history is gonna change" and that seems central to the Flux-Series, which emphasizes the capacities of growth and development to the human experience of time's passing. But as the film imagines history changing, it does so in racially problematic ways. Having sidelined Sider's concerns over the logical rigors of time travel narratives, our screenwriters and authors might have been better schooled not in philosophy but in constructing time travel narratives that remain responsive to history's disruptive moments in time.

Notes

1. Sider, Theodore. 2016. "Time." *Science Fiction and Philosophy*. Susan Schneider (ed.). Wiley Blackwell.

2. Smith, Nicholas J.J. 2024. "Time Travel." *The Stanford Encyclopedia of Philosophy.*
3. McTaggart, J.M.E. 1908. "The Unreality of Time." *Mind* 17: 457–73.
4. See, for instance, Andrew Shail and Robin Stoate's discussion of the film's treatment of the birth of rock and roll in 2010, *Back to the Future*, British Film Institute.

Doc Brown and the Erotic Ideal

JUSTIN KITCHEN

Watching *Back to the Future* when I was younger, I never once thought that Dr. Emmett L. Brown was *remotely* erotic. I've since reconsidered, and I'm now ready to argue my case: Doc Brown is the *quintessence* of eroticism! He displays an expertise in eroticism more pronounced than any other character in the franchise and perhaps more than most people in general.

You may be relieved to hear that the potential or actual sexual escapades of the eccentric scientist aren't relevant to my discussion and will not be explored in this essay. Instead, I'll establish different ways to conceive of love and eroticism and then relate these to the behavior and personality of Doc Brown. We will quickly discover expressions of love that go beyond the sexual and conventionally romantic—love reminiscent of the activities and feelings of good friends, trusted companions, intimate confidants, and lifelong partners. Keep an open mind and let's explore these important ideas together. By the end, Doc's erotic expertise will be made clear.

"*This is for all you lovers out there*": Intro to Eros

The first thing we must do is understand and expand our concept of "love" and "erotic." We get the term "erotic" from the Ancient Greek word *erōs*, which is usually translated as "love." Eroticism has a complex history in Western culture, so it will make things easier for us if we focus on an authoritative voice in Western Philosophy itself—specifically, the voice of Socrates in the works of Plato. *More* specifically, it would be fruitful to focus on one of Plato's most beloved works on love, the *Symposium*. This work consists of a series of conversations and speeches about *erōs* taking place at a drinking party in Ancient Athens.

We'll focus on two or three competing images of love found in the

Symposium. The first is the romantic love presented by two characters: Aristophanes and Alcibiades. The second image of love is the so-called "Platonic love" presented by the character of Socrates. This is all in the hope of explaining the kind of love that Doc seems to exemplify.

"You're my density": Aristophanic Love

Aristophanes was a famous comic playwright in Ancient Greece (you can find his plays at your local bookstore). In Plato's work, the *character* of Aristophanes gives a speech in the form of a mythology of the human race and how they came to experience love. He describes ancient humans in a comical fashion:

> The shape of each human being was completely round, with back and sides in a circle; they had four hands each, as many legs as hands, and two faces, exactly alike, on a rounded neck. Between the two faces, which were on opposite sides, was one head with four ears.[1]

The gods became afraid of the power and ambitions of these humans, and so Zeus cracked a plan. He would cut the humans in two with his lightning bolt and let them roam around the world with two legs and two arms. And so the gods made the human race not a collection of *individuals*, but a collection of *pairs*, separated by cruel fate and with a longing to reunite. This longing is love:

> This, then, is the source of our desire to love each other. Love is born into every human being; it calls back the halves of our original nature together; it tries to make one out of two and heal the wound of human nature.[2]

This image of love has continued for 2,500 years in pop culture, saturated as it is with themes like "true love," "the one," and "destiny." Turn the radio dial to any pop music channel and you'll hear refrain after refrain on these themes. Rewatch *Back to the Future* and you'll hear Marty's advice to George, hitting on this familiar theme:

> MARTY: Tell her that destiny brought you together. Tell her that she is the most beautiful girl that you have ever seen in the world. Girls like that stuff.... What are you doing, George?
> GEORGE: I'm writing this down; this is good stuff.

But this scene is telling because both the characters and the audience know there's something wrong with it (that's what makes it funny). Marty admits that his advice is deceptive, but that it may be useful because "girls like that stuff." And George immediately recognizes it as a work of good fiction—perhaps material for his future novel.

And what happens when George confronts his crush, Lorraine, with this "good stuff?" Instead of speaking from the heart, he tries to put on a schmaltzy voice and fails *spectacularly*:

> GEORGE [glancing at his notepad outstretched before him]: Lorraine, my density has brought me to you.
> LORRAINE: What?
> GEORGE: Oh. What I meant to say was....
> LORRAINE: Wait a minute. Don't I know you from somewhere?
> GEORGE: Yes! Yes. I'm George. George McFly. I'm your density.... I mean, your *destiny*.

Doc will not have any of this romantic nonsense. The only pop culture works that he references—the works of Jules Verne—are much, much older and don't really contain such themes. And his advice for George (via Marty) is more practical: have him ask Lorraine to a rhythmic ceremonial ritual.

But we must admit that Doc feels and expresses love—towards Marty and Clara and towards science and the pursuit of knowledge—so we must move on to our next character in the *Symposium* and our next interpretation of love in order to expand our understanding. In comes Socrates...

"Doc, she's beautiful": Stages of Platonic Love

In response to Aristophanes' portrait of love, Socrates steps up and begins his speech. Despite the common belief that Socrates said "I only know that I know nothing" (a misquote), Socrates did indeed claim to know about "matters of love"[3]—or, a more literal translation from the Greek, "the erotic" (*ta erōtika*).

Socrates continues and says that he learned "matters of love" from a mysterious and wise woman named Diotima.[4] She taught that true lovers move through progressive stages of love—each stage directed towards a higher form of beauty, each sublimated or abstracted from the lower form. These stages collectively make up Diotima's so-called "Ladder of Love."

"He's an absolute dream": Conventionally Romantic Love

The first rung represents conventional romantic love, similar to the Aristophanic image of love already presented: the lover's attention and desire are directed towards the beauty of a *body*.[5]

The love at this first level is dream-like, which is in keeping with what Lorraine constantly shouts about Marty throughout the first film: "Isn't he a dreamboat!" ... "Oh my god, he's a dream!" ... "He's an absolute dream!" ... It seems too good to be true!

Again, this is the romantic nonsense that Doc flags in *Part III* when he dismisses the notion of "love at first sight." It seems that such a condition would have to be based on a superficial impression of another person's beautiful body and face. This superficiality is what makes it a poor candidate for a meaningful experience of love, and it's what prompts Doc to dismiss the idea outright:

> DOC: The idea that I can fall in love at first sight is romantic nonsense. There's no scientific rationale for that.
> MARTY: Aw, come on, Doc. It's not science. You meet the right girl, it just hits you. It's like lightning.

It may be like a bolt of lightning in its power but also in its brevity. It's a flash in the pan and very often unsustainable. The dream often ends as suddenly as it began. The prime example of this is at the end of the first film when the object of Lorraine's desire is actualized with a kiss:

> LORRAINE: This is all wrong. I don't know what it is. But when I kiss you, it's like I'm kissing ... my *brother*.

The lesson that Diotima is imparting here is twofold: first, this is a common place to *start* our education on "matters of love"; and second, we cannot stay at this level, but must continue to advance up the ladder.

"Your friend in time": Companionate Love

The second rung of Diotima's Ladder of Love represents companionate love, in which the lover's attention is directed towards the beauty of an individual *soul*:

> After this the lover must think that the beauty of people's souls is more valuable than the beauty of their bodies, so that if someone is decent in his soul, our lover must be content to love and care for him and to seek to give birth to such ideas as will make him better.[6]

A helpful way to think about this is when you love someone for their beautiful character or integrity and see their body as secondary or irrelevant to the beauty you're attracted to. Lorraine manifests this a bit when she takes Marty's character as something that *enhances* his beauty. On the other hand, she takes a lack of character (for example, a lack of moral courage) as a reason *not* to love someone: "George McFly? He's kind of cute and all but ... well, I think a man should be strong. So, he can stand up for himself and protect the woman he loves."

136   IV. Matters of Value

This is definitely the kind of love Doc displays. First, towards Marty, to whom he wrote a touching letter ending with these heartfelt sentiments:

> You've been a good, kind, and loyal friend to me, and you made a real difference in my life. I will always treasure our relationship and think on you with fond memories, warm feelings, and a special place in my heart. Your friend in time, "Doc" Emmett L. Brown.

Doc demonstrates companionate love time and again by helping Marty acquire a more coherent understanding of reality and by helping him preserve the best version of their future. This is just what Diotima means when she says that lovers will make each other better. Doc encourages Marty time and again by insisting, "If you put your mind to it, you can accomplish anything." This encouragement is passed on to a 1955 George, which then returns to Marty in 1985, proving the positive influence of Doc Brown on the entire McFly family.

Of course, Doc also displays companionate love towards Clara. We discover at the end of *Part III* that they become companions in time the way that Doc and Marty were. Presumably, they make each other better people—giving each other clarity of meaning and happiness, which they pass down to their children.

We have to admit, though, that the love Doc expresses towards Clara is more substantial than the love he has towards Marty. Can Socrates and Diotima continue to help us capture this special kind of love?

"I love science": Intellectual Love

The next rung of Diotima's ladder represents a kind of *intellectual* love, in which the lover's attention is directed towards the beauty of *ideas*. Presumably, the ideas that the lover saw actualized in the soul of their companion in the previous rung of the ladder are then abstracted and loved for their own sake:

> Our lover will be forced to gaze at the beauty of activities and laws and to see that all this is akin to itself, with the result that he will think that the beauty of bodies is a thing of no importance. He will see the beauty of knowledge and be looking mainly not at beauty in a single example but the lover is turned to the great sea of beauty, and, gazing upon this, he gives birth to many gloriously beautiful ideas and theories, in unstinting love of wisdom, until, having grown and been strengthened there, he catches sight of such knowledge, and it is the knowledge of such beauty.[7]

Doc has certainly reached this rung of the Ladder of Love, but it seems he did it well before the events of *Back to the Future*. I don't think it's inaccurate to describe the love Doc has for scientific ideas and knowledge as *unstinting*. We find Doc living in a garage after spending all his family wealth and selling off his family's property in pursuit of scientific breakthroughs. He admits to Clara in *Part III* that this passion was ignited when he was eleven after reading *Twenty Thousand Leagues Under the Sea*: "That's when I realized that I must devote my life to science."

But then he meets Clara and wants to devote his life to her. Does Doc then reach an even higher rung on Diotima's "Ladder of Love"? I'm not so sure. We may have to kick Diotima's ladder away and come back to the ground.

"Love like that doesn't happen too often": Philosophic Love

The highest rung of Diotima's ladder—the highest form of Platonic love—represents what we'll call *philosophic* love, in which the lover's attention is directed towards *beauty itself*:

> This is what it is to go aright, or be led by another, into the mystery of Love: one goes always upwards for the sake of this Beauty, starting out from beautiful things and using them like rising stairs: from beautiful bodies to learning beautiful things, and from these lessons the lover arrives in the end at this lesson, which is learning of this very Beauty, so that in the end he comes to know just what it is to be beautiful.[8]

No, this won't do. It sounds majestic and … beautiful, but it doesn't seem to capture what Doc is experiencing with Clara. Platonic love moves further and further away from the world of concrete objects and people, but Clara *grounds* Emmett: she brings him back to the world of people—horse rides, town festivals, dancing, star gazing, and flower picking.

Likewise, what brings Socrates back to the ground in Plato's *Symposium* is … Alcibiades. This character becomes the last in Plato's *Symposium* to give a speech (a notable position in the work). But the image of love he presents is fixed squarely on the ugly mug of Socrates himself. Alcibiades proceeds to give a speech *about Socrates*—the exemplary philosopher—and portrays him as the very embodiment of love:

> If I were to describe for you what an extraordinary effect his words have always had on me (I can feel it this moment even as I'm speaking), you might actually suspect that I'm drunk! Still, I swear to you, the moment he starts to speak, I am beside myself. He makes me admit that all that matters is just what I most neglect: my personal shortcomings, which cry out for the closest attention.[9]

There are two interpretations of this idea of love, and both ask us to return to the love of an *individual*. The first asks us to return to the second rung where the lover is attracted to the beauty of one's soul—their moral character. This is awkward in Platonic philosophy and seems to contradict the advice of Diotima, who insists that "one goes always upward."[10] The second interpretation takes us away from Platonic philosophy entirely and towards another school of philosophy—Stoicism (capital "S," not lowercase "s"). This second interpretation makes more sense, and it better portrays Doc as an expert in matters of love.

"One in a googleplex": Stoic Love

The love that Doc ultimately manifests is not Platonic. As it develops, it starts to move up into the world of ideas (so to speak), but then grounds itself in the world of people and one specific person: Clara Clayton. If we stick to Plato's framework, Doc seems to go back to the first or second rung of Diotima's Ladder of Love when he encounters Clara. One may even think he topples down into Aristophanic love: Doc admits to his drinking companion that he thinks Clara is "one in a million. One in a billion. One in a *googolplex*. The woman of my dreams." So the best tack for us to interpret his love as something admirable and praiseworthy is to use Stoic philosophy to frame it instead of Platonic philosophy.

Love is a difficult topic to discuss in Stoicism, partially due to a lack of primary sources. On the one hand, all the Stoics whose works have survived—Seneca, Epictetus, Marcus Aurelius—often speak of love as a harmful form of desire, a kind of insanity (akin to Aristophanic love). It's something that must be avoided if one is to be truly happy. On the other hand, a more positive *erōs* is clearly described by the early Greek Stoics. And it's listed among healthy emotions by several ancient sources.[11]

> They say that love is an effort to form a friendship because of an impression of beauty.... That is why the wise person is also an erotic person and will fall in love with those worthy of love.[12]

All love is characterized as directed towards a relationship with someone or something you find beautiful—that's in keeping with Platonic love. But the kind of relationship and the kind of beauty is what makes the difference. Bad love is an impulse directed exclusively towards outer beauty (physical attractiveness) and sexual intercourse. But good love, the only love worthy of the name according to Stoics, is an impulse directed towards inner beauty (virtue) and friendship. This is the love that Doc experiences at the end of the franchise; it is Stoic love. And it is the sight of Clara's inner beauty that hits him like a bolt of lightning and electrifies his life. More importantly, this is the love that can be maintained and even *grows* over time.

Stoic love is a kind of friendship akin to companionate love. It's an ongoing kind of impulse called an *epibolē* (translated as either "effort," "resolve," or "inclination"). Its defining feature is that it anticipates a future relationship where both parties are wise and virtuous. True love entails true friendship, where both parties push each other to be better. As we know, our future is whatever we make it, so we best make it a good one. This is not the lower rung of a ladder or one of many steps on a staircase: it is certainly the ideal of a loving relationship.

So, there we have it. We can say that Doc moves through Platonic love easily enough. He apparently jumps towards the top of Diotima's Ladder of Love as young as eleven years old when he fosters a strong love of science and the pursuit of knowledge. In doing so, he skips over Aristophanic and romantic love. He very clearly fosters companionate love for Marty, in which they both help each other become better. And then all these disparate pieces are collected into a beautiful whole when he meets Clara. His first glimpse of her seems to ignite a kind of love that is best explained using Stoic philosophy: a wonderful blend of romantic, companionate, and intellectual love focused on a single person. This Stoic love that Emmett and Clara foster is a lifelong friendship prompted and maintained by their impression of inner beauty in the other.

Surely, we can no longer deny the eroticism of Dr. Emmett L. Brown. Throughout the *Back to the Future* franchise, he has displayed an expertise in love—many different types of love—more prominently than most. We can only hope to reach the heights of eroticism that Doc has reached. Only time will tell.

Notes

1. Plato. 1997. *Plato: Complete Works*. Nehamas, A.; Woodruff, P. (trans.). Cooper, J.M. (ed.). Hackett. 190d. The cited numbers in parentheses are Stephanus pages, which are found in many translations of Plato.
2. *Ibid.*, 191d.
3. *Ibid.*, 177d–e.
4. *Ibid.*, 201d–207a.
5. *Ibid.*, 210a.
6. *Ibid.*, 210c.
7. *Ibid.*, 210c–e.
8. *Ibid.*, 211c.
9. *Ibid.*, 215d–216a.
10. Nussbaum, Margaret. 1986. *The Fragility of Goodness*. Cambridge University Press. In Chapter 6, Nussbaum discusses the dilemma Plato seems to present us: do we follow beauty away from the love of an individual (as Diotima suggests)? Or do we stay and limit ourselves (as Alcibiades seems to suggest)? Doc seems to show us a path between the horns of the dilemma.
11. See especially Cicero. 1927. *Tusculan Disputations*. King, John Edward (trans.)

140   IV. Matters of Value

Harvard University Press. 4.62–79. Other examples include Diogenes Laertius, Arius Didymus, and Pseudo-Andronicus.

    12. Didymus, Arius. 1999. *Epitome of Stoic Ethics*. Pomeroy, A.J. (trans.). Society of Biblical Literature. §11s. The translation was modified to maintain consistency in terms.

V

Sex and Gender in *Back to the Future*

"Regress" to the Future

Catherine Villanueva Gardner

> "Time traveling is just too dangerous, better that I devote myself to studying the other great mystery of the universe—women!"
> —Doc Brown, *Back to the Future Part II*

In 2022, Michael J. Fox suggested that, for any reboot of the *Back to the Future* series, the main character should be female. It was in an interview with *ET* that Fox pitched this potentially progressive update, saying, "I actually had this thought that if they did the movie again, they should do it with a girl as Marty."[1] Initially, such a shift would seem like a breath of fresh air in an industry that is still problematically male-dominated. Indeed, even as recently as the 2024 Oscars, both critics and fans criticized the apparent male bias in both the selection of the nominees as well as the winners. Moreover, as renowned science fiction author, Pamela Sargent has noted, the science fiction genre does not just focus on scientific possibilities; it can also be called "the literature of ideas."[2] In other words, science fiction allows us to ask "what if?" In fact, for many years, the back cover of *Asimov's Science Fiction Magazine* included an advertisement asking just that—"What if?"—to solicit membership,[3] so the genre of *Back to the Future* would seem to be wide open to the possibility of a gender switch in its main character.

Fox's suggestion of "what if?" Marty was a woman is both intriguing and courageous as recent gender-switched movie reboots have typically lacked commercial and/or critical success. The 2018 *Ocean's 8*, a re-gendered spin-off of the *Ocean*'s franchise, was reasonably successful at the box office, mainly due to the star power of the lead characters and their ensemble interactions. However, the movie is an example where the narrative drive of the movie is only ostensibly generated by the female main characters, but as critics have argued, these women are never allowed to be fully agents in their own story, as their "man troubles" disrupt the narrative of their woman-led caper.[4] In contrast, *Terminator: Dark Fate*, with its introduction of a female terminator, was fairly well received by critics, but tanked at the box office, although Linda Hamilton's reprisal of her role as Sarah Connor has been seen as progress for representations of older women and female lead characters in general. The 2016 *Ghostbusters* movie, a reboot of the 1984 original, essentially followed the narrative of the original film, but with the "twist" of an all-female team of ghostbusters. Despite this adherence to the original, it received mixed reviews, and—ultimately—failed to make a profit at the box office. Significantly, much of the public's criticism of this *Ghostbusters* reboot, especially on social media, appeared to be driven by the gender switch of the lead characters.[5]

Thus, the lack of both critical as well as box office success of these gender-switched reboots appears to be a combination of poor aesthetic quality on the part of their creators and thinly veiled sexism on the part of the audience. Merely switching the gender of the main characters is no substitute for a well-written plot and dialogue, whereas the reaction to these re-gendered movies demonstrates something about fixed gender expectations in our culture. Science fiction narratives, such as battling robots or ghosts, or cheeky criminal capers, tend to be associated with men and masculinity.

Can Marty Be "Martina"?

Unlike the examples mentioned thus far, a reboot of the *Back to the Future* series would appear to be more open to a gender switch in its main character, but ultimately, as we shall see, the gender system is buried too deep in these movies, as gender ideology—not time—often drives the story's narrative. As we are well aware, gender itself is not fixed in reality: the ideals of masculinity and femininity have changed over time and culture. Indeed, Kate Bornstein in *Gender Outlaw* (1994) points out that even individuals who are cisgender throughout their lives undergo subtle shifts—at work, with their partners, as they age, etc.—in their gender and gender expression.[6]

However, I will show that, even if *Back to the Future* fans would accept a gender shift in a reboot of the series, it is not clear that the movies *themselves* could allow such a shift to take place. Unfortunately, the movies in the series, and especially the original movie, rely for their narratives on the construct of gender being remarkably fixed in order for their plots to remain coherent. This is an important point, as the characters in the movies can move through time and experience significant psychological development due to their adventures in the past or future; for example, we see by the end of *Part III* that Marty learns to control his temper and Doc overcomes his fear of women as he finds the love of his life. Thus, the movies allow for temporal questions of "what if?" as Marty and Doc travel backwards and forwards across time, it is less certain—as I shall demonstrate—that we can ask "what if?" Marty was "Martina"? Examining Fox's recommended gender shift as it would play out in new and alternate narratives for the movies, especially the original *Back to the Future*, we can see the problematic nature of gender in the fantasy universes of the *Back to the Future* series. Just as Doc and Marty are committed to maintaining the fabric of the past, so do the movie narratives—*albeit unintentionally*—reenforce the construct of gender.

In brief, the *Back to the Future* trilogy *actively* relies on gender as a narrative driver: Marty cannot become "Martina." While contemporary movies *do* allow for a new trope of the "tough female fighter" (for example, Uma Thurman's highly-trained assassin in Quentin Tarantino's *Kill Bill* films), Marty's altercations with others in all three movies usually stem from having his masculinity questioned and his resulting overreactions. Various generations of Tannens—the McFly family nemeses—throughout each of the three movies call Marty a chicken or "yellow," typically precipitating a fight or even physical harm for Marty. It is only in the third and final movie that Marty is able to resist the challenge of a road race with local bullies and thus avoid an accident that would ruin his life.

If a reboot were to have a female character as its star, how would questioning "Martina's" femininity look such that it would provide a similar narrative driver? There are no obvious "opposite" feminine characteristics on the socially constructed gender binary to Marty's pride in his masculinity, and his aggression in maintaining this pride, that would generate the action in what is also part of the "action movie" genre. A quick mental check of the stereotypical list of—typically passive—"feminine" attributes associated with women yields little. Women are supposed to take pride in their physical appearance, be polite and accommodating, and be generally given to emotionality. Yet, it is hard to imagine that competitive modeling or aggressive bouts of crying could support the narrative weight of an entire movie.

In addition, other rehearsals of male gender performance, such as ambition and career success, occur throughout the trilogy as indicators of both the problems of—and solutions *to*—the personal difficulties of Marty and his father. In the first act of the original film, George McFly is an emasculated loser in a dead-end job, bullied by his supervisor, Biff. When Marty travels back to 1955, he finds that George is a socially awkward loner and a peeping tom. Despite Doc's portentous warnings that

Marty shouldn't try to alter the past, Marty's active participation in *maintaining* the narrative arc of the past does alter what we once saw as the present (in 1985). By the end of the movie, George has become a successful science fiction author and his marriage to Lorraine, who is no longer a depressed alcoholic, is now happy and thriving. Yet this "new"—or is that "corrected" or "real"?—present that we see at the end of the movie has less to do with breaking gender roles and expectations for Marty's parents and more to do with the McFly family's change in socio-economic class status, a rise in status that seems to be due solely to Marty's father and his success as an author. Lorraine still appears to be a homemaker, albeit far happier with this role now that George has money. The changes in the McFly family fortunes are clearly coded with their new class status. The house reflects these middle-class values in its décor: it is organized with serene beige furnishings and a white (so 1980s!) piano. Marty's brother, Dave, is now a professional, wearing a suit and tie, which he says he always wears to the office. Marty's parents return from playing squash (or tennis, or a similar-enough yuppie athletic activity).

Much of the humor and surreal nature of the original movie is derived from Marty's mother, Lorraine, developing a crush on him in 1955. If the gender of Marty is switched to "Martina," then Lorraine would desire a queer relationship with her own daughter, which—while offering a contemporary take on gender relationships—is unlikely to be marketable to the average movie-goer. Alternatively, George McFly, Marty's father, would develop a crush on his own daughter: "Martina." This second option does not have the "cute" quotient of Lorraine's puppy-like crush on Marty. Rather, George, who we already know is a peeping-tom, having a crush on "Martina" could produce a serious "ick" response in the movie's audience.

Significantly, part of Lorraine's attraction to Marty is that she sees him as a man who stands up for himself and will protect the woman he loves: a pre-packaged heterosexual romantic ideal that still lingers even to this day. However, it is clear that if Lorraine's crush on Marty means that she's not interested in George, then Marty and his siblings will not exist in the future. Luckily, George rescues Lorraine from being sexually assaulted by Biff, thus simultaneously fulfilling her gender ideals and solidifying the existence of her future children. It is interesting to notice that Marty's confidence grows in the movie to the point that he plays guitar on stage at the Fish Under the Sea dance, but his new confidence does not stem from being the masculine protector Lorraine wants. Rather, it is the protection of his family: the people he loves. It could be argued that this protection of loved ones—rather than protection against others through violence—is true masculinity, not the warped ideals of toxic masculinity that Marty appears to hold. And indeed, we see by the end of *Part III*, with Marty not accepting the challenge of a road race with Needles, that he has come to see that masculinity can be equated with self-control, that courage can be expressed in knowing when to walk away.

Unfortunately, however, even if it were possible for the movies to allow for a gender-shift in the main character of Marty/Martina, a surprising amount of the plotting of the movies takes place both *within* a misogynist world and *requires* that misogynist world for their narrative drivers. Even when we are offered different timelines, each of them consistent with the past, they are all premised on the workings of a misogynist world, as we shall see below in the varying fortunes of Lorraine and Jennifer. With this in mind, I'd encourage die-hard *Back to the Future* fans not to throw up their hands in horror but to read ahead to the final section of this essay to see that the goal here is not to criticize the movies themselves but to question the rigid system of gender ideology!

Time Travel May Be the Easy Part...

Again, returning to 1955 in the original movie, Lorraine is sexually assaulted by Biff. Yet, she appears profoundly unaffected by this incident to the point that, after Marty's return to 1985, we see that George and Lorraine have hired Biff to detail their cars. It is tempting to consider the dismissal of sexual assault as a continuity glitch with the movie script itself. Certainly, given the centrality of the assault for the narrative of Lorraine and George's teen romance, the past cannot be changed in any significant way. But perhaps we should consider whether this component of the movie contains outdated attitudes, even though the rest of the *Back to the Future* narratives have held up well over the decades. Lorraine, as a teenager, is quite "fast" (in '50s terms) or "thirsty" in contemporary terms, even physically pawing at Marty. Are we perhaps supposed to think that she somehow brought on Biff's assault due to her behavior?

It is, however, easy to forget in our post-#MeToo world that attitudes toward sexual assault in the 1980s (and certainly in the 1950s) were quite different. In the '80s, many feminists were still in the grip of the individualistic thinking of second-wave feminism, and attitudes regarding sexual assault tended toward encouraging masculine strength in overcoming the sexist realities of the world around them. Thus, Lorraine's attitude toward Biff at the end of the first movie, bolstered by her class status, especially in relation to Biff's lower status, seems to be an example of this second-wave individual empowerment rather than a glitch in narrative continuity.

Another reflection of 1980s attitudes about sexual assault occurs in

Part II, when Jennifer accompanies Doc and Mary into 2015, as Doc claims she is asking too many questions in the present. Jennifer is not essential to Doc's plan for the future, and in order to preserve the passage of time, she is essentially roofied by Doc and left in an alley to be found by two female police officers who show little surprise or concern over what we would nowadays see as her precarious situation. At this stage, the preservation of time is more important to Doc than Jennifer's safety, something that changes after he meets Clara in *Part III*. Just as Marty has to revise his attitudes about masculinity, Doc needs to learn not to value obtaining his own ends over connection with humanity.

Later, Marty and Doc rush Jennifer back to 1985, which they find to be an alternate, dystopian version of the present. Lorraine, now a widow, is stuck in an abusive, unequal, and toxic marriage with a cartoonishly wealthy Biff who assaults Lorraine and threatens her children. She seems to stay largely because, as Biff tauntingly reminds her, were she to leave, he'd cut off his financial support for her and her children. Even more worrying, Lorraine defends Biff's assault to Marty, claiming that she only has herself to blame. Given Biff's penchant for bullying and assault, it is easy to believe that he would grow up to become an abuser (with or without excessive amounts of wealth). Overall, *Part II* was not well received by critics, and this injection of the cold reality of the system of gender as part of the plot in an otherwise charming fantasy could be the reason.

Perhaps surprisingly, *Part III*, set in 1885, has the strongest portrayal of women, with both Maggie McFly, the Irish pioneer woman, and Clara Clayton, the scientist-teacher, portrayed as adventurous, independent thinkers. Also in the film, Doc breaks his own rules about preservation of the past when he rescues Clara from falling into a ravine; he comes to realize he has altered the past, as she was supposed to die. In a parallel narrative, Marty starts to learn to move beyond his concerns about the preservation of his perceived masculinity. Even though Buford "Mad Dog" Tannen challenges Marty to a gunfight by questioning his masculinity and calling him "yellow-bellied," Marty suddenly realizes how ridiculous the whole situation is. When cornered by a gun-toting Buford, Marty refuses to draw his own gun and suggests they should settle things "like men." After Marty returns to 1985 one last time, Needles challenges him to a drag race at a stoplight, calling him "chicken." However, instead of actively accepting the challenge, Marty puts his truck in reverse and explains to Jennifer that he's not stupid enough to race. He then sees that had he done so, he would have crashed into a Rolls-Royce, which we know from 2015 would have been the start of a physical and psychological downward trajectory for him.

Thus, as the trilogy comes to a close, we start to see gender being depicted in a less rigid manner as part of the narrative driver for the movie. Significantly, this relaxation of the gender system has no effect on the aesthetic appeal of the movie, as it is simultaneously both charming and gripping to watch. However, despite this relaxation of rigid gender boundaries, it is still unclear how this narrative finale would play out if Marty were "Martina." First, it is hard to find a good example of exaggerated femininity that could similarly ruin "Martina's" life in the way that Marty's road race does/could have done, perhaps botched cosmetic surgery to enhance her modeling career? Even if a surgical accident did have the narrative drive to conclude the series, what lessons about gender would "Martina" learn that are similar to Marty's? Whereas Marty learns to value family, relationships, and personal fulfillment, growth that ultimately leaves the gender system intact, "Martina" can only truly achieve psychological and moral growth if the gender system *as a whole* is toppled.

However, let us consider this other possibility for a moment. Within the *Back to the Future* universe, Marty cannot become "Martina," but is there a possible alternate *Back to the Future* universe in which he/she could exist: a "what if?" universe? How much would this alternate universe need to differ in order for "Martina" to exist as a meaningful being affecting change in the world? All the "nuts and bolts" of this alternate universe could stay the same as those of the original *Back to the Future* universe: the time machines, the school dances, the guitars, etc. But we—or the script writers—would need to re-imagine this universe as one where gender is no longer significant or gender differences—if they remain—have little or no value. In many ways, it is far easier to envision oneself hurtling into a different time period than living in a world where gender is non-existent or radically different enough for "Martina" to have the same narrative impact as Marty. Why is that the case? We are gendered from birth and this gendering is constantly reinforced, making it quite mind-bending to conceive of this alternate universe. Yet—importantly—this conception is not just an intellectual puzzle; rather, it is also an ethical puzzle. Gender is not an innocent system; rather, inequality between men and women is baked into the system of gender itself. And this inequality lies at the foundation of the problems with a gender switch to "Martina."

Time Travel and Gender

For philosophers, the *Back to the Future* series appears to be an unambiguous example of what time travel could look like (whether it is physically or logically possible is for other authors in this collection to decide). In this particular case of time travel, the travel is instantaneous, as demonstrated by the first experiment with Doc's dog, Einstein. The past and future are treated as places, if you will, with Doc and Marty (and Einstein) moving from one place to another. The travelers do not get older or younger, either in the past or present. They are "outside" time looking in, as it were. Time travel in both typical philosophical discussions and in *Back to the Future* is treated as moving backwards and forwards across a fixed temporal landscape. But we are warned by both philosophers and as movie audiences that we *cannot*—or, if we can, *should not*—change the past. And a central theme to all the movies, especially the first movie, is the importance of keeping the past unchanged, or if the characters do participate in past events, it is only as much as necessary to ensure that the future remains unchanged. In the first movie, Marty cannot change (nor does he want to change) his parents falling in love at the school dance, and he struggles to ensure that he does not disrupt the past any more than his presence in 1955 already has done.

However, when he returns to 1985, Marty finds that the social class of his family has changed, even though their gender roles have not: George is still the provider, albeit a successful one, and Lorraine is still a housewife, albeit a contented one. Thus, in the efforts by the movie characters to ensure that they do not change the past, do they also treat masculinity and femininity and their accompanying roles as immutable? In order to maintain the past—and thus offer the McFly family decent possible futures grounded in this past—the construct of gender, and especially masculinity—needs to be preserved.

Back to the Future fans, I am not claiming that the movie series *itself* is misogynistic; instead, I am merely pointing out that it is hard to break free from the system of gender. Indeed, it would appear that—conceptually—it is easier for humans to understand the possibility of time travel than to question our established gender constructs. In theory, it is possible to visit the past, but it would appear that gender needs to remain reasonably static. We can swap time lines, but not gender, so Marty can never become "Martina." Moreover, we need to ask what the time travelers learned during their adventures. Marty does learn that his conception of masculinity can be altered, leading to an improved future, and that this can happen without any disruption to the passage of time. But, as I have already asked, what would a parallel learning experience be for "Martina"?

Thus, a significant further question for any discussion of the *Back to the Future* series is, assuming time travel is possible, can we achieve gender progress when we are required to preserve the past? There are multiple possible futures for Marty and his family, but they are all grounded in a problematic past and within a problematic social construct.

Notes

1. Kile, Meredith. 2022. "Michael J. Fox Shares His Idea for 'Back to the Future' Remake and Talks Christopher Lloyd Reunion." *Entertainment Tonight*.
2. Sargent, Pamela. 1976. "Introduction." *More Women of Wonder: Science Fiction Novelettes by Women*. Vintage Paperbacks, xiii–lxiv.
3. Asimov, Isaac. "1977-present." *Asimov's Science Fiction Magazine*. Dell Magazines.
4. Dargis, Manohla. 2018. "Review: 'Ocean's 8' Women Walk Away with a Male Franchise. Sort Of." *The New York Times*.
5. Sims, David. 2016. "The Ongoing Outcry Against the *Ghostbusters* Remake." *The Atlantic*.
6. Bornstein, Kate. 1994. *Gender Outlaw: On Men, Women, and the Rest of Us*. Routledge.

The Feminist McFly

LEIGH E. RICH *and* MICHAEL N. ROBINSON

It was perhaps fortuitous that the theme song to *Back to the Future* ended up being "The Power of Love" by Huey Lewis and the News. Lewis initially hesitated when asked to write a song for the time-bending mis(ad-venture) of a music-loving teen, his eccentric intergenerational friend, and a "slacker"-riddled family. Worried about penning something too "on the nose," Lewis simply delivered his next single.[1] Nevertheless, "The Power of Love" captures the essence of the 1985 blockbuster (and its two sequels), which catapults Marty McFly into the past and then back to the future as a guitar-playing, too-cool-for-his-family hero. This is because the films are a coming-of-age story, not only about *eros* (romantic love) but also *philia* (friendship), *storge* (familial), *philautia* (self), and *agape* (love for everyone). And with a focus on time travel and the dissociations it creates, *Back to the Future* illustrates how the self is co-constituted through relationships with the particular others in our lives.

On the surface, the films are male-driven adventures. Marty and Doc travel through time, defraud Libyans, and escape the predicaments their careless actions cause in a plutonium-powered DeLorean. Much in the trilogy alludes (and illudes) to what is often associated with the "masculine": science, sports cars, rock and roll, futurism, the Wild West, and besting rivals. The trilogy also emerged as America turned politically toward a nostalgia-fueled conservatism, which whitewashed the social revolutions of the previous decades, and American television viewers consumed en masse sitcoms such as *The Honeymooners*, *Leave It to Beaver*, and *Happy Days*.[2] But while *Back to the Future* indulges in the outward charms of post–World War II suburbia (and, in *Part III*, a sanitized West), it doesn't venerate the past or the patriarchy but pokes fun at the limitations of these eras and our fictionalized conceptions of them. At its core, the trilogy speaks to compassion, community, and the development of a moral self—exploring emotion, the "household," and "mothering" that

Western philosophy tends to dismiss as irrelevant (or even counterproductive) to what it means to live a good life.[3]

While Marty and Doc are not feminists *per se*, their narrative arcs exemplify an ethic of care—a model of moral development introduced by Carol Gilligan and others in the 1980s (with aspects related to Eastern philosophy and Confucius). Rather than a rivalrous struggle toward maturity (like Sigmund Freud's Oedipal complex) or an individualistic "Man of Reason" (found in Lawrence Kohlberg's stages), care ethics prioritizes attending to, nurturing and (most importantly) esteeming relationships. Gilligan's *In a Different Voice* traces a trajectory from selfishness to selflessness and then to goodness as caring for (and not harming) others or the self.[4] Placed against other ethical frameworks, Gilligan's feels "messier" because it addresses the intimate and social contexts in which moral quandaries arise, acknowledging that these often cannot be fully resolved. But moral development and ethical action likely begin no other place, and both an ethic of care and *Back to the Future* emphasize the relational embeddedness of the human condition. Mature adults aren't Hobbesian mushrooms "sprung [separately and fully formed] out of the earth."[5]

Relationships form the heart of the trilogy—a web of coming-of-age stories that begin with Marty but include his parents and even Doc. Who the characters become is conditional: co-constituted through their interactions and changing as choices, connections, and communication fluctuate. Though the films present an epic journey pitting free will against fate, *Back to the Future* tells a feminist tale of discovery which reminds us that "*to be* a person is to be in relationships."[6]

Care for Self

When we first meet Marty, he's seventeen and reluctantly finishing high school under the stern, authoritative eye of Principal Strickland. Trying to distance himself from his ne'er-do-well family—and not become a "slacker" like his father, George—Marty assumes a cool independence that suggests he's grown up, ready to chase his rock-star dreams and a deeper relationship with his girlfriend, Jennifer. But, in many ways, this is not actually the case, and Marty remains overly focused on himself. In Gilligan's initial stage of development, this is a means for "survival."[7] For instance, Marty immaturely frets that he's just "not cut out for music" after the school's band auditions (where he's critiqued for being "just too darn loud"), and when Jennifer suggests sending his tape to a record label, he dejectedly wavers, "What if they say I'm no good? What if they say, 'Get out of here, kid. You got no future'?" He's also more concerned that the newly wrecked family car ruins his plans to take Jennifer to the lake, rather than how this problem affects his struggling parents. "I *needed* that car tomorrow night," Marty grumbles (despite being too "chicken" to tell his folks about Jennifer). "Do you have any idea how important this was to me? Do you have any clue?" All the while, he longs for a shiny four-by-four truck and a different family.

The adults in Marty's life aren't much better. His best friend, Doc, wakes him in the middle of the night to document his scientific success, though the much older Doc should be concerned with the teen's need for sleep and mounting tardies at school. Doc does care for Marty, encouraging him, along with Jennifer, to develop confidence and that if he "put[s] [his] mind to it, [he] can accomplish anything." But Doc's self-centeredness dominates the trilogy's opening scenes: he fuels his time machine with stolen plutonium, placing Marty, himself, and all of Hill Valley in danger, while nonchalantly explaining how he took possession of the plutonium after conning a group of Libyan nationalists who wanted him to "build them a bomb." At this stage, for Doc, it's innovation that matters, regardless of the consequences (which are far-reaching and vast): Doc is shot dead by bazooka-wielding Libyans, and Marty is inadvertently transported to 1955.

In this way, *Back to the Future*'s parable begins even before Marty is a gleam in his father's eye. In 1955, when George, Biff, and Lorraine are teenagers, they exhibit aspects of Gilligan's self-focused first stage. Biff, the quintessential egotist, doggedly bullies George and paws at Lorriane, concerned only about his own desires. Stunted in his growth, he'll worsen in *Part II* and reveal in *Part III* (in the guise of his great-grandfather) the relational roots of violence. For Biff, becoming "his own man" means winning a zero-sum game similar to the play of young boys. Gilligan references the work of other scholars to describe how games are "the crucible [for] social development during the school years," where "children learn to take the role of the other and come to see themselves through another's eyes."[8]

Boys in particular play more aggressively, driven by rules and "the ways rules can be made or changed,"[9] whereas girls compete "indirect[ly]"—where "one person's success does not necessarily signify another's failure."[10] When disputes arise, boys employ "legal elaboration"; girls "subordinat[e] the continuation of the game to the continuation of relationships."[11] Lorraine offers an example. When her timeline changes after Marty (not George) is hit by her father's car, she amorously pursues her future son. Marty tries to refocus her attention on George, but she has little interest. Still, she treats George kindly even as others tease him: "He's kind of cute and all, but [...] a man should [...] stand up for himself and protect the woman he loves."[12]

In both timelines, George pursues Lorraine from self-interest—creepily peeping into her bedroom window and engaging her only when threatened after "Darth Vader" tortures him with Val Halen. Marty prods his father for selfish reasons as well—his future existence—a selfishness that expands in *Part II* when he buys a sports almanac in 2015 that he plans to use to enrich himself upon his return to 1985. The relationships are toxic, and the violence physical, emotional, and verbal. "Victories" come at the expense of others, some through brawn, others through guile. Even Strickland bags a "win," as he smugly tells Marty near the beginning of the story to skip the auditions: "You don't have a chance. [...] No McFly ever amounted to anything in the history of *Hill Valley*!"

Perhaps anticipating the transition to Gilligan's second stage of moral development, Marty replies, "Yeah, well, history is gonna change."

Care for Others

While self-care offers benefits, a life solely self-centered is "solitary, poore, nasty, brutish, and short."[13] For Gilligan, such realization "signals a new understanding of the connection between self and others which is articulated by the concept of responsibility" and "seeks to ensure care for the dependent and unequal."[14] Significantly, such responsibility and care are not a mutually beneficial contract as in Thomas Hobbes' *Leviathan* or a scientific calculation of overall pleasure and pain, but an appreciation that others matter and one is not the center of the universe. Rather, the self is enmeshed (and realizable) in a net of particular others, caring for whom develops one's morality and extends (rather than is abstracted) to the "generalized other" of utilitarian and deontological ethics. As Virginia Held explains: the "'others' in the picture [...] are not what a universal point of view or a view from nowhere could provide. They are, characteristically, actual flesh and blood other human beings for whom we have actual feelings and with whom we have real ties."[15] This is the realm in which the characters of *Back to the Future* grow as morally and emotionally responsible beings.

In traveling to 1955, Marty is ripped from his dysfunctional family and learns that his (along with their) existence depends upon relationships. His dissociation disrupts his navel-gazing and galvanizes his growth along Gilligan's path, not only externally but internally as he confronts the fear and anger his dismissive family provokes. He risks his life to save George, taking the blow from his grandfather's car and forging a kindness for his dad that's absent in 1985. He also intervenes on behalf of his mother, standing up to a tyrannical Biff. The dangers are immediate and existential, since Marty has replaced George in front of an oncoming car and (thus) as the object of Lorraine's desire.

Mentored by a young Doc—who's not (yet) responsible for the chaos but befriends Marty anyway—Marty mentors George, not simply trading father-son roles but engaging in what feminists deem "mothering," where the "value in the relation cannot be broken down into individual gains and losses for the individual members" but what matters is the health, growth, and "development of the relation-and-its-members."[16] In *Part II*, an older Doc will attempt something similar for Marty and Jennifer (when they prevent Marty Jr. from engaging in crime with Griff),[17] and Marty will travel to 1885 in *Part III* to stop Biff's great-grandfather from killing Doc (and the relationships that spur Doc's new family). Care is on display: Marty clad in his "life-preserver" amid a sea of frail connections.

But, as Gilligan notes, caring for others comes at a cost. Marty's actions rile Biff, an antagonist who dogs him in all timelines, and his plan to re-couple his parents involves deception and Oedipal peril—escorting his mother to a dance and acting lasciviously so that George can become her hero. The problem of prioritizing goodness-as-self-sacrifice is "the illogic of the inequality between other and self," where "others are legitimized as the recipients of [one's] care" but self-care is selfish.[18] Taken to an extreme, persons and relationships suffer. In 1985, before Marty travels back in time, Lorraine wearily plays the housewife, serving a ready-made meal for dinner and palliating the "problem that has no name"[19] with alcohol. Almost in pantomime, she coaxes her kids to care about their Uncle "Jailbird" Joey and admonishes them to act "properly" in romantic pursuits. George, whose youngest son begs him to just once try saying "no" to Biff, spinelessly avoids confrontation himself. No better than when he was a teenager, he completes Biff's work instead of eating or engaging with his family. In this way, self-abnegation doesn't nurture relationships or the person; it destroys them. As Lorraine tries to connect with her husband and kids about how she and George met, George is distracted, cackling at an episode of *The Honeymooners* he's no doubt seen before.

This lesson-on-steroids emerges in *Part II*, after Biff acquires Marty's almanac and the one's artifice and others' avarice create an alternate 1985.[20] Biff has murdered George and coerced Lorraine to become his wife, sacrificing her well-being for the sake of her kids. When she attempts to leave, Biff manipulates her love for her family—threatening to leave Linda McFly financially destitute and to see to it that Dave and Marty end up in prison just like their Uncle Joey: "one big happy jailbird family." Little more than a trophy, Lorraine is disfigured and doused in clothes, jewels, and liquor. "Who's going to pay for your cosmetic surgery, Lorraine?" Biff taunts. Lorraine despairs, pointing to her breasts, "You were the one who wanted me to get these, these *things*. If you want them back, you can have them."

As Held notes, while relationship development may be more significant than self-development, the two cannot be disentangled,[21] and Gilligan emphasizes how "the exclusion of [the self]" when caring for others "gives rise to problems in relationships, creating a disequilibrium" that's unsustainable.[22] *Back to the Future* portrays this in nuanced ways as well. As Marty repeatedly attempts to forewarn Doc about his death at the hands of the Libyans, Doc refuses to listen, tearing up a postdated letter Marty leaves for him. "No man should know too much about his own destiny," Doc explains. "Information about the future [tempts consequences that] could be disastrous!"—endangering particular others and the "generalized other."[23] These are also connected: "Particular others can be actual children in need in distant continents, or the anticipated children of generations not yet even close to being born," even "the well-being of the globe."[24] Marty begs Doc to "take that risk" because his "life depends on it," but Doc sacrifices himself. "No! I *refuse* to accept the responsibility!"

Others and Self

Gilligan's third stage "focuses on the dynamics of relationships and dissipates the tension between selfishness and responsibility through a new understanding of the interconnection between other and self."[25] The concept of responsibility transforms, and the question becomes whether it's "possible to be responsible to [oneself] as well as to others and thus to reconcile the disparity between hurt and care."[26] Marty and Doc grow toward this phase as the trilogy progresses. At the end of the initial film, Marty realizes he can save Doc by returning to 1985 before the Libyans arrive. This means two distinct Martys will likely meet (which could disrupt the space-time continuum), but he accepts the risk and proceeds with his plan. However, a mechanical problem with the DeLorean delays him, and he arrives just in time to see Doc killed all over again. Thankfully, Doc instead comes to, revealing a bulletproof vest and Marty's aged, taped-together letter. Marty looks skeptically: "What about all that talk about screwing up future events? The space-time continuum?" To which Doc replies, "Well, I figured, what the hell!" Though Doc seems carefree, events suggest he and Marty have attempted nonviolence: not so much has altered in 1985 that both perhaps safeguarded their familiarity with the future to care for others and themselves.

The transition from the original film to *Part II* drives home the allusion. Sending the past-trapped Marty back to the future requires "1.21

gigawatts," and "in 1955, [plutonium's] a little hard to come by." Young Doc exclaims, "How could I have been so careless?" and tells Marty, "I'm afraid you're *stuck* here." The solution, however, emerges not through duplicity or a conquering of forces but an embracing of nature and social history. "See this?" Marty points to the note Jennifer wrote on the "Save the Clock Tower" flyer. Because of love and the Hill Valley Preservation Society, Doc can predict the moment lightning will strike, with no risk of radiation or terrorists.

Such perils are resolved in the cliffhanger, after Doc augments the DeLorean, allowing the flux capacitor to run on household waste. All three films (not unlike Mr. Fusion) elevate what Western moral philosophy tends to degrade. By the end, George's authentic concern for Lorraine frees his family from division and abuse, and Marty learns the difference between being a "slacker" who pities himself and a "fighter" who harms himself and others when taunted as "chicken."[27] Marty's investment in relationships, and thus himself, grows across the narrative, whether he's caring for Doc and his parents, cradling his infant great-grandfather, performing at the Enchantment the Sea dance, or even empathizing with Biff.[28] Helped by his great-great grandparents in 1885, Maggie calls him "a strange young man," though Seamus predicts, "I've just got a feeling about him. [...] Look how the baby takes to him."

The Relational Self

"Mothering," in fact, is a recurrent gag in the trilogy. After Marty is struck by his grandfather's car, his (teenage) mother tends to his wounds, reassuring him his "nightmare" is over and "[e]verything's going to be fine." An adult Lorraine does the same in the alternate 1985, as does Maggie on the McFly farm in the Old West. Each nurses Marty, promising he's "safe and sound now" though he's lost in time. That Marty keeps hitting his head may be symbolic of the limitations of "reason" without "care." Like Gilligan, *Back to the Future* critiques the gendered biases of Freud, Kohlberg, and others and even turns *Oedipus Rex* on its head: by attending to relationships with propriety and reverence,[29] Marty saves his father, avoids wooing his mother, and escapes tyranny and fate.

His self- and moral development flourish when he nurtures his relationships, regardless of the timelines in which they exist. Gilligan underscores this "reiterative" paradox: "[a]ttachment and separation anchor the cycle of human life," and to care for others we must recognize the self, yet only through relations do we become separate selves.[30] Held adds that "mothering" creates not just "*new* persons" but "new types of *persons* [...]

the most transformative human activity of all."[31] Who each of us is, and who the characters in *Back to the Future* are, depend upon our interactions. "[O]ur relationships are not generic," says John Santiago, referencing Confucius; "they are specific and come with traits unique to them."[32] Whether George is a "slacker" or a thriving writer and family man is not a matter of fate but affiliation. So too with the others.

As Elizabeth Grosz notes in *Time Travels*, "the present is that which acts and lives, which functions to anticipate an immediate future in action," while the reality of the past is "virtual," exerting "influence indirectly, only through its capacity to link to and thus to inform the present."[33] Although *Back to the Future* is a story centered around men, it celebrates care and the facets of life often fused with the feminine. Several characters could be called proto-feminists, including women who leave their marks though they play lesser parts: Jennifer exhibits care throughout her scenes. Clara, a teacher in 1885, challenges Doc in life and science, becoming a mother and partner in discovery. Lorraine in 1955 resists the gendered strictures of her time, chasing her desires and advising Marty, "Don't be such a square." As the first film concludes, a vivacious middle-aged Lorraine suggests she's nurtured herself as she's nurtured her family (and maybe even read Friedan and Gilligan in between). Western ideals of the "Man of Reason" that prioritize independence over interdependence "might make us *in*capable of morality, rather than capable of it."[34] As *Back to the Future* teaches, "to be a person is intrinsically and constitutively social. That is, a person is never alone, could never exist alone […] 'unless there are at least two human beings, there can be no human beings.'"[35]

Notes

1. Blistein, Jon. 2019. "The Breakdown: Huey Lewis and the News on 'The Power of Love.'" *Rolling Stone*.

2. The three films overlap with the Reagan–Bush "We Can Make America Great Again" era (1980–1992), which dismissed the AIDS crisis and tried to turn back the clock on civil rights, gay and LGBTQ+ rights, and second- and third-wave feminism. While *The Honeymooners* and *Leave It to Beaver* nudged at certain social issues in nuanced ways in the 1950s, *Happy Days* in the 1970s is notable for the racism and sexism it painted as "cute."

3. It's also telling that, a year later, Francis Ford Coppola released *Peggy Sue Got Married*, an award-nominated movie with a similar arc but a female protagonist and concern for relationships in the title. Peggy's counterpart, Charlie, even desires a career in music, though the film skips the machinery of *Back to the Future* and accomplishes Peggy's time travel through more "feminine" approaches of fainting and ritual.

4. Gilligan, Carol. 2003. *In a Different Voice: Psychological Theory and Women's Development*. Harvard University Press. Originally published in 1982.

5. Hobbes, Thomas. 1651. *Philosophicall Rudiments Concerning Government and Society*. J.G. for R. Royston, at the Angel in Ivie-lane. On page 127: "Let us return again to the

state of nature, and consider men as if but even now sprung out of the earth, and suddainly (*like* Mushromes) come to full maturity without all kind of engagement to each other."
    6. Santiago, John. 2008. "Confucian Ethics in the *Analects* as Virtue Ethics." *Philosophical Ideas and Artistic Pursuits in the Traditions of Asia and the West: An NEH Faculty Humanities Workshop*. http://dc.cod.edu/nehscholarship/8, ¶3 under "The Confucian Person," *emphasis original*.
    7. Gilligan, 74.
    8. Ibid., 9.
    9. Ibid.
    10. Ibid., 10.
    11. As Gilligan highlighted in the original publication of her book, care ethics is not a gendered voice but a "human voice." Citing the work of Jean Piaget, George Herbert Mead, Nancy Chodorow, and Janet Lever, Gilligan's depictions of gendered play are generalizations, nuances of which may have altered in the decades since. For instance, social psychologist Jonathan Haidt describes how, with the rise of the internet and smartphones, boys today gravitate toward the "coalitional violence" in multiplayer video games, while girls "spend a lot more time on social media [...] Instagram, Tumblr, Pinterest—the visual platforms. And their interactions are asynchronous." The former, while still aggressively competitive, maintains elements of the "social"; the latter "is not play. It's performance. It's brand management. [...] It plays on their insecurities." Cited in Remnick, David. 2024. "Jonathan Haidt Wants You to Take Away Your Kid's Phone." *The New Yorker*, April 20, ¶30–¶31.
    12. It is, however, Lorraine in the first two 1955 timelines who takes action, initiating her relationship with George and even undressing Marty, despite the gendered ideas that "[a]ny girl who calls up a boy is just asking for trouble."
    13. Hobbes, Thomas. 1904. *Leviathan or the Matter, Forme, & Power of a Commonwealth, Ecclesiasticall and Civill*, edited by A.R. Waller. Cambridge University Press, 84. Originally published in 1651.
    14. Gilligan, 74. By being honest and fair, an individual in the first stage recognizes that others exist and that a self-centered life, though pleasurable and profitable, is "selfish."
    15. Held, Virginia. 1990. "Feminist Transformations of Moral Theory." *Philosophy and Phenomenological Research* 50, Supplement: 321–344, 338.
    16. *Ibid*.
    17. "Attempt" because, rather than "mothering" the child and helping him grow morally, Doc and Marty paternalistically solve the problem by swapping Marty for his son. Additionally, Marty's narcissism in *Part II* is highlighted in both his decision to buy the sports almanac and the future naming of his children: Marty McFly, Jr., and Marlene McFly.
    18. Gilligan, 74.
    19. Friedan, Betty. 1963. *The Feminine Mystique*. W.W. Norton. On page 15: "The problem lay buried, unspoken, for many years in the minds of American women [...] a strange stirring, a sense of dissatisfaction, a yearning that women suffered" when patriarchal ideals bullied them to care more about making their children's "peanut butter sandwiches" than something of themselves—too "afraid to ask [...] 'Is this all?'"
    20. And certainly "the darkest timeline." Melman, Jeff, and Chris McKenna. 2011. "Remedial Chaos Theory," *Community*, season 3, episode 4. NBC, October 13.
    21. Held, 338.
    22. Gilligan, 74.
    23. Under a powerful Biff, "the darkest timeline" in *Part II* isn't fun for anyone.
    24. *Ibid.*, Held, 333 and 340.
    25. *Ibid.*, Gilligan, 74.
    26. *Ibid.*, 82.
    27. An underdeveloped theme that arises in *Part II* and *Part III*, future Marty in "the darkest timeline" ruins his ability to play guitar and thus pursue his best self because he didn't back down from a schoolyard provocation. This Marty also loses his dead-end job and creates additional harm for his family when his boss goads him into doing something illegal.

160   V. Sex and Gender in *Back to the Future*

28. In *Part II*, Marty gets a glimpse of Biff's rough home life and the relationships that reproduce bullies.
29. See Santiago.
30. Gilligan, 151.
31. Held, 335, 337–338, *emphasis original*.
32. Santiago, ¶6 under "*Ren*: The Confucian Exemplary Man."
33. Grosz, Elizabeth. 2005. *Time Travels: Feminism, Nature, Power*. Duke University Press, 102.
34. Held, referencing Alison Jaggar, 344, *emphasis original*. Care ethics does not disregard autonomy or the agency of the person. As Gilligan notes (on page 95): "The willingness to express and to take responsibility for judgment stems from a recognition of the psychological costs of indirect action, to self and to others and thus to relationships. Responsibility for care then includes both self and other, and the injunction not to hurt, freed from conventional constraints, sustains the ideal of care while focusing the reality of choice."
35. Santiago, citing Herbert Fingarette, ¶3 under "The Confucian Person."

Making Sense of Masculinity in the Past, Present, and Future

BEN ALMASSI

Good science fiction expands our sense of what's possible; it challenges conventional wisdom about the world and how it has to be. This applies not only to hoverboards and plutonium-powered DeLoreans but also to how we (re)construct our intimate relationships and personal identities.

Nobody embraces both technological and domestic speculative fiction quite like Robert Zemeckis, Bob Gale, and their collaborators on the *Back to the Future* trilogy. Marty McFly travels thirty years into the past, and what does he gain? An alternate perspective on who his parents are and who they could be. Marty splits his time in 1955 Hill Valley with Doc Brown working on the engineering problem (to get "back to the future!") and with his father, George, working on the romantic problem of restoring the precarious McFly family unit. In a way, then, this unlikely blockbuster franchise may seem more conservative than revolutionary, using futuristic tech to try to put things back as they were. Yet, for all his efforts, the future Marty gets back to (at the end of the first film, and again at the end of the trilogy) isn't quite the one he had left. Things have changed—not the technology as much as the men and their relationships.

Marty's main job in the first film seems to be getting George (back) on track, as the son tries to (re)make his father into a (better) man. The sequels meanwhile, center more on Marty's fragile sense of self, how it affects his decisions, and the alternate pasts, presents, and futures that result. How do the *Back to the Future* films make sense of masculinity: its normative demands, toxic implications, and alternate possibilities? Are Zemeckis and Gale using science fiction for old-fashioned patriarchal ends, where manhood means driving monster trucks, winning fights, besting bullies, and never backing down when challenged? Or, are they asking us to look twice at toxic masculinity (in 1950s and 1980s suburbia, in 1880s Old West tropes, and even the 21st century "future") and to imagine something better?

Thinking philosophically about manhood and masculinity can help us make sense of the narrative arcs of characters as different as George, Marty, Doc, and Biff (and their past, present, and future variants), their relationships with one another, and their relationships with Lorraine, Jennifer, and Clara. It can also help us appreciate the curdled mix of conservative and feminist expressions of masculinity across these films and what we might draw from them for our own lives.

Toxic Men from Pluto

Manhood in 1985 Hill Valley is in a pretty sorry state. Biff is a bully, George is a wimp, and Marty lacks confidence. As he admits to Jennifer, unknowingly echoing his father, "What if they say 'Get out of here, kid, you've got no future'? I just don't think I can take that kind of rejection." At least Doc Brown has achieved his life's work, even if it took 30 years and his family's fortune to do so. And to be fair, Doc is in pretty much the same place when the first film ends as when it began (bulletproof vest notwithstanding), rearing and ready for time-travel. But Biff has been humbled and George is self-assured, with his first novel hot off the press and his relationship with Lorraine thriving. Have Marty's adventures replaced toxic masculinity with a healthy alternative?

Toxic masculinity poisons us all. It's not that masculinity is really bad for men *rather than* women; it's that some apparent refutation of feminism (baked into the concept itself) is harmful to men as well as women and other people.[1] And we can see that play out at the McFly residence, as middle-aged Biff bullies George just as he did in high school, and even though Lorraine still loves George, three decades into their relationship, she's tired and worn down. She recounts their love story yet *again* for her kids. "It's so stupid," Linda protests. "Grampa hit him with his car!" Later, we learn Lorraine's romantic tale has a rotten foundation, one George has never admitted, which Marty only discovers when he saves his peeping tom of a father from an oncoming car—and in so doing, changes the story.

Social scientist Sam de Boise observes that "the term 'toxic masculinity' potentially increases receptivity to the notion that there are harmful and non-harmful forms of masculinity."[2] Like rainy days and blood diamonds, the phrase invites the inference that there are other, better ways that men can be. But what are those ways, exactly? "It's quite clear what we mean by 'toxic masculinity,'" writes Andrea Waling; "there is less consensus as to what we might mean by a 'healthy masculinity' despite more pressing needs to encourage it among men and boys."[3]

A notable philosophical reclamation of masculinity can be seen in Mary Wollstonecraft's *A Vindication of the Rights of Men* and its sequel *A Vindication of the Rights of Woman*,[4] where she argues for "a kind of masculinity into which women can be invited rather than enlarging or inviting a positive kind of femininity."[5] Indeed, Wollstonecraft is inviting men *and* women to be masculine. But here she is not suggesting that women should join men in hunting and gaming or abandon their duties as wives and mothers. In fact, she says, by cultivating masculinity, they can be better wives and mothers than under conditions of sexual inequality. "The two sexes mutually corrupt and improve each other," Wollstonecraft writes. The problem as she sees it is too much sentimentality and not enough rationality, all around, in the education and enculturation of both women and men.

Yet, for better or worse, at no point in their narrative arcs are the McFly men especially reasoned or rational. Courageous, sure, but not rational. George is a writer, but he's not making arguments, and he doesn't stand up to Biff by reasoning with him. When Marty convinces his father to join in the narrative-resetting ruse at the big dance, it's not by talking things through. Headphones, a Van Halen cassette, a radiation suit, and a midnight threat to melt George's brain are Marty's tools of persuasion. Mary Wollstonecraft would not be impressed.

"It's just an act!"

Developing a virtue of rationality is only one way philosophers have understood masculinity. In *Gender Trouble* and elsewhere, Judith Butler draws attention not to virtues, nor other character traits, but actions.[6] Gender isn't something we *are* so much as something we *do*—something we perform. Butler's performativity theory of gender has been influential in the late 20th and early 21st centuries. If this phrasing calls to mind theatrical performers, that's intended: masculinity and femininity are roles we play, scripts we follow, or performances we give where all the world's a stage, and all men and women are merely players.

Marty is assuredly more comfortable with performance than reason. He's on stage with two different bands in two different decades at Hill Valley High School. He films Doc and Einstein in the inaugural test of the DeLorean at the Twin (Lone) Pine(s) Mall with an eye for the dramatic. And he coaches his hapless father to perform masculinity; to play out a script, win over Lorraine, and restore their family unit: "…we've got to show her that you, George McFly, are a fighter. You're somebody who's gonna stand up for himself, somebody who's gonna protect her." When all of this makes George anxious, Marty assures him, "It's just an *act*, right?"

While Marty is writing this script (the planned sequence of events, the blocking, George's line, etc.), he himself seemingly can't resist playing out a script of fragile masculinity when other men taunt him. "*Nobody* calls me chicken!" he insists to Biff's grandson, Griff, in 2015, getting drawn into a conflict he had just resolved. On that very same day, middle-aged Marty says the same thing to Needles, who goads him into a disastrous scheme which immediately gets Marty fired. This wacky, futuristic scene shows that Marty's insecurity has been reified over the years, again and again, as he predictably responds to taunts from Needles and generations of Tannen men. Such barbs are as effective on a future, middle-aged Marty as they are on a teenage Marty when Needles challenges him to a race that injures him and totals his truck thirty years prior. In the Old West, the insults may be different ("What are you, yellow?" Mad Dog Tannen sneers), but Marty follows the same script of thin-skinned bravado. "*Nobody* calls me yellow!"

Interestingly, even when Marty tries to write his own story in *Part III*, he falls back on Hollywood westerns. The manly cowboy name he gives himself? Clint Eastwood. And when he refuses to follow through on the gunfight with Mad Dog at 7 o'clock (excuse me, 8 o'clock—Clint/Marty does his killing *after* breakfast), Marty protects himself with a concealed iron plate, just like Clint's Man with No Name does in *A Fistful of Dollars*.

Refusing and Reclaiming Masculinity

In *Refusing to Be a Man*, John Stoltenberg applies the insights and values of radical feminism to the lives of men.[7] His position is clear: manhood is not worth saving. We would be better off without it. For Stoltenberg, being a man essentially requires us "to deny someone else's selfhood—over and over again."[8] A man worried about his manhood worries about what other men think of him, measuring himself against them and valuing their judgments more than his authentic self. This can be tempting, seeking other men's validations. It is ultimately both inauthentic and immoral, Stoltenberg argues, because a person simply cannot make genuine ethical decisions and submit to the imperatives of manhood. "So long as we continue to try to act in ways that keep us still 'men,' we are doomed to paralysis, guilt, self-hatred, inertia."[9] The good news is that we can resist. Manhood is a hoax, and refusing to perform it can be an act of resistance to the injustices done in its name.

Having raced across time and perennially performed insecure masculinity for three films, in the penultimate scene of the trilogy, Marty refuses Needles' dare. He throws his truck in reverse and avoids the fateful crash. This is real progress—but what now? With what will Marty replace his toxic insecurity? What is his healthy alternative? Here, we are reminded of Harry Brod's critique of Stoltenberg on masculinity: "what is lacking is precisely the standpoint from which to practice a transformative politics that being profeminist as men provides. One is left with only an ungendered individual moral identity, rather than a gendered collective political identity," Brod says, "essential for sustained political action."[10] For her part, visionary feminist philosopher bell hooks urges us not to conflate patriarchy and masculinity. "Until we make this distinction clear, men will continue to fear that any critique of patriarchy represents a threat"[11]; hooks describes herself as a visionary feminist for a reason. The assumption that feminism has nothing to offer men and men nothing to offer feminism is founded upon the absence of a clear vision of what feminist manhood can look like. Patriarchy is invested in obscuring such a vision, she argues. "How can you become what you cannot imagine?"[12]

This emphasis on our need for alternative forms of masculinity is rooted in both love for men and solidarity with women. hooks believes that both men and women can and do benefit by challenging presumptive gender roles. The challenge she envisions can't just reshuffle traditional masculinity nor just refuse it. "To offer men a different way of being, we must first replace the dominator model with a partnership model that sees interbeing and interdependency as the organic relationship of all living beings."[13] *Back to the Future* presents George and Lorraine's restored relationship as an intriguing yet uneasy blend of partnership and domination. When they last see Marty in the school stairwell (before he goes back to the future), George and Lorraine are now together. They are partners. When we next see them thirty years later, they are happy and flirty as they return from playing tennis. But, if George is no longer dominated by Biff as he was in high school and the initial version of 1985 we see at the beginning of the film, neither has the domination model been fully replaced.

"Rather than defining strength as 'power over,'" hooks says, "feminist masculinity defines strength as one's capacity to be responsible for self and others."[14] When George opens the car door in 1955, he's playacting; when he finds not Marty but Biff inside, his voice falters on his scripted line as things quickly become real. But Lorraine clearly and explicitly asks George for help, and he responds. In calling out Biff, standing up for Lorraine, George is *caregiving* as feminist ethicist Joan Tronto describes it, attentive and responding to another person's actual needs.[15] And with Biff about to break his arm, it is satisfying when George knocks him out with one mighty punch, satisfying enough to look past the fact that he is using his strength here as power-over *and* to protect himself and another.

The persisting theme of domination and strength as power-over is harder to overlook later, at the dance, when a nameless boor steals Lorraine away ("Scram McFly; I'm cutting in!") and George reasserts himself with a brusque shove. On its face, this later scene mirrors the former, with Lorraine calling out and George unexpectedly overpowering another man physically to save her. However, with lower stakes (Marty's disappearing photograph notwithstanding), the use of violence over reason and George's growing confidence and romance with Lorraine through defeating male adversaries become more apparent. It is no surprise that thirty years later, in the near-utopian version of 1985, George and Biff are not friends or even coworkers. The tables have turned, and their statuses have flipped as George now comfortably looks down on the bully turned toady waxing his car.

Harriet & John and Emmett & Clara

For a partnership approach to masculinity closer to bell hooks' description, let's go back to 19th-century England, when intellectual and romantic partners John Stuart and Harriet Taylor Mill were arguing for both individual liberty and sexual political equality. If their predecessor Mary Wollstonecraft had advocated for a world where men and women alike were more masculine, John and Harriet sought to deconstruct the artificial divide between so-called masculine and feminine qualities. As a young John Stuart Mill asked Thomas Carlyle in 1833, "Is there really any distinction between the highest masculine and the highest feminine character?"[16] John had praised Harriet not because she was an exemplary woman nor because she was "as good as any man" but because she had "much feeling and much thought." As John wrote in his preface to Harriet's essay "The Enfranchisement of Women" in 1851, "the foundation of her character was a deep seriousness, resulting from the combination of strongest and most sensitive feelings with the highest principles."[17]

John and Harriet met in the early 1830s, he a bachelor, she a mother of three, five years married. Harriet's first husband died in 1849; Harriet and John Stuart Mill wed two years later. Seven years after that, Harriet herself died in 1858. But if their marriage was brief, their philosophical partnership was not. Together they wrote newspaper articles and philosophical texts, including *Principles of Political Economy* and *On Liberty*. After Harriet's death, John wrote *The Subjection of Women*, a landmark work of liberal feminist philosophy, building on the epistemological and social-political arguments for sexual equality, they had developed in concert. There we find a depiction of an ideal marriage as an equal relationship between people of similar interests and abilities, with intimacy and mutual influence, neither with power over the other, neither in control. In unequal marriages, the family becomes "a school of despotism, in which virtues of despotism, but also its vices, are largely nourished," John wrote; when justly arranged, it could serve instead as a school for sympathy, "the real school of the virtues of freedom."[18]

In *Part III*, an untimely bolt of lightning sends Doc and his DeLorean back to 1885, sixteen years after the publication of *The Subjection of Women*. The book was probably not known to many cowboys or barmaids in the Old West town of Hill Valley, California—save perhaps for the town's new teacher, Clara Clayton. We can imagine it on young Clara's bookshelf alongside *Twenty Thousand Leagues Under the Sea* and her telescope. While Doc and Marty save Clara from plunging to her death in Clayton (or rather, Shonash) Ravine, it is really the telescope which unites the two science lovers, Doc and Clara. They share their mutual interests in astronomy and Jules Verne, and they later dance together at the Hill Valley Festival before stargazing late into the night. When Doc allows himself the vulnerability necessary to share his fantastical time-traveling story, as a woman of reason, Clara is fittingly skeptical. However, when she later overhears confirmation of Doc's sincere love on the train leaving town, as a woman of *feeling*, she is moved to trust and return to him.

To be sure, Zemeckis and Gale have written a script in which Clara needs to be physically rescued not once but twice. She is also a woman who knows her constellations and can ride a horse at full gallop to catch a speeding train. She is also almost certainly a better collaborator for Doc in building a (steam-powered!) time machine than Marty would have ever been. Their relationship enables Doc to enact and embody a kind of masculinity previously unknown to him. Jules and Verne, their precocious pair of boys, will have an undeniably unique childhood traversing the past, present, and future, but with parents as real partners, their family should serve as a fairly good school for young men living unstuck in time.

Notes

1. Sculos, Bryant. 2017. "Who's Afraid of 'Toxic Masculinity'?" *Class, Race, and Corporate Power* 5(3): 1–5.

2. De Boise, Sam. 2019. "Is Masculinity Toxic?" *NORMA International Journal for Masculinity Studies* 14: 147–151.

3. Waling, Andrea. 2019. "Problematising 'Toxic' and 'Healthy' Masculinity for Addressing Gender Inequalities." *Australian Feminist Studies* 34(101): 362–375.

4. Wollstonecraft, Mary. 1790. *A Vindication of the Rights of Men.* Joseph Johnson; Wollstonecraft, Mary. 1792. *A Vindication of the Rights of Woman.* Joseph Johnson.
    5. Johnson, Claudia. 1995. *Equivocal Beings: Politics, Gender, and Sentimentality in the 1790s.* University of Chicago Press.
    6. Butler, Judith. 1990. *Gender Trouble: Feminism and the Subversion of Identity.* Routledge. Butler, Judith. 1988. "Performative Acts and Gender Constitution." *Theatre Journal* 40(4): 519–531.
    7. Stoltenberg, John. 1989. *Refusing to Be a Man: Essays on Sex and Justice.* Taylor & Francis.
    8. Stoltenberg, John. 1993. *The End of Manhood: A Book for Men of Conscience.* Dutton.
    9. Stoltenberg 1989.
    10. Brod, Harry. 1998. "To Be a Man, or Not to Be a Man—That is the Feminist Question." In *Men Doing Feminism,* ed. Tom Digby. Routledge.
    11. hooks, bell. 2004. *The Will to Change: Men, Masculinity, and Love.* Atria Books.
    12. hooks, bell. 2000. *Feminism Is for Everybody: Passionate Politics.* Pluto Press.
    13. *Ibid.,* hooks 2004.
    14. *Ibid.*
    15. Tronto, Joan. 1993. *Moral Boundaries: A Political Argument for an Ethic of Care.* Routledge.
    16. Mill, John Stuart. 1833/1962. "The Early Letters of John Stuart Mill." In *The Collected Works of John Stuart Mill,* ed. Francis E. Mineka. Toronto University Press.
    17. Rossi, Alice, ed. 1970. *Essays on Sex Equality.* University of Chicago Press.
    18. *Ibid.*

VI

Issues of Personal Identity

Past, Present, and/or Alternative Selves

Jeremy C. DeLong

In *Back to the Future*, Doc Brown repeatedly warns Marty about the dangers of time-travel, whether it be changing the timeline in the past or providing past-selves knowledge of the future. Marty's own experience makes these dangers clear enough, as his interference with the original 1955 timeline nearly results in him and his siblings being wiped out of existence. *Part II* and *III* also demonstrate the dangers of time-travel. The entire trilogy, one could argue, might simply be understood as a cautionary tale about such dangers.

However, let's focus on the end of the first film. Having seemingly "set things right," saving himself and his siblings, Marty returns to 1985, arriving a few moments before his past-self originally left for 1955. Marty *again* sees Doc gunned down by the Libyan terrorists, and is certain Doc has been killed, as Marty previously witnessed Doc destroying the letter (warning Doc of just these events), believing it too dangerous to have such knowledge.

Yet, Doc isn't dead. Sometime between Marty's exit from 1955 and his reappearance in 1985, Doc figured "What the hell?!," reconstructed the letter, and gained the foresight to wear body armor the night in question. So, while the risks of altering time may be quite real, *Back to the Future* also invites us to consider the possibility that, if done properly, knowledge of the future can allow us to *improve* the future.

Nevertheless, Doc *himself* otherwise seems to be the *same person* throughout the movie. He was only provided future knowledge of one event, which would occur very late in his life. Thus, this very minor change to the timeline did not seem to greatly affect *who* Doc is. However, the same cannot so readily be concluded for Marty's own family, especially his siblings.

The (New? and Improved) McFlys

Upon waking the morning after his return to 1985, Marty begins to notice major differences in the circumstances and personalities of his own family and their associates. The family home is far more luxuriously and tastefully decorated, indicating the McFlys' significantly greater financial success than what Marty is used to. His brother (New-85 Dave) now appears to be a highly-motivated, well-dressed, and successful businessman who is ready early in the morning to go to work at "the office"—a far cry from Old-85 Dave, a Burger King employee who needed to catch the bus for his night shift. Marty's sister, Old-85 Linda, was a socially awkward and ill-dressed teenager, unpopular with boys; New-85 Linda is a confident socialite, who is having trouble keeping track of her many suitors. As surprising as Marty finds these differences, the changes in his parents are even more extreme.

Old-85 George was cowardly, deeply scared of rejection, socially awkward, and thought to be a "slacker," (at least by Principal Strickland). In contrast, New-85 George is well-dressed, confident, and clearly successful. While Old-85 George would've never risked the rejection of letting anyone read his science-fiction stories, New-85 George has just published his first novel. Old-85 George had a pat, frequently-used excuse to justify his cowardice, that he's "just not very good at confrontations." New-85 George has an altogether new and positive mantra (which he picked up from Marty earlier in the film): "If you put your mind to it, you can accomplish *anything*."

Old-85 Lorraine was an overweight and depressed alcoholic, trying to make the best of her relatively unfortunate life that was "meant to be." After noting "we all make mistakes in life," in reference to her incarcerated brother, she clearly feels the same about her marriage to George, as she recounts the story of realizing she was going to spend the rest of her life with him not long after they met. Old-85 Lorraine was also quite prudish and unsupportive of her children actively seeking romantic relationships. In contrast, New-85 Lorraine is fit, active, and sober. She seems truly happy with her life and marriage and is far from prudish as she encourages her teenage son to go on a weekend camping trip with his girlfriend. In stark contrast to Old-85 George ignoring Lorraine (while distracted by a rerun of *The Honeymooners*), the New-85 loving couple share a real comradery.

The icing on the cake is that the Old-85 family bully, Biff Tannen, is no longer George's abusive work supervisor. Instead, he is a self-employed blue-collar worker, desperate for acceptance and approval by the entire McFly family. Marty is perhaps most surprised when Biff hands him the keys to the car of his dreams: a customized, black Toyota pickup.

After Marty's girlfriend Jennifer appears, she notices Marty's shock and asks him if everything is all right. Looking at his happy family, he replies: "Oh yeah, everything is great!" And, of course, everything does seem great. Despite the near calamities, it seems as if the ultimate result of Marty's interference in 1955 is that he's made his own life, and the lives of those he cares about most, far better in the new 1985. It's a perfect Hollywood happy ending.

Or is it? Did Marty really *improve* the lives of his Old-85 family? In order to say *their* lives were improved, we would of course have to say that the Old-85 family members are the *same persons* as the New-85 family members—that the old versions still *exist* in some meaningful way and that *their own* lives have been made better. If the people in these variant timelines are not the same persons, this would not be so. Were that the case, Marty wouldn't have improved the lives of his Old-85 family. Instead, he would've *destroyed* and *replaced* them (in whole or in part) with (albeit happier and more successful) alternate versions. Considering this question further requires considering the philosophical topic of *personal identity over time*.

Personal Identity Over Time[1]

The question of personal identity over time is a metaphysical question concerning what it means for any unique individual (i.e., a person) to exist *through* time (or even at different times) as *that same unique* individual. Attempts to answer this question can be understood as identifying the *necessary and sufficient conditions* for any particular person to exist, at any particular time. In this regard, we might ask, for instance: "What *must* occur (i.e., what is necessary), and what *is enough* to ensure (i.e., what is sufficient), that 1955-George will be the *same unique person* as 1985-George?"

It's important to note here that philosophers asking these questions do not intend to suggest that there can be no changes *at all* to a person when asking if the "same person" still exists. The very concept of "a person changing" in some way *presumes* that the same person still exists and is the same entity that has undergone the change. Saying that Old-85 Lorraine has gained weight, in contrast to 1955-Lorraine, presumes that personal identity has been maintained over those 30 years. Both are Lorraine, and it is *Lorraine* who has changed (i.e., gained weight). Similarly, we don't typically think that a unique person dies when they go in to get a haircut or that a new person has come into existence after the haircut.

The point here is not limited to physical changes. We also typically think that people can undergo substantial mental changes (e.g., becoming more educated) or even psychological changes (e.g., becoming more patient). When such changes occur, these people are clearly no longer *entirely* the same as they were before, leading us to colloquially say things like: "they are a new person" or "they are not the same person they were before." Yet, these are just a manner of speaking, as it seems that the changed individual is still the same person in the metaphysical sense that they have maintained their personal identity (i.e., no one died, and no new person has started to exist). Again, it is *that* unique (metaphysical) self who is the person who underwent the changes.

So, if our standard intuitions are correct, many changes/differences in or about a person can occur while that person's identity is maintained. That said, there do seem to be limits. We typically take the death of our body to be one of the more obvious limiting changes for maintaining the existence of our personal identity. But that might be due to historical limitations of technology. For example, imagine that in addition to a time-traveling DeLorean, Doc Brown invents a perfect cloning machine which he uses to create a perfect clone of Marty (Marty-2). Marty-2 looks, thinks, and acts just like the original. If the original Marty were then to die in an unfortunate accident, would the original Marty's personal identity persist in Marty-2? Would "Marty" himself still exist? If Doc treats Marty-2 to an even better life, would the original Marty's life have been improved?

In such cases, people's intuitions often differ, so we need further philosophical inquiry to help establish what changes are permitted (and which are not) in order to maintain personal identity. Numerous views on the appropriate condition(s) for personal identity have been proposed, but none are obviously correct. They all seem to involve trade-offs. All such views have both their own explanatory benefits, as well as their own theoretical costs.

Genetic and Birth History Views

One might initially be tempted to say that Marty's family members *are* the same people (metaphysically) in the new 1985, via appealing to a *genetic* view of personal identity. The 1955 versions of George and Lorraine had been born approximately seventeen years prior to Marty's interference, which doesn't seem to have changed their genetics in any way. At most, their lives simply took a different track. That seems consistent with our intuitions about our freedom of will, the possibility of making different choices, and thus having (even very) different lives. Similarly, Marty's siblings have the same general physical appearance; this strongly suggests that their genetic make-up is also the same in both their Old-85 and New-85 iterations. Thus, we might therefore conclude that all of them are the same persons (metaphysically).

However, there is a fairly clear counterexample to the "same genetics, same person" view. Identical twins also have the exact same genetics. But if you'd been born an identical twin, you wouldn't think of your twin as *you*; you're a *distinct* individual.

Appealing to some sort of necessary "historical birth" account of identity will also hardly work either. Eggs and ova can be viable for a range of time (about a week normally; indefinitely if frozen). Actual birth can thus "naturally" or artificially occur much earlier or much later. And it seems we wouldn't want to say you were born an entirely (metaphysically) "different person" than you would have been, if your mother had gone into labor earlier. Thus, requiring exactly the same historical account of birth for personal identity also seems to fail. So, while the Old-85 and New-85 McFlys all seem to have the same genetics and at least relatively historically-similar births, it's problematic to rely on either of these criteria for establishing a reliable theory for personal identity.

Body-Brain Views

Rather than *genetics*, we might point to the *bodies* (i.e., the same living organism, same person), or even just their *brains* (i.e., same brain, same person) as a basis for establishing personal identity; these are in fact very distinct criteria. However, since the trilogy never separates anyone's brains from their bodies, let's initially just consider these a joint criterion here, "same brain and body, same person," as both are always present whenever the other is in *Back to the Future*.

Again, the 1955-versions of George and Lorraine had been born a little under two decades prior. As far as we know, they've have had the same body-brain combination since birth. There is also no reason to think there were any changes to their body-brain combination in the ensuing 30 years. So just as the Old-85 persons were simply the older versions of each person's original 1955 body-brain, so the New-85 persons would also simply be older versions of those original 1955 bodies-brains. While the bodies-brains might have undergone *different experiences* in the ensuing years, and thus might have turned out differently in some ways (e.g., they are fitter, thinner, more successful, etc.), it would still clearly have to be *those very same bodies-brains*, or those *very same living organisms*, that continued to exist through time.

So, if "same body-brain" is what determines personal identity, it seems they would once again be the same persons. And thus, it would be those same persons who underwent the alternate events and experiences. Similar to the genetic view, we would simply say that their unique lives, as the unique living body-brain sharing organism they are, simply went down "different tracks" in the alternative timeline Marty created. And similarly, if we are granting the same *genetics* for Marty's siblings, we should also be willing to grant the same body-brain combination between Marty's Old-85 and New-85 siblings. All of the same points above (about the older generation) would also then apply, and when we again reflect upon how it seems we could make many different choices in life as ourselves and still be *our same selves*, or "us," even if those variant choices led us to live very different lives, this seems perfectly sensible.

By itself, the body view of personal identity (or some version of it) is quite attractive for a number of reasons. In many ways, we feel that our own *selves* are closely tied to our own bodies in our normal experience of the world. It makes perfect, *naturalistic* sense to say that we *just are* the living organism that is our body, and nothing more. Of course, this also entails that when our body dies, we also die, and there is no "second-chance" or "afterlife." But there is no good reason to think those things are available to us anyway, as mortal creatures in a naturalistic world.

However, when we start thinking about possible ways in which our brains might be separated from our bodies, the "body view" seems to lose much of its intuitive appeal. Just as it's possible to replace various other important bodily organs to keep them functioning, it is possible (in-principle) to replace a brain as an organ, to keep our original body functioning. When we get a successful kidney transplant, we don't hold a funeral. No one has died! The same body/organism clearly continues to persist, and we tend to think the same "person" also thus continues to exist, though with a change to the origins/source of their bodily organs.

Similarly, the brain is also a "bodily organ." Were we to replace your brain with a *new* brain taken from the failing body of someone else, would the walking/talking living organism that got off the table be *you*? The same overall living organism/body that was born to your parents would clearly still be alive and functioning. But the original "stream of consciousness" would have been replaced, in addition to the "mental content" (memories, experiences, psychology, etc.) of our lives from the past. Many people would understandably find it implausible that such a being would still be "them." Thus, body views come with a number of problems of their own, in terms of being necessary and sufficient for personal identity in all situations.

Given the possibility of "brain transplants," it intuitively seems as if the brain should be treated as a far more important organ than a kidney. In fact, were our brains to be removed entirely from our bodies, and kept alive in some "vat," many would have the intuition that we still existed *as ourselves*, even *without* the rest of our bodies. This thought experiment provides a lot of intuitive support for the brain view ("same brain, same person"). While our lives might be totally different if restricted to a "vat," perhaps even far less rewarding and enjoyable, it's plausible that *we* would still exist, *as ourselves*, even as just a brain in a vat.

Nevertheless, the brain view is still a *physicalist* view. Like the body view, it requires the sameness of some physical thing persisting, in order for personal identity to persist. And, physical things are often divisible, with similar functionality. Consider that a liver transplant with even just a small part of a healthy liver can be enough to serve the function adequately in the new host. What might be surprising is that brains also do not seem to require being "whole" to serve their function adequately. The two (left and right) hemispheres of the brain can be separated, and life can be maintained with relatively high functionality. This has already been demonstrated by actual brain-surgery patients who had half of their brain (i.e., one hemisphere) removed. They continued to live more or less normal lives, and they are generally considered to be the same person. However, if our personal identity is based upon having the "same brain," and our personal identity can be maintained by one-half of our brain, we don't need the entire brain. So far, so good. But what if we halved your brain and gave the other half to someone else's body? Are there now two of *you*? This seems absurd. And thus, the brain view of personal identity also runs into substantial theoretical problems.

While the body and/or brain views of personal identity would seem to grant that Marty's family are the same persons, these more *physicalist* views of personal identity have been shown to be problematic. Thus, even though these criteria would support the view that Marty has indeed improved the lives of his family (because they are the *same persons*, albeit different in many ways), rather than replaced/destroyed them for new versions, perhaps we should not be so hasty.

Physicalist vs. Content/Data Views

What likely seemed attractive about the brain view was its focus on our *mental* lives, as the brain is the organ which controls all such aspects. However, perhaps it was a mistake to focus on the *organ* that is responsible for our mental lives, when we should have been focused on the *content* and *experiences* themselves. Perhaps what makes "us" be *us* at any given time is the ability to *remember our* lives, and *experience our* lives, *as ourselves*—and to even *respond* to such memories/experiences in a way that psychologically fits who we are.

While the brain may be a necessary organ for accomplishing these tasks under the limited, ordinary and historical circumstances for humans—and that is why its importance for personal identity *seems* so crucial—perhaps it is not truly necessary. Perhaps all we need is *some* "brain-like thing" in which to *store* and *access* our memories and psychology. So, whether we have a typical "human brain," or some other "brain-like structure" that serves a similar function, what really matters is the *content* of our mental lives.

Memory and/or Psychology Views[2]

The weak memory/psychology view might be summarized as "*some* sufficiently overlapping amount of the same memories and psychological traits, caused in the right way, result in the same person." Once again, the older generation of 1955 persons seems to be relatively safe on this view. Old-85 George and Lorraine likely all *remember* things from earlier in their own lives, and their psychological *continuity be*tween 1955 and 1985 would likely have an appropriate causal relationship (i.e., earlier experiences and attitudes in their lives cause later experiences and attitudes in later versions of themselves). While the New-1985 persons seem to have ended up with very different memories than their Old-85 counterparts, the New-85 older generations' memories and psychology could still be *causally* linked back to those 1955 counterparts. And, thus once again, we can simply say they are the "same persons," but their lives went down very different tracks, due to the new timeline.

However, the situation for Marty's siblings is now far more problematic. We do not know anything concrete about how the lives of Marty and his siblings were changed in the ensuing years, but we can deduce they had to be quite different in order to have such different outcomes in personal character and general standards of living. And there is no baseline of memory and psychology for them to be causally linked back to, prior to the changes in the timeline—they didn't yet exist.

One might argue that, perhaps if their lives were somewhat similar to their Old-85 counterparts, at least early on in their lives, then there would possibly be some sufficient grounds for saying that the Old-85 and New-85 siblings were the "same persons" in a similar way to the older generation. But that is a misapplication of this view of personal identity. The issue is not whether or not Old-85 and New-85 siblings had any *exactly similar* memories or psychological traits that overlapped at any time. Rather, it is whether either of these 1985 versions of his siblings can both be causally traced back to a common "prior self," which shares *some* memories and psychological states. That seems impossible since the timeline was changed prior to their birth/existence. There simply is no common "person" that existed in the past to which the old and new versions of his siblings can be causally linked. On this memory/psychology view, they seem to be *completely different persons*.

So, even if we were to compare memories and psychological traits for each sibling across timelines, this won't demonstrate the same identity. New-85 Dave and Old-85 Dave are about as different as one can imagine. Even if their memories/experiences and psychological make-up were completely identical in both timelines up to age 10 (highly unlikely, given the major timeline shifts) before any radical diversion, the Old-85 and New-85 versions could then causally trace back to when they were ten years old. But we still haven't demonstrated that their 10-year-old selves are identical. And once again, that seems impossible, given that there is no being that was *them*, prior to the timeline shift, to causally link back to.

There is an even stronger view of mentalistic content for personal identity. But if the weaker version fails, then the stronger version will certainly fail in the case of the siblings. And it will also even fail in the case of the older generation. This view is that we need all the *exact* same memories/experiences and psychological traits to be the same person. The opening passages of this essay clearly demonstrate that the Old-85 and New-85 persons in *Back to the Future* must be radically different. And thus, they could not possibly be the same persons. Instead, they would all be *new persons*, in an alternative timeline.

Concluding Thoughts

The *Back to the Future* trilogy is fairly clear and consistent in regard to its warnings about altering time. While the original film might seem to present a typical Hollywood happy ending, our discussion here has revealed a reason to be skeptical of such a cheery outlook. Though things initially seem great for the McFlys after Marty's time-travel adventure, it might be too good to be true. Perhaps Marty did make the lives of his family better in the New-85 timeline. Or, maybe it simply appears that way, and Marty did in fact essentially destroy his original parents and siblings, replacing them with alternate (albeit improved) versions of themselves. At the very least, we should remember that time-travel is risky and not just for the time-travelers.

Notes

1. For some additional non-technical and entertaining philosophical works that treat these same criteria for personal identity, the following are recommended. See Dennett, Daniel. 2008. "Where Am I." *Philosophy Now*. Anja Publications; Perry, John. 1978. *A Dialogue on Personal Identity and Immortality*. Hackett.

2. John Locke is typically credited with first championing the "Memory View" of personal identity. See Locke, John. 1690. *An Essay Concerning Human Understanding*.

From Density to Destiny

Casey Rentmeester

What makes you who you are? Aristotle argues that your character is a reflection of the actions you consistently repeat. While there is no doubt truth in this account, it also seems to be the case that there are pivotal moments in your life that substantially define you. We find the importance of decisive moments in the character of George McFly in *Back to the Future*. In 1985, George is a downtrodden father who has been mercilessly bullied by the belligerent Biff Tannen for decades. His son, Marty, inadvertently travels back in time to 1955 and stumbles upon a younger version of his father at Lou's Cafe. As a teenager, George lives in perpetual doubt, exuding no confidence in any of his social interactions, traits he will carry into adulthood. By happenstance, George falls out of a tree he's climbed to watch his classmate Lorraine[1] undress, which leads George to get hit by a car driven by Lorraine's father. As a result, Lorraine takes pity on George and goes on a first date with him, eventually leading to their marriage and ultimately the conception of Marty.

In the alternate universe that Marty's time travel creates, George is no longer hit by the car and thus is no longer the receiver of Lorraine's pity. As such, in order to ensure his very existence, Marty needs to convince George to win over Lorraine by being confident and forthright with her, traits he utterly lacks. At first, George completely fails, captured well by his classically awkward pick-up line to Lorraine, "I'm your density." Eventually, though, with the help of some clever manipulation by Marty, George finds a way to win Lorraine's heart by intervening in Biff's drunken molestation of her. This event is nothing less than life-changing for George, who goes on to become a confident and successful science fiction writer by the time Marty returns back to the future of 1985. What are we to make of this shift philosophically? Is there merit to the idea that certain events can be so significant as to alter one's life so much as to change the sheepish George at the beginning of the film into the supremely confident version of himself showcased by the film's end?

Exploring Martin Heidegger's distinctions between leaping in (*einspringen*), leaping ahead (*vorausspringen*), and leaping forth (*vorspringen*), I think through what it means for George to make a fundamental shift in his existence through this act of courage. Leaping in occurs when someone handles a situation for you, as when Marty confronts Biff in the cafe, while leaping ahead has to do with another's ability to open yourself up to possibilities that you could not have imaged without the other person's help, as when Marty convinces George to take a stand on Lorraine, a stand that simultaneously required a confrontation with Biff. Finally, leaping forth occurs when you enact your own possibilities and thus take ownership for your life, as when George finally stands up for himself in the film. Ultimately, I argue that the Ancient Greek philosopher, Aristotle, is right that character becomes defined by consistent actions, but certain events in which a person takes a leap outside one's comfort zone can prove to be especially definitive.

Character Development

In this analysis of *Back to the Future*, character development has not only to do with the ways in which the characters unfold in the movie and its sequels, but also the very ways in which any person's character is formed and developed in the first place. Aristotle, whose philosophy is so influential that it can be said without hyperbole that "there were whole centuries when the civilized world lived in Aristotle's shadow,"[2] was the first Western philosopher to develop a systematic theory of character development. Thus, his philosophy is the most obvious starting point to launch our analysis.

In his *Nicomachean Ethics* and his lesser-read *Eudemian Ethics*, Aristotle's primary question is "what is the good life?" Having surveyed several answers to this question, he comes upon the ultimate conclusion that the good life consists in the cultivation of virtues, which he defines as the "states of character" of a good man.[3] For Aristotle, "moral virtue comes about as a result of habit," such that "states of character arise out of like activities."[4] Humans are unique from all other animals for Aristotle in that we are rational, which means we can think and choose, thus giving us the ability to conduct our lives. Even though he acknowledges that everyone has inborn dispositions of character (e.g., some are prone to timidity, while others to brashness; some are prone to idleness, while others are busybodies, etc.), he states directly that "virtue is in our own power, and so too vice."[5] This means that even if one's natural tendency is to be sheepish and cowardly, as George clearly is when Marty goes back in time to meet him, one can choose to change this through consistently engaging in acts that call for courage. Eventually, these acts start to form into one's character through habituation "when [a habit] becomes operative in a particular fashion as the result of ... repetition."[6]

While Aristotle's theory of character development does provide a fitting general lens to understand how persons form characteristic traits, it seems there are some especially significant events in life that can nearly entirely alter a person. The George McFly at the start of the movie based in 1985—a man engrossed in his own insecurities, accepting insult upon insult as if it is to be expected—is not the same man at the end of the film when Marty goes back to the future. His old, wrecked Chevy Nova has been replaced with a new BMW (being waxed by none other than Biff). George casually grabs Lorraine's ass to showcase his supreme confidence, an act nearly impossible to imagine being performed by the version of George we meet earlier in the film. We come to learn that George's intervention of Biff's molestation of Lorraine is indeed the reason they fell in love and that George has been keeping Biff in line since high school. While Aristotle doesn't explicitly focus on how one moment can change a person's character in his ethical treatises, the German philosopher Martin Heidegger provides some helpful insight as to how the entire trajectory of a life can be altered due to one especially meaningful event. Thus, an analysis of George's character development requires a foray into Heidegger to complement our overarching Aristotelian lens.

Heidegger was deeply influenced by Aristotle—indeed, he once advised his students (half-seriously, it seems) to study Aristotle for ten to fifteen years if they were to really understand Western philosophy.[7] In the early 1920s, in fact, before he became a giant of philosophy in his own right, most of his lectures were on Aristotle. In 1927, though, Heidegger establishes himself as much more than a mere interpreter by publishing his *magnum opus*, *Being and Time*, which is easily one of the most important philosophical works of the 20th century. The fundamental question of this work is "what does it mean to be?" and, since we must necessarily approach this question from a human lens, Heidegger dives into one of Aristotle's primary questions—"what does it mean to be human?"—to come upon an answer. Although his answer to this question is complex, at the core of our being is a trait he refers to as "care" (*Sorge*), a sub-feature of which is "solicitude" (*Fürsorge*), which literally means "caring-for" others in the original German. Because he agrees with Aristotle that we are fundamentally social beings—Aristotle famously thought that "man is by nature a political animal"[8]—caring for others is a basic human trait in his system.

Aristotle believed that the end—or, in the original Greek, the *telos*— of human life lies in living well (*eudaimonia*), which means performing one's function well. This required not only cultivating our rational nature but our social nature as well, the former of which is formed by intellectual virtues (i.e., thinking well), and the latter of which is formed by moral virtues (e.g., courage, patience, etc.). Heidegger interprets Aristotle's *telos* as follows: "to the extent that a being reaches its *telos* and is complete, it is as it is meant to be, *eu*."[9] In other words, to be good (*eu* simply means "good" or "well") at being human is to live towards one's *telos* or proper end. We do so in the realm of our social nature by engaging with others, and it matters *how* we do so if we are to cultivate the proper virtues.

Heidegger distinguishes two extreme possibilities of demonstrating solicitude, that is, care for others, namely, leaping in (*einspringen*) and leaping ahead (*vorausspringen*). He defines leaping in as "tak[ing] away 'care' from the Other and put[ting] [oneself] in [another's] position in concern."[10] This amounts, essentially, to stepping in and taking over a situation for another, even if that situation would ideally have better been taken on by that individual for his or her own sake. After George's awkward "I'm your density" line to Lorraine, Biff attempts to further humiliate George by shaking him down for money before Marty trips him in front of the packed cafe, a considerable slap in the face. In that moment, Marty recognizes that George isn't going to stand up for himself; Marty therefore needed to handle the situation on behalf of George. This is a classic case of leaping in. While we can surely admit that this was a noble act on the part of Marty, the problem with having other people solve your own problems regularly is that you don't cultivate the requisite virtues to take on challenges yourself.

To actually change one's character into something better, a moral agent must do the actions themselves in both Aristotle's and Heidegger's philosophies. Heidegger thus contrasts leaping in with leaping ahead, which doesn't take another's care away "but rather give it back to him authentically as such for the first time ... [thereby helping] the Other to become transparent to himself *in* his care and to become *free for* it."[11] Leaping ahead entails helping others open themselves up to possibilities that they didn't even realize they could achieve. Marty plays this role for George later in the film by concocting a scheme to make him out to be heroic, which inadvertently leads to George confronting Biff head-on. The *plan* was for George to sweep in and save Lorraine from Marty's *feigned* abuse as they "parked," but Biff steps in and has his cronies rough up Marty while he jumps in the car with Lorraine. After George gets to the car and sees Biff molesting Lorraine, his demeanor soon turns from helplessness to rage, and he lands a powerful left hook directly to Biff's face. To everyone's surprise, George has conquered his menace while landing a spot in Lorraine's now-adoring heart. Marty's plan—although not perfectly executed—still worked, and in an even better way since George finally put Biff in his place.

The results of the Biff altercation are nothing less than life changing for George, as his former pathetic self gets transformed, and he is now being roundly congratulated and asked to run for class president. Marty later tells Doc that he never knew his old man "had it in him." From George's look of amazement in the moment, it's clear that George didn't know he had it in himself either. But once that part of him was disclosed, it unleashed an utterly new version of himself, eventually catapulting him into confidently pursuing a career as a successful science fiction writer in the last scenes of the movie. Heidegger talks of opening oneself up to such possibilities as a "freeing up" or a "liberating," since you are liberated from the insecurities that once plagued you and opened up to a new version of yourself that you didn't even realize was possible. As is common in Heidegger's philosophy, he maintains the notion of "leaping" (*springen*) to capture this idea of projecting one's own possibilities in order to show the etymological connections. In this case, Marty's leaping ahead (*vorausspringen*) led to George's leaping forth (*vorspringen*), which is when one takes one's own leap into a new version of themselves and projects new possibilities in accordance with that leap. Just as Heidegger once said that "only the leap into the river tells us what is called swimming,"[12] only a leap into new possibilities allows one to take them up and allow them to inform one's character. Similarly, Aristotle argued that "a man has practical wisdom not by knowing only but by being able to act."[13] Unlike intellectual virtues that can be honed merely by thinking well, moral virtues require practice. George had to face his fear in order to overcome it, which thereby opened him up to a life he couldn't have dreamed of before doing so.

Cultivating a Second Nature (or, Choosing Destiny)

Back to the Future doesn't show us what happens between George's altercation with Biff and Marty's arrival back in 1985. It is clear, though, that George's life trajectory is fundamentally better for him and those around him, including Lorraine and their children. The interesting question is how George could turn his default nature as a "loser" (as Principal Strickland describes him) into an obviously successful and happy person. For Aristotle, certain persons are "not best equipped by nature for all the virtues."[14] George is naturally slavish and timid—and he clearly becomes uncomfortable in taking on any conflict head-on when we meet the younger version of himself. He regularly says "I'm just not a fighter," as if his weak nature is already set in stone. However, Aristotle argues that we can change our nature and form a second nature through the repeated performance of habit, even though it is not easy: "it is easier to change a habit than to change one's nature; even habit is hard to change just because it is like nature."[15] Although it seems as if George's character changed on a dime in the film, in reality, building a second nature takes time.

In Marty's first encounter with his teenage father, he witnesses Biff yelling at George for not having his homework done in time for Biff to recopy it. The dynamic of dominance is obvious: Biff is a bully, and George doesn't even think to stand up for himself. Aristotle is quite clear that some persons, through cowardice, "shrink from doing what they think best for themselves,"[16] a comment that perfectly fits George. He is also explicit that "to endure being insulted and put up with insult … is slavish" and that it is, in fact, more praiseworthy to get angry "at the right things and with the right people"[17] than to simply accept insult. Therefore, in order to actually achieve one's end, namely, *eudaimonia*, one must make a choice, which he defines as "a deliberative desire for something that is in our power."[18] In this initial scene, George simply doesn't have it in him to transcend his nature and make that choice.

Inspired in part by Aristotle, Heidegger spends a lot of time talking through what it means to transcend your given nature. He argues that humans always understand themselves "in terms of existence [*Existenz*]—in terms of a possibility to be itself or not itself."[19] The word existence [*Existenz*] has a specific meaning for Heidegger in that it signifies the distinctive possibility of choosing one's possibilities against the background of thrownness (*Geworfenheit*), that is, against the background of the world as given that one has not chosen. Since humans *ex-sist*, we literally stand out ("ex" means "out" and "sist" means to take a stand in Latin) from all other beings in that we are capable of taking a stand on our life through our actions. This is why Heidegger says that Dasein (his word for the being of humans) "is what it becomes."[20] Unlike rocks or even animals, humans have a choice in the trajectory of their lives, and those who choose to be a certain way and own that choice against their unique background of thrownness are said to have achieved *Eigentlichkeit*. That word is typically translated as "authenticity" by English translators, but a better translation is "ownedness": the person who takes hold of one's own particular life in one's own particular way has owned it (*eigen* means "own" or "particular"). The person who fails to do so and gets carried along by the crowd, or by bullies like Biff, for that matter, has not.

As it turns out, George's heroic intervention during Biff's assault of Lorraine was the leap he needed in the sense of *vorspringen* to start to own his life on his own terms and stand up for himself, thereby catapulting him into a path of ownedness. He literally transformed the pitiful Peeping Tom in the initial 1955 scene to the supremely confident husband totally at ease in playfully grabbing Lorraine's ass in the alternate reality at the end of the film, the sheepish and pathetic butt of Biff's jokes to the successful author ordering Biff around, and the timid and awkward father into a man who is perfectly comfortable telling Marty at the end of the film, "Like I've always told you: you put your mind to it, you could accomplish *anything*." With the unbeknownst help of Marty, George indeed chose his destiny.

Notes

1. It's not explicitly obviously that George is peeping on Lorraine specifically. The issue is something of a debate among the *Back to the Future* fandom.
2. Lerner, Max. 1943. "Introduction." *Aristotle's Politics*. Jowett, Benjamin (trans.). Random House, 16.
3. Aristotle. 2011. *The Eudemian Ethics*. Kenny, Anthony (trans.). Oxford University Press, 86.
4. Aristotle. 2009. *The Nicomachean Ethics*. Ross, David (trans.). Oxford University Press, 22–23.
5. *Ibid.*, *The Nicomachean Ethics*, 46.
6. *Ibid.*, *The Eudemian Ethics*, 18.
7. Heidegger, Martin. 1968. *What Is Called Thinking?*, Wieck, Fredd D.; Gray, J. Glenn (trans.). Harper & Row, viii.
8. Aristotle. 1943. *Politics*. Jowett, Benjamin (trans.). Random House, 54.
9. Heidegger, Martin. 1997. *Plato's Sophist*. Rojcewicz, Richard; Schuwer, André (trans.). Indiana University Press, 84.
10. Heidegger, Martin. 1962. *Being and Time*. Macquarrie, John; Robinson, Edward (trans.). Harper & Row, 158.
11. *Ibid.*, 159.
12. *Ibid.*, *What Is Called Thinking?*, 21.
13. *Ibid.*, Aristotle, *The Nicomachean Ethics*, 134.
14. *Ibid.*, 117.
15. *Ibid.*, 135.
16. *Ibid.*, 169.
17. *Ibid.*, 73.
18. *Ibid.* Aristotle, *The Eudemian Ethics*, 33.
19. *Ibid.*, Heidegger, *Being and Time*, 33.
20. *Ibid.*, 186.

Does Marty Commit Temporal Manslaughter?

Joe Slater

We all know the story. After we meet the McFlys in 1985, including their somewhat pitiable, mostly forgettable patriarch, George, we follow his son Marty on an adventure back in time where he bumps into his parents' younger selves. Marty's mother, Lorraine tries to seduce him and almost doesn't fall in love with George (which would eliminate Marty from existence!). But through some careful scheming and a lot of luck, Marty gets them together, saving himself. What's more, having stood up for himself against the McFly family nemesis, Biff, George becomes a more confident, self-assured person, so much so that when Marty returns to 1985, the McFlys are considerably happier and successful as a result. It's a picture-perfect, almost fairy-tale-like ending.

However, it's not that simple. We might *think* that George is the same guy at story's end, just with a vastly improved life. But is he *really*? They (i.e., George at the beginning of the film and George at the end of the film) might be the same age and have the same DNA, but they have wildly different memories, relationships, and outlooks on the world. So are they really the same person? If not, does that mean Marty inadvertently killed his actual father? At the risk of putting a damper on the whole story, I'm going to argue that he did.

Preliminaries

Let's think a bit more about what happened. Early in the film, when Marty arrives home from school in 1985, he sees the family car being towed. Biff—who's just crashed the car while drinking beer—is shouting at George about a fictional "blind spot" and bullying him about work. George is meek, submissive, and obsequious. In his own words, he's "not good at confrontations." George is a doormat. The rest of the family also has its troubles. Marty's brother Dave works at Burger King; his sister Linda can't get a date. Lorraine, their mother, seems to have a drinking problem and disapproves of Marty's relationship with his girlfriend, Jennifer. For simplicity, let's stick with George (though I think the important bits will apply to the whole family). Time travel makes it tricky to know who we're talking about, so when I'm talking about *this* George, from now on, I'll call him George$_{A1}$ (for Adult George 1).

Again, when Marty eventually travels back in time, he meets younger versions of his parents, and almost prevents himself from being born. In 1955, George is obviously younger, timid, and is bullied by Biff, but he has a secret passion for writing science fiction stories. Let's call this version of him George$_Y$ (for Young George).

By the end of the film, as Marty puts it, "everything is great." The house is nicer, Linda has a number of suitors, Dave has a professional job, and George and Lorraine are active and happy. The car is fine and being waxed by Biff, whom George now stands up to. George is also a successful science fiction writer. Emboldened by his experience of standing up to Biff in 1955, *this* George has made the best of his life. Let's call this version of him George$_{A2}$ (for Adult George 2).

Now that we've sorted out our George terminology, we can return to the question raised at the start of this essay: does Marty kill his dad? Obviously, he doesn't kill George in any ordinary sense (e.g., by shooting or poisoning him). But time travel allows for a variety of strange ways of changing the world. And it allows for weird ways someone could *kill* people. Time travel allows for the possibility of temporal assassins (e.g., who could go back in time and kill baby Hitler). But it also allows for the possibility of killing someone accidentally. Let's call this—when via time travel, you change the world so that someone from your timeline ceases to exist within that timeline—*temporal manslaughter*.

Is this what happens to George$_{A1}$? George$_{A2}$ looks like George$_{A1}$, has the same blood type, and similar childhood memories, but could George$_{A1}$ be killed and replaced by George$_{A2}$ through the events of *Back to the Future*? To answer this question, it seems as if we need to know if George$_{A1}$ and George$_{A2}$ are the same person. If they *are*, then George$_{A1}$ wasn't killed. He's still with us at the end of the film, just with a few changes. This brings us to the topic of personal identity.

Personal Identity Through Time: The Physical View

When philosophers talk about personal identity, they might be raising a few different issues. One thing we might wonder about identity is how any object can change (while retaining its identity). A classic example, discussed by Thomas Hobbes (1588–1679), concerns the "Ship of Theseus."

Theseus has a ship, but the sea being a dangerous place, bits of the ship occasionally fall off or need repair. If one plank of the ship is replaced, is it still the same ship? How about two planks? What if half of the planks which make up the ship are replaced with completely *new* planks, is it still the same ship? Suppose that eventually, every plank of Theseus's ship has been replaced, so the ship now has *none* of the same parts with which it started. Is Theseus still sailing on *the same* ship on which he began sailing? To make this more puzzling, suppose also that someone picked up all of the old discarded ship parts which Theseus discarded as he was making repairs over the years and builds a ship out of them. Now we have one ship, made of new parts (the one on which Theseus is still sailing), and which has some *temporal continuity* with the original ship, and another entire ship (made of all the parts of the original ship). Which one is the *real* ship of Theseus?

It might not seem like much of a real problem, but the cells that make up our human bodies are being damaged and replaced all the time. As you read this, your body won't have any of the same cells as it did 15 years ago (if you're that old). However, you probably think you are, in some meaningful sense, *the same person* as you were any number of years ago. Similarly, we think George$_Y$ is the same person as George$_{A1}$.

This question—about what makes someone the same person through time—is sometimes known as the *reidentification question*.[1] One simple answer we might give to this question is that what it means for George$_Y$ to be the same person as George$_{A1}$ is that they have the same body. Sure, when we look at George$_{A1}$, he's gone through some changes, but there's a *physical continuity be*tween them. There have been physical changes in those 30 years—his hair has grown, skin cells have died and fallen off, being replaced by new ones, and so on—but if someone were to observe him for the entirety of that time (as difficult as that might be) they'd see one human being (i.e., they'd see *George*) who simply seems to undergo some changes.

This is one of the answers we might give to the reidentification question: a person at one time (t_1) is the same person at another time (t_2) if and only if there is a *bodily continuity be*tween them at t_1 and t_2. Let's call this the physical view, which might look appealing. You're a human being—a human animal. And, so we might reason, you're a physical thing. You have organs and limbs and a brain which are all physical parts. And these things can change a bit through time, but you are still the same *organism.*

If we accept the physical view, what should we say about George$_{A1}$ and George$_{A2}$? Well, they don't really have any bodily continuity with each other. They *both* have continuity with George$_Y$ (in their respective timelines) but not with each other, so it looks like they're different people. This would of course mean that George$_{AI}$ has been removed from existence, and thus that Marty *has* committed temporal manslaughter.

But maybe this is too quick. A number of philosophers have thought there are big problems for the physical view. One such philosopher was John Locke (1632–1704). Locke gave an example that has attracted a lot of attention, involving a cobbler and a prince.[2] I'll present essentially this same case with a bit of a twist. Suppose Doc Brown decides to do some weird brain science and asks Marty to volunteer in an experiment. He puts a special helmet on Marty and another on his dog, Einstein, then presses a button. There's a strange, discomforting sound, a flash of light, and when it's over, the mental states—the memories, desires, beliefs, and so on—of Marty and of Einstein have been swapped. Marty's human body runs around trying to chase his (now non-present tail). Einstein simply sits there and looks puzzled.

If we're watching Marty while this happened, we would have seen the same body (i.e., the same physical thing). If we didn't know what had happened, we'd say that Marty just started to act in a very peculiar fashion. And if we accepted the physical view, that would be how we should understand what happened. Marty was a (fairly) normal teenager, but at some point, he started to chase his tail, bark, eat dog food, etc.

However, according to Locke, this isn't the right way to think about it. Rather, we should say that the *person* has changed. We might say, for instance, that Marty is *in* Einstein's body, and Einstein is in Marty's body. If we're right about that, then what keeps you the same person *isn't* the physical stuff, but something *psychological*. Of course, *usually*, these things go together, but in weird cases that philosophers like to think about, they might come apart, so the physical view is wrong.

Here's another kind of case that might lead us to the same conclusion. Imagine Doc develops technology to transfer your consciousness into a machine; maybe he builds you a cool robot body. Instead of aging and dying, you could live for hundreds or thousands of years, with a cybernetic brain. If you think that this could really be *you*—that you would have lived for a bit in a human body, then after that in the robot body—then this is also a fairly devastating problem for the physical view.

And it's not *just* weird philosophical or sci-fi cases that suggest problems for the physical view. It's common for family members of sufferers of severe dementia, where they genuinely don't know who they are anymore, to say that they're *not the same person* anymore, or that they're not really there. They've lost what made them *them*. So we might think we need a different kind of view—one that incorporates *psychological* features.

The Psychological View

Again, Locke thinks that what's important for personal identity is psychological features. So, instead of identity depending on physical factors (i.e., bodily continuity), it depends on *psychological* continuity. Now, one issue for this kind of view is that people don't always have psychological continuity. When, in 1955, Marty gets run over by his grandfather, he seems to be knocked unconscious, so there is a *break* in his psychological continuity. But obviously we wouldn't say that he's literally a different person after he then wakes in his mother's bedroom (despite the fact that she calls him "Calvin"). So, if we think it is a psychological relationship that makes someone the same person at two different times, we have a challenge of specifying what this relationship is.

Locke thought that the important thing was really *memory*. If Marty and Einstein swap minds, the Marty-body has Einstein-memories, so we could think that's what makes it really *Einstein* in there. But even this doesn't really work. Imagine that Biff gets really drunk and kills someone, but he was so drunk he can't remember it. Surely it was still *Biff* that did it. We definitely don't excuse people committing horrible crimes if they can't remember doing them. And you don't have to be drunk to forget things—we all forget things all the time. This clearly doesn't mean we're not the same people.

Derek Parfit (1942–2017) takes on this challenge.[3] He says we can think of different psychological connections that we hold over time. Memories are important, but desires, beliefs, hopes and dreams, and things like this are also important. Just thinking about memories—while I write this, I remember a lot of things about my life, but I can't even remember what I had for breakfast yesterday! But I *do* remember lots of things. I have a *lot* of the same memories as I had yesterday (probably over 99 percent of them). And comparing yesterday and the day before, that's probably true as well. Day-to-day, there are very strong psychological connections. And going back day by day, we can see that I am *connected* to myself as a toddler, even though, *right now*, I might have very little in common with my toddler self psychologically.

Parfit suggests that we think of psychological continuity as obtaining when there are overlapping chains of strong connectedness. We can therefore say that I'm the same person as toddler-me, because there are these overlapping chains that connect us. Thinking back to the Einstein-Marty mind swap—here we could say that it *is* Marty in Einstein's body, because he still has the right psychological connectedness.

And this view might look quite appealing. However, we get a problem with a different sort of sci-fi case. Now, let's imagine that Doc Brown invents a teleporter like those in *Star Trek*. So, if you step into the machine, it takes detailed scans of you and makes a copy in some other place (e.g., a different planet). Since a copy is made of you in another location, the original body gets painlessly vaporized. On the psychological view, as we've been thinking about it, that copy *is* you. It has all your memories, desires, beliefs, and so on; therefore, it has psychological continuity with the original body. And that's what this view says we need for personal identity.

So far, so good. But imagine that one day you decide to use the machine to teleport on holiday—somewhere warm, maybe. And on this occasion, something goes wrong. It still makes a copy—let's say in Hawaii—but instead of vaporizing the original, it has a malfunction, and the person in the machine is still there. *Now*, what should the view say about who is the real you?

Surely, it can't be *you* in two places. Imagine this happened, and you didn't find out until years later. And your newly created doppelganger—the person who looks like you—goes on to develop some evil tendencies, while you become (or continue to be) a really good person. If they commit a gruesome murder, it would clearly be unreasonable to blame *you* for it. This is sometimes called a *branching* case. Branching cases give a problem for the psychological view, because both branches have psychological continuity. Parfit argues that if we have a branching case, *neither* of the resulting individuals is identical with the first, because picking any one of the branches would be arbitrary.

And this looks like a problem for our case, because George McFly looks like a branching case. Consider the figure below.

We have 1955 George$_Y$ going about his life. Before Marty goes back in time, he lives his life on Timeline 1, and becomes George$_{A1}$. But then, Marty goes back in time and causes a branch. In *that* timeline, he becomes George$_{A2}$. But as we can see the big picture, seeing this branch, maybe we shouldn't say he's really *either* of them. There are lots of other ways someone holding the psychological view might respond, but for simplicity, let's say we accept this implication. If we did think of it this way, then George$_{A1}$ isn't George$_{A2}$—he's not *really* even George$_Y$! So, once again, Marty's influence would have killed George$_{A1}$.

But surely something has gone wrong here. One of the reasons we care about personal identity is attributing responsibility to people. If Biff killed someone in 1955 before Marty arrived, then we wouldn't think that Marty bringing Timeline 2 into reality means that Biff in that wasn't responsible for the murder in Timeline 2. So perhaps thinking just about the reidentification question—what makes a person at one time (t_1) the very same person as an individual at another time (t_2)—doesn't help us out when we're asking the questions we *really* care about when we think about personal identity.

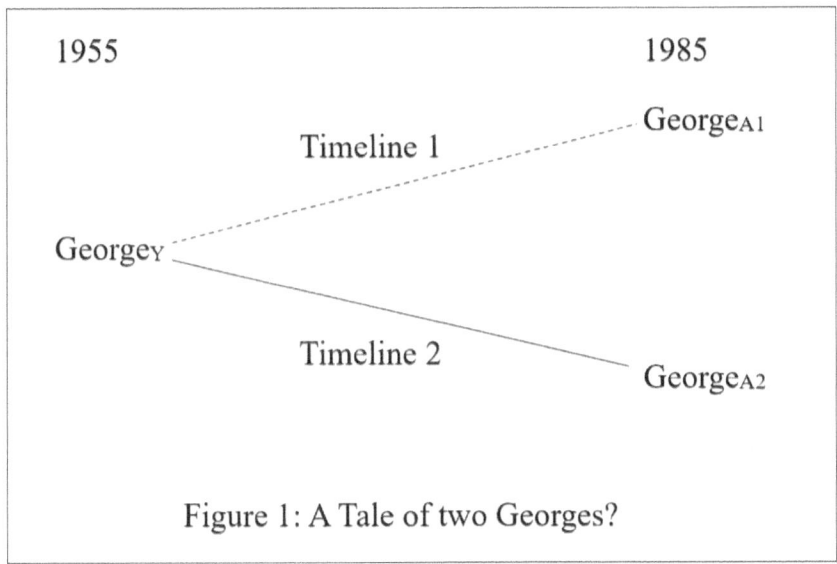

Figure 1: A Tale of two Georges?

The potential lives George_Y might have.

The Characterization Question

In her book, *The Constitution of Selves*, Marya Schechtman argues that by focusing on the reidentification question, philosophers have overlooked a different, important question. She calls this the *characterization question*. Instead of asking under which conditions a person at one time and a person at another time are the same individual, the characterization question asks what "characteristics" *really be*long to a person. By "characteristics," we mean not only things like beliefs, memories and desires (which the psychological view focuses on), but also things like *actions, experiences* and *character traits* (e.g., being brave or cowardly, witty or dull, and so on). What is it that makes it appropriate to say that a particular person *possesses* these characteristics?

Maybe it's *this* question we should ask when asking whether George$_{A1}$ is really gone and thus whether Marty inadvertently killed him. By this I mean we should ask whether we have lost the person who it would be appropriate to attribute George$_{A1}$'s memories and desires and belief, actions, and experiences and character traits.

As is often the case with philosophy, people have given a number of competing answers to this question, but we'll just think about Schechtman's own answer, which she calls the *narrative self-constitution view*. Very roughly, the idea is that *persons*—people like you and me, who have self-awareness and an idea of who we are—have a role in determining our identity. We are not simply passive agents that things *happen to*. We do things, and we make clear our own sense of self by giving *reasons* for why we have made certain decisions. When we do this, we can think of our lives as having a *narrative*—we can tell a story about how our lives go, and this will involve us offering an *explanation* for why we have done certain things. And in this sense, you *create* your identity. Your narrative is a story that explains how some events from your history connect to other events in your history. But you can't just tell yourself *anything* and have that be part of your identity. Schechtman says the story you tell must cohere with an "objective" account of your life, which she understands as requiring that the story make sense alongside the stories that others around you would tell.

What makes it the case that some achievement *belongs to you* is that it fits within your narrative explanation of your life. This also explains which things you might be *responsible for*. So, when we think about George$_{A1}$, the narrative he might embrace about his life would go a certain way. It is likely important for him that he was run over by Lorraine's father's car (while being a peeping tom and falling from a tree!) and that Lorraine fell in love with him after they kissed at the Enchantment Under the Sea dance. And lots of things happened since then, too. He has certain *relationships* which he will see as major things in his life. He will have many memories of doing things with his wife, and with his children. He might still love science fiction, but has never had the courage to show anyone else his writing. Perhaps he is not as successful in his career as he would like and wishes that he weren't still associated with Biff Tannen.

Now, we can compare that to George$_{A2}$. His story may be very similar to George$_{A1}$'s, as far as their childhood is concerned. But he seems to have been emboldened after standing up to Biff, and really taken control of his life. He is eager to put himself out there. He doesn't let people like Biff take advantage of him. He keeps fit. He also has relationships with his children, but they are (or at least seem to be) healthier. His wife and children respect him. He is successful. These are important components of *his* story.

While there are striking similarities between their stories, the narratives of these stories are very different. It isn't the superficial features of the stories that differ, but important features of the nature of the relationships they have. To George$_{A1}$, George$_{A2}$ would seem like a completely different guy—maybe the sort of life he would fantasize about having but one with a very different life story. So, thinking about personal identity in this way, too, it looks like George$_{A1}$ is dead, killed inadvertently through his son's time-traveling adventure.

Mourning George$_{A1}$

This conclusion might sound sad, but imagine you're Marty at the end of *Back to the Future*. You have lots of memories of George$_{A1}$. Maybe you bonded over certain TV shows like *The Honeymooners*. Perhaps you've got memories of going on holidays together. And there might be certain features about him that made him the man who raised you, and you loved him for that. You might have been frustrated by how he capitulated to Biff at every opportunity, and might have wished that he would stand up for himself and take some risks. But this is the man you've known for your whole life up to your time travel adventure.

But this new guy—George$_{A2}$—didn't actually *do* any of those things with you. Maybe George$_{A2}$ took Marty from that timeline (whatever happened to the Marty that *did* all the things in this timeline, by the way?!) on extravagant holidays and maybe was a wonderful parent and husband to Lorraine. You don't remember *any of this*. Sure, he might seem cool, but he's not *your dad*.

We can imagine Marty having thoughts like this and feeling devastated. His dad is gone—and it's all because of him ... and so is *his* mom, brother, and sister. His "new family" (while perhaps much happier than their counterparts) are strangers to him but with familiar faces. And every time he sees them, he might be tragically reminded of who he lost on the way. I suppose these are the dangers of time-travel.

Notes

1. This terminology describing the types of questions comes from Schechtman, Marya. 1996. *The Constitution of Selves*. Cornell University Press.
2. Locke, John. 1689. "Of Identity and Diversity," Chapter XXVII of *An Essay Concerning Human Understanding*, 2nd ed. available on Project Gutenberg.
3. Parfit, Derek. 1984. *Reasons and Persons*. Oxford University Press, Chapter 10.

VII

Traveling Through (the) History (of Philosophy)

Back to the Future ... of an Illusion

LEONARD KAHN

At first glance, *Back to the Future* appears to be no more than an especially successful science-fiction comedy. Similar movies from this era and genre (e.g., *Ghostbusters*, *Weird Science*, and *Bill and Ted's Excellent Adventure*) attempted to entertain their audiences but avoided challenging them.

Yet, only a moment's reflection on *Back to the Future* shows its fundamental peculiarities. It's particularly surprising that an American film featuring a woman overtly lusting for her own time-displaced son would do so well at the box office. This is odd, perhaps especially since *Back to the Future* was released in the middle of a decade known for its ascendancy of political and cultural conservatism. *Great Scott!* What's going on here; how was any of this possible? In order to answer this question, we, not unlike Marty, will need to go on a trip to the past, so let's activate the flux-capacitor and prepare to hit 88 miles per hour. Our first stop is ancient Greece.

Back to the Past: Oedipus and Freud

Meet Oedipus. Much of what we know about this semi-mythological character comes from the play *Oedipus Tyrannus* written by the Athenian, Sophocles (497–406 BCE). According to Sophocles, Oedipus was the child of Laius and Jocasta, the King and Queen of Thebes. When Oedipus is born, an oracle prophesies that his fate will be to kill his father and marry his mother, so King Laius orders one of his subjects to leave the infant on a hillside to die. However, the subject takes pity on Oedipus and brings him to the King and Queen of Corinth, who raise Oedipus as their own, without telling him that he *isn't* their biological child.

As a grown man, Oedipus learns from another oracle of the prophecy that he would kill his father and marry his mother. Since Oedipus believes that the King and Queen of Corinth are his birth parents, he flees Corinth for Thebes. While on his journey, Oedipus ends up quarreling with and killing King Laius without realizing Laius is his birth father. Oedipus arrives at Thebes only to find that a terrible monster guards the entrance to the city and requires anyone who wishes to enter to solve a riddle: what creature walks on four legs in the morning, two legs at noon, and three legs in the evening? The monster devours all who cannot solve the riddle, but Oedipus sees that the answer is a human, since we crawl when we are young, walk upright when we are adults, and require the aid of a cane when we are old. The importance of the riddle for our purposes is that its answer involves a human's development as the human travels through time. By solving the riddle, Oedipus frees Thebes from the monster's terrible curse, after which he marries Jocasta, replacing Laius as the King of Thebes, without Oedipus or Jocasta realizing that Jocasta is his birth mother. So Oedipus ends up fulfilling the prophecy, just as the two oracles foretold.

Now, let's reset our time machine and flash forward to Vienna, the capital of the Austro-Hungarian Empire, in the late 19th century. Here, we meet a young Sigmund Freud who is about to develop *psychoanalysis*, a form of clinical therapy that identifies and treats mental illness, which is constitutive of a set of theories which has a profound influence on the way we understand the mind still today. Perhaps Freud's greatest insight was in the role that unconscious mental activities play in our lives. These activities are often available only in dreams; this point is sometimes paraphrased by saying that dreams are the "royal road" to the unconscious mind.[1]

Perhaps coincidentally, Freud's insight seems tailor-made for a film in which dreams are regularly being discussed on screen. After Lorraine meets Marty in 1955, she refers to him three times as "a dream." In 1985, Doc Brown tells us that he "always dreamed of seeing the future." And, most importantly, on three separate occasions, Marty explicitly considers the possibility that his time-traveling has all been a dream.

Nevertheless, somewhere around 1900, Freud attended a performance of *Oedipus Tyrannus*, which led him to repurpose the story to advance a general theory which centered around the idea of the "Oedipus complex." According to the theory (which actually applies to *all* human beings), boys between the ages of four and six enter what Freud called the "Oedipal phase," the most important phase of their sexual development before they begin puberty. Prior to it, boys desire love from both their parents, but during the Oedipal phase, boys develop *new* feelings toward them. They begin to have erotic desires for their mothers. They are too young at this stage to understand what those desires entail, but what they *do* know is that the existence of their fathers prevents them from exploring those desires. As a result, boys develop a further desire to kill and replace their fathers.[2] These developments plunge boys into a dilemma. They are too weak to kill and replace their fathers. And, even if they could do so, they would be killing someone from whom they desire love.

Indeed, to the extent that they hold onto the desire to kill their fathers, they will come to fear that their fathers will harm or even castrate them.[3] Furthermore, boys come to understand that there is (what Freud thought to be) a universal taboo against erotic relationships between family members.[4] Even if they *could* overcome their fathers, their societies (to say nothing of their mothers!) would not allow them to pursue these erotic relationships.[5]

The only way for children to successfully resolve the Oedipus complex is to *repress* their erotic desires for their mothers while learning to identify with their fathers and overcome their hatred toward and fear of them. In the process, boys set the stage for the healthy erotic relationships they will have with others after they begin puberty. They also begin to develop a superego (roughly, Freud's term for the voice of conscience) by internalizing societal norms against incest. Though it has rather mundane origins, the superego is the ultimate source of our ability to live up to high standards and ideals.[6]

Unfortunately, some males fail to fully resolve their Oedipus complex. First, if boys are unable to repress their erotic desires for their mothers, then they are likely to develop unhealthy (what Freud would call "neurotic") attachments to them. Worse, when they grow up, they will be unhappy in their erotic relationships with others precisely because these new partners are not their mothers (the *true* object of their erotic desires), even though they will not recognize the cause of their unhappiness. Second, if boys are unable to identify with their fathers, they will have difficulty relating to authority figures and acting in accordance with societal norms; they'll likely project the anger and fear they feel toward their fathers onto others (especially those who enforce these norms). The result is poor relationships with members of *both* sexes and a life full of many reasons for unhappiness.

Though Freud, not unlike Oedipus, thought that he had solved a great riddle about how humans develop over time, we need to pause here. Freud claims that boys desire at some level to break what are among the most basic taboos in society: patricide and incest. It is tempting to reject any theory which casts one in such an unflattering light, and many give in to that temptation and dismiss everything Freud had to say.

But, before we too give in to this temptation, it is useful to consider

Freud's conception of an illusion. As Freud saw it, any belief is an illusion just in case the reason we hold it is that it fulfills a wish.[7] Freud's point is not that all illusions are false. Rather, his point is that if we realize that we hold a belief *because* it fulfills a wish, then we should suspend that belief until we have evidence one way or another. For example, Freud held that the belief in an all-powerful god who will reward us for our good deeds and punish others for their bad deeds is an illusion. But Freud did not maintain that it was an illusion because he thought there was no such being (though he thought that too). Instead, he maintained that it was an illusion because many people believe it to be true for the reason that it addresses an immature desire for a father figure who will make things right for us. Only by recognizing the nature of this desire and its role in supporting an illusion can we overcome it and put ourselves in a position to make things right for ourselves. Freud would add that our belief that the Oedipus complex is false is also a good candidate for being an illusion, since that would fulfill our wish to not have patricidal and incestuous desires.

Putting Marty on the Couch

So let's now imagine that we use the DeLorean to bring Marty by Dr. Freud's office. What would Freud make of Marty's relationship with his mother, Lorraine? It seems as if Freud would notice signs of an unresolved Oedipus complex.

In 1985, Marty is only too willing to offer an opinion about his mother's sexual availability ("I think [Lorraine] was born a nun!"). Lorraine herself reinforces this story: "When I was [a teenager] I never *chased* a boy, or *called* a boy, or *sat in a parked car* with a boy." Of course, Marty eventually learns of his mother's dishonesty. In 1955, Lorraine tells Marty, "I'm almost eighteen years old, it's not like I've never parked before." Marty also learns that she smokes and drinks, and when he suggests that Lorraine might regret this later in life, she chides him with a wonderfully Freudian response: "you're beginning to sound just like my *mother*." Marty is clearly shaken by this exchange, which echoes Marty's own remark earlier in the film: "I'm beginning to sound like my old man." There are several layers to these exchanges, but for now, what's most important is to see Marty's investment in his image of his mother as chaste. In 1985, there is no threat to this image, and if she is not available to him, she is not available to anyone else either. Marty can simply act out half of his Oedipal drama with his girlfriend, Jennifer, who bears a striking resemblance to young Lorraine and whose last name (Parker!) makes her role as a sexual surrogate all too obvious. However, Marty's trip back to 1955 completely destabilizes his illusion.

What about Marty's relationship with his father, George? Freud would likely say that it provides more evidence of an unresolved Oedipus complex. There are a number of similarities between Marty and George, but Marty self-consciously avoids identifying with George, and it's easy to sympathize with him. George's life is a disaster, and he has allowed himself to be bullied by Biff Tannen for over three decades while his dreams of being a writer of science fiction withered. However, the parallels between Marty and George are there. Both share a fear of rejection, and at different points admit, "I don't know if I could take that kind of rejection" in reference to having others judge their creative work.

Marty also has many poor relationships with male authority figures of the sort Freud believed were characteristic of an unresolved Oedipus complex. In 1985, he is at odds with Mr. Strickland ("You got a real attitude problem, McFly. You're a *slacker*!") and Old Biff ("What are you looking at, *butthead*?"), and he immediately alienates the high school audition band judge ("I'm afraid you're just too darn loud"). In 1955, he immediately gets on the wrong side of the preening alpha that is young Biff. Marty does likewise with Lou Caruthers, the owner of the cafe ("You want a Pepsi, pal? You're gonna pay for it!"), Sam Baines, his future grandfather ("He's an idiot."), and even Old Man Peabody ("You space bastard! You killed my pine!"). Doc Brown is the only adult male in either time period with whom Marty has a good relationship, and it is no accident that Doc doesn't play the role of an authority figure for Marty. In general, the Marty we meet as the story begins lacks agency and control over his own life, something that is clearly conveyed by the fact that Marty is only able to make his way around Hill Valley of 1985 by skitching.

We're now in a place to appreciate that Marty's trip back to 1955 is an opportunity for him to visit an Oedipal fantasy and to overcome it. First, Marty encounters his mother as a young woman, but it is *she* who has erotic feelings for her son. Second, Marty's father, George, is no barrier to Lorraine. George is initially uninterested in her, and he is no threat to Marty, who is immediately popular with all of George's peers.

Yet, in order to ensure his own birth, Marty must destroy this Oedipal fantasy. The logic of resolving the Oedipus complex requires Marty to overcome the desire to kill his father. But Marty takes the opportunity to go one step further and not only to defeat this desire but to save his father in at least two ways. Marty does this initially by preventing George from being run over in the street. While doing so puts Marty's own future in jeopardy, it also opens the possibility of a much healthier relationship between George and Lorraine.

Recall that in 1985, as we see it at the beginning of the film, the reason Lorraine fell in love with George was his passivity. As Lorraine puts it, George "seemed so helpless, like a little lost puppy, my heart just went out for him." Marty initially prevents Lorraine from falling in love with George for the wrong reason and then helps to put George in a position to win Lorraine's love through his heroism in preventing Biff from raping her. For this reason, it is George's agency, rather than his passivity, that helps define his relationship with Lorraine. As we see when Marty returns to 1985, this change allows George and Lorraine to live happily together for decades. Moreover, George becomes a successful science fiction writer as well as the kind of person with whom Marty not only can identify but the kind of person with whom he *should* identify. The logic of resolving the Oedipus complex also requires Marty to suppress his erotic feelings for his mother, but here too Marty takes this logic even further than Freud. Since it is Lorraine's (rather than Marty's) erotic feelings that are manifest, he can work on getting Lorraine to transfer these feelings from him to George. Marty doesn't simply repress his feelings for his mother; he gets Lorraine herself to admit "this is all wrong." When Marty returns to 1985, he is no longer dependent on others to get from place to place. He has the truck of his dreams and is literally in the driver's seat, capable, like his father, of exerting his own agency.

Is This Trip Really Necessary?

We seem to have resolved the riddle with which we began: why does *Back to the Future* have an incestuous love story in it? The answer is that the film is an engagement with and exploration of Freud's Oedipus complex and its resolution. But this answer only raises a further question. Why choose to engage with the Oedipus complex at all? In order to unravel this second riddle, we need to appreciate two points.

The first point concerns the nature and limits of the Oedipus complex. We previously said that it would be a mistake to dismiss the theory simply because it paints us in an unflattering light. But it would also be wrong to accept the theory uncritically. Indeed, there are many reasons for wariness about the Oedipus complex. For one, it appears to presuppose that heterosexual relationships are normal while homosexual, bisexual, and queer relations are not.[8] It also seems to presuppose that so-called patriarchal middle-class nuclear families—families with a father, mother, and one or more children—are normal, while other types of families are deviant or defective.[9] Neither of these presuppositions is defensible, and Freud's theory seems far better suited to understand the development of heterosexual men who are raised in patriarchal middle-class nuclear families (such as Marty). Furthermore, the complex itself was theorized without much empirical evidence[10] and the search for that evidence has been mixed at best.[11] Even some of Freud's most creative interpretations seem to want to get "beyond Oedipus."[12]

Nevertheless, the key insight for us is that Freud originally thought of the Oedipus complex as a perfectly general phenomenon that applied to *all* humans. Again, Freud believed that he was solving a riddle about all of humanity. But the last century or so of scientific research has demonstrated that humans and human forms of life are too varied and complex to be captured by any theory that is as simple as the Oedipus complex. Still, the fact that the Oedipus complex doesn't apply to *every* human hardly means it applies to *none* of them. Both the complex and the larger mythology around Oedipus remain a fruitful source of reflection with regard to some humans and some human institutions.[13]

The second point we need to appreciate involves the historical context of the film. We noted earlier that the film hit theaters at the crest of a wave of political and cultural conservatism. Ronald Reagan had just been elected to his second term as President (a fact that ends up as a punchline in the film). A return to the values and norms of the 1950s was a central theme in Reagan's vision for America.[14] As Reagan himself put it, "Going around this country, I have found a great hunger in America for spiritual revival, for a belief that law must be based on a higher law, for a return to traditions and values that we once had."

With these two points in mind, I'd like to suggest that the film engages with Freud's theory in order to identify an unresolved Oedipus complex that was being suffered by American culture during the 1980s. Like a child going through the Oedipal stage, 1980s-America desired to embrace and reproduce with one of its parents, 1950s-America. Yet, this desire is based on a mistake. Just as Marty had false beliefs about what his parents were like in the 1950s, so too Americans had false beliefs about the decade and its values. When Marty first arrives in that decade, things appear to be better than they are in the 1980s. There is, for example, no trash on the street and no graffiti on the walls. But we should all be aware of the many problems that existed during this era throughout the nation. First, racism was shamelessly widespread. Just within our brief peek into 1955 Hill Valley, Biff refers to George as an "Irish Bug" and one of Biff's lackeys calls a member of the all–Black band, the Starlighters, a "spook." The best job that the African American future mayor Goldie Wilson can get in 1955 is sweeping up in Lou's Cafe. And, though the high school is integrated by 1985, it seems to have been almost entirely white just three decades earlier.

Second, patriarchy and misogyny are (subtly though clearly) in evidence. When Marty visits his future grandparents, Sam emphasizes that he's the breadwinner by bragging about the family's new television that he's purchased, and he's the one to decide what they watch. Sam is also quick to replace Stella's judgment about Marty (Stella says only that he's "a very strange young man," but Sam corrects her, insisting that Marty is "an idiot"). Less subtly, Sam even threatens to "disown" Lorraine if she displeases him, taking on the role of the *paterfamilias*. Less subtly still, Biff sexually harasses Lorraine in the school cafeteria and later attempts to rape her in a parking lot full of (seemingly uninterested) people coming and going. Biff insists his friends not watch ("This ain't no peep show!"), but he isn't worried about being stopped. Indeed, Biff's concern about being observed reminds us of Marty's discovery that George is a "peeping Tom," who is spying on Lorraine.

Third, the 1950s are haunted by the specter of nuclear war as a result of heightened tensions between the United States and the Soviet Union. After young Doc sees Marty's radiation suit, he assumes that Marty wears it "because of all of the fallout from the atomic wars," and when Doc reflects on the power the flux capacitor requires, he infers, "I'm sure that in 1985, plutonium is available at *every* corner drug store!" In fact, in an earlier version of the script, the film begins in 1985 with Marty's class watching a 16mm documentary about nuclear tests in the 1950s.

The conclusion we are meant to draw is clear: if 1950s-America is mother to 1980s-America, then our love for it must be moderated with an understanding of its many flaws. It is not a proper object for our desires for reproduction. Rather, it is a complex time and place that we can love platonically for its virtues and evaluate critically for its vices while leaving it behind, as all of us must do with our parents, if we too are to mature into psychologically healthy adults.

However, if 1950s-America is the mother to 1980s-America, then who is its father? To answer this question, we need to look outside the film itself. The original audience members of *Back to the Future* knew only too well what came between 1955 and 1985. The period from the late 1950s to the early 1970s saw massive transformations in America. For the sake of simplicity, we'll call this period the "transformational era." One aspect of the transformational era was its impact on race relations and the addressing of racial oppression. This included legislation and judicial decisions that brought about desegregation in public schools, fair housing laws, the prevention of laws banning interracial marriage, the securing of voting rights, and a host of other important changes.

Another aspect of the transformational era was its impact on the relations between sexes and genders. The period saw the rise of second-wave feminism, which championed a broad range of issues that were especially relevant to women and brought attention to the many ways in which women were treated as second-class citizens. The period also saw significant advances with respect to reproductive rights. During the transformational era, the Sexual Revolution also meant that young women like Jennifer and Marty's sister, Linda, didn't have to lie to adults about their erotic interest in members of the opposite sex, as Lorraine had to in the 1950s.

And yet another aspect of the transformational era was the attempt to demilitarize the United States and de-escalate the nuclear arms race between the U.S. and the USSR, while a grass-roots anti-war movement helped to end America's involvement in the Vietnam War.

If 1980s-America was a child of 1950s America, then its other parent was surely the transformational era. The 1980s are just as unimaginable without one as they are without the other. True to the nature of the Oedipus complex, 1980s-America, at least in the mind of cultural conservatism, blamed the transformational era for preventing its union with 1950s-America, and it sought to destroy it for this reason. In this regard, the Reagan Administration repeatedly took aim at the advances in civil rights that were made during the transformational era.[15] Reagan's own *Abortion and the Conscience of the Nation* chronicles his vision for rolling back the transformational era's advances in reproductive rights.[16] And Reagan rode to election on the back of bellicose rhetoric regarding the use of nuclear weapons against the Soviet Union, and, as late as 1984, was joking that "we begin bombing in five minutes." Reagan also oversaw Able Archer 83, a military exercise undertaken only two years before *Back to the Future* was released, which nearly started a nuclear exchange in central Europe.[17]

If *Back to the Future* is successful, then audience members can recognize that its passion for 1950s-America can be put behind it, and its hostility toward the transformational era can be let go, since it did not ruin a past utopia. Now, only wishful thinking can maintain this belief—a belief that has become a paradigm example of what, as we have seen, Freud called an "illusion." On the contrary, by seeing a world that is bereft of the reforms of the transformational era, we can come to identify with it. In short, they can overcome the Oedipus complex into which their culture had fallen. If these lessons are learned, then audiences can set aside the script from another age and acquire their own agency. Instead of trying to get back to the past, they can aim for a better future. If they do so, then they have an open future before them, rather than an illusory past which is the result of wishful thinking, not mature consideration. They can go anywhere they want and are not required to follow any preset path or predetermined road. Let's get back into the DeLorean one last time with the audience, since we are now in a place where we can fully understand the final line of *Back to the Future*: "Roads? Where we're going, we don't need roads."

Notes

1. More precisely, according to Freud, "the interpretation of dreams is the royal road to a knowledge of the unconscious activities of the mind."
2. Freud appears to have discovered the Oedipus complex as early as 1897, but his first systematic statement of it is in Freud, Sigmund. 1923. *The Ego and the Id.* Norton.
3. Freud, Sigmund. 1995. "From the History of an Infantile Neurosis" Gay, Peter (ed.). *The Freud Reader.* Norton.
4. Freud, Sigmund Freud. 191., *Totem and Taboo.* Routledge. 2009.
5. Freud's thinking on this subject is much more complex and nuanced than I have suggested here, and it developed significantly over the course of his career. Even at the end of his life, Freud continued to revise the theory. While the theory is meant to apply to children of both sexes, its application to male children seems a better fit than to female children. On this point, see Chodrow, Nancy, J. 1989. *Feminism and Psychoanalytic Theory.* Yale University Press. I limit myself to the version of Freud's theory that applies to male children since Marty is male. Also, relevant here is the Electra Complex, as developed by Carl Jung. See Jung, Carl. 1961. "The Theory of Psychoanalysis." *Freud and Psychoanalysis*, Vol. 4 of the Collected Works of C.G. Jung, Princeton University Press.
6. Freud, Sigmund. 1995. "Fragment of an Analysis of a Case of Hysteria." Gay, Peter (ed.). *The Freud Reader.* Norton.
7. Freud, Sigmund. (1927) 1989. *The Future of an Illusion.* Norton.
8. *Ibid.*, Freud, 1995.
9. Deluze, Gilles; Guttari, Félix. 1977. *Anti-Oedipus: Capitalism and Schizophrenia.* Viking Press.
10. Grünbaum, Adolf. 1984. *The Foundations of Psychoanalysis: A Philosophical Critique.* University of California Press.
11. Daly, Martin; Wilson, Margo. 1988. *Homicide: Foundations of Human Behavior.* Routledge.
12. Greenberg, Jay. 1991. *Oedipus and Beyond: A Clinical Theory.* Harvard University Press. See also Mitchell, Stephen A.; Black, Margaret J. 2016. *Freud and Beyond: A History of Modern Psychoanalytic Thought.* Basic Books.
13. Lear, Jonathan. 1998. *Open Minded: Working out the Logic of the Soul.* Harvard University Press.
14. Marcus, Daniel. 2004. *Happy Days and Wonder Years: The Fifties and the Sixties in Contemporary Cultural Politics.* Rutgers University Press. See also Rossinow, Doug. 2015. *The Reagan Era: A History of the 1980s.* Columbia University Press.
15. Shull, Steven A. 1993 *A Kinder, Gentler Racism? The Reagan-Bush Civil Rights Legacy.* Routledge.
16. Reagan, Ronald. 1984. *Abortion and the Conscience of the Nation.* Thomas Nelson.
17. Ambinder, Marc. 2019. *The Brink: President Reagan and the Nuclear War Scare of 1983.* Simon & Schuster.

A Sartrean Time Machine

Elad Magomedov

The universe of *Back to the Future* is constructed in accordance with the principle that treats the unexpected as something disruptive and the expected as something restorative. If Marty anticipated what he did not expect from the onset, then the story would never begin: he would save Doc *before* the occurrence of the catastrophic attack by the terrorists that serves as a catalyst for the sequence of events in the rest of the story. In fact, the narrative of Marty's character moves precisely in this direction, namely from the lack of anticipation to anticipation, so that his main task always consists of turning the unexpected into something that is expected.

Confronted by the unexpected love of his younger mother, he can only diffuse its detrimental consequences by *anticipating* and evaluating them in the light of a desired outcome that does not yet exist but is nonetheless awaited—that is, the romance between his mother and his father. It is only to the extent that Marty can expect or anticipate something that his character possesses the power of an oracle, the ability to see the future as if it were the past, so as to "fix," or restore it to an original state, that which is disrupted in the first place. What ultimately saves Marty, in other words, is the idea that the future can be shaped into a *particular* future, provided that certain conditions in the present are met. Let us call this idea about the relation between the present and the future "stable futurality."

That such stable futurality is not the only way to think the relationship between the present and the future is suggested by Sartrean ontology. We may accordingly ask: what would happen if Doc's time machine operated in accordance with the Sartrean laws of time, rather than those offered to us by the movie? The short answer is that Marty's universe would collapse. The more nuanced answer involves all kinds of unexpected twists and turns that are not always easy to make sense of. In what follows, we'll explore the idea that if Marty's universe were governed by the "unstable futurality" as contained in the Sartrean laws of time, his expectations would be in vain, for there would be no way to guarantee the transition from cause to effect. In other words, even if Marty ensured that all the conditions for a certain outcome were present, the laws of Sartrean freedom dictate that he still would have no guarantee that Lorraine, George, or Doc would act as they're "supposed to" by the laws of stable futurality. Under the rule of Sartrean ontology, consciousness is condemned to be free, always retaining its ability to act other than expected. This results in a time paradox that corrupts not just Marty's own existence but the existence of the universe as such.

Consciousness and Freedom

Sartre's idea that consciousness is free in the absolute sense can be understood when contrasted with the order of things.[1] The DeLorean, like any other "thing" in the surrounding world, is not free. It is subject to the mechanical laws of causality which allow Doc, the physicist, to predict with certainty how the DeLorean will behave if it reaches 88 miles per hour before hitting the cable at the precise moment of the lightning strike. Since this thing moves not of its own accord but only through an external cause, nothing about it can interrupt its embeddedness in the web of causality in which it is entangled. In fact, even this formulation, namely that its movement is "not of *its own* accord," is not entirely accurate, since to have any accord at all, the thing must be able to *relate* to itself and something other than itself.

This ability to relate to something is a characteristic of consciousness. The DeLorean on the road does not "relate" to itself or the road unless it does so *for* some observer. In itself, independent of observing consciousness, the thing is neither "near" nor "far" with regard to the road, but simply *is* what it is, fully coinciding with its own identity. It "is" no more and no less than its factual determinations, such as its weight, shape, color, and material. Due to this full positivity of being condensed in the thing, the DeLorean cannot experience itself as lacking in any sense. When it runs out of plutonium to generate the 1.21 gigawatts of power required for time travel, it does not experience itself as *not* being fueled. Instead, due to its absolute coincidence with its factual characteristics, it is always already determined *to be* something by some cause acting upon it—for example, if it is hit by lightning under specific conditions, it is determined by the laws of gravity to *be* no more and no less than a portal from October 26, 1985, to November 5, 1955.

The situation is entirely different when it comes to consciousness. Unlike the surrounding things that exist in themselves, consciousness is always consciousness *of* something: it is either a consciousness of itself or of something that it is not. In perceiving the skateboard, Marty has a consciousness of the skateboard appearing *to* his consciousness, and in this sense, he stands in relation to something that his consciousness is not. This ability to relate to what consciousness is not allows consciousness to be in a world and disclose an entire horizon of what appears as a "this" or a "that" *for* it. At the same time, this "relating to" is itself not a thing among things. It is not "in" the world like the flux capacitor is "in" the DeLorean, but instead serves as the light that shines on the world and allows it to appear. In relating to what it is not, consciousness always finds itself fleeing *out* of itself and *towards* the world; this flight "out" of itself and towards the world already entails the flow of time, in which every instant in the present glides away into the past, resulting in consciousness constantly being separated from what it was by the emergence of a new instant. This is why one's past cannot *determine* one to do anything. Think of the promise that Doc in 1955 makes to get Marty back to 1985: as soon as he promises himself to do something, the one who promised slips away into the past at that very instant. In order for him to keep the promise by acting upon it, he must commit himself to the promise again and again. In other words, he must recover the promise from the past, where it remains impotent, and reaffirm it in the present at each instant. Thus, it is not the past that determines consciousness to act in a certain way, but rather own commitment to take up the present, as reaffirmed by that consciousness with every new instant.

The same counts for all the "factual" determinations from which one is constantly separated by a void: whereas the skateboard does not choose to be or not to be what it is, Marty can refuse to coincide with his factual characteristics. He may not undo the fact that he was born as an American rather than a German, but these factual characteristics do not determine him to be in a certain way, like the DeLorean is determined to *be* a portal through time under specific conditions. Such factual characteristics as nationality, ethnicity, gender, and so on—always already belong to the past and can only make a transition into the present to the extent that consciousness takes them up as a project and takes them with it towards the future, thus carrying them over into every new instant of the present, projecting them in the constant self-regeneration of the fleeting now-moment. But this movement toward the future is simultaneously a movement toward what is *not yet*: the future too consists of pure negativity, pure absence of being, which can only appear as an imaginary possibility to which consciousness can relate but which, as such, does not (yet) possess any positive being. Consciousness is thus constantly suspended between two kinds of nothingness: one lying behind it as something that consciousness is no more, and one in front of it, as something that is not yet. Under such conditions, consciousness can only be limited by itself and therefore remains free in the absolute sense of the word.

Free Once Again

What does all this mean for Marty's journey back in time? First, it means that by traveling back to 1955, Marty instantaneously undoes all the actions those around him committed in the past. Their consciousness, once again animated and resurrected from the past into the present, regains its radical freedom. Without knowing it, they are bound to act once again, and just like before, there is no necessary reason for why they should repeat their decisions and actions in the same manner. This becomes evident from Lorraine's refusal to fall in love with George, revealing not only that history should not necessarily repeat but, foremost, that Lorraine is, once again, free.

The Sartrean undertone of the film surfaces in the behavior of other characters, too. George cannot be determined to kiss Lorraine like a billiard ball can be determined to follow a particular trajectory upon impact; as a conscious being rather than a thing in itself, he can only be motivated, but ultimately everything depends on whether or not he *chooses* it. For Sartre, it is conceivable that George might not make the expected choice even if all conditions for that choice are present. Thus, the Sartrean notion of freedom introduces the unexpected into every choice that must be made in 1955—or, more precisely, every choice that must be *remade*. The situation when Marty travels back in time and thus brings everyone back to life by reinjecting freedom into them is comparable to what occurs on a film set: the actors stand still and wait for the cue, and as soon as the director calls them for action, everyone comes to life. Even though there is a script, and everything is meant to unfold exactly according to it, no two takes will be the same; there will always be minor or major variations, and each of these variations will produce a different future.

By introducing the unexpected, freedom compromises the general illusion of those characters who insist on the necessity of the past. We see this illusion, for example, when the older Lorraine declares that her encounter with George was "meant to be," or when Doc refuses to change the future for his own good because he is convinced that whatever has not yet occurred is also already set and was meant to be. Doc's conviction is particularly interesting because his future is simultaneously a past for him—it has already occurred once—and it is only in that sense that it can contain any necessity associated with destiny. After all, the main characteristic of the future is precisely that it is *not* yet: it can neither be changed nor accepted because, at least within the domain of consciousness and its effects, it has no fixed content.

This absence of necessity of the future establishes a frightening consequence of Sartre's ontology, namely that once Marty travels back, there is absolutely nothing that can guarantee that the future from where he came should occur again. To regain it, Marty must bring about a situation in which not only everyone around in 1955 makes exactly the same choices as in the original timeline but also keeps making choices that sustain that timeline every step of the way until Marty's birth. This means that as soon as he reanimates the inhabitants of the past by making them free again, he is bound to disappear at any moment unless he follows every one of them to the very end, persistently finding himself on the brink of annihilation while also escaping it by constantly convincing them to do the right thing.

It's not easy to understand why it should be the case that upon coming back to consciousness, the inhabitants of the past are not bound to act as expected despite the presence of conditions for an otherwise fixed outcome; but this difficulty arises only if we treat consciousness as if it were a thing. It is indeed true that we can expect things to behave in accordance with necessity, which is the foundation of natural sciences. But the reason why psychology could never be a natural science is precisely that a thing that is determined by natural laws is not temporal. It appears "in" time, but is itself not capable of relating to anything in temporal terms: it does not anticipate the future or remember the past, nor does it have a present that constantly separates it from what is no more and what is not yet. Consciousness alone has this modality of being. To the extent that the reanimated characters become conscious again, they find themselves by that very fact on neither side of necessity.

Admittedly, one cannot deny that conscious beings are "determined" if one reduces this term to what "happens" to us by accident: if a tile slips from a roof while I happen to pass underneath and kills me *by consequence*, one might say that even though I was conscious, I was causally determined to die. But this accident was not a project, not a commitment to the realization of a not yet existent possibility on the part of consciousness. Freedom does not refer to the contingent nature of that which happens to us, but rather to the fact that what we commit ourselves to is realized through a choice affirmed in every step of realizing that project. Sure enough, I may be physically forced to stay locked up in a prison without any possibility of escape—but the very fact that my consciousness can *conceive* or *imagine* an alternative to the situation already means that I do not coincide with my being imprisoned, the way the falling stone coincides with its being acted on by gravity.

The Time Paradox

If we pursue the idea that providing the past with a new present through temporal reanimation injects freedom into all conscious beings, then the problem of freedom does not occur only in others but in Marty too: while the original Marty is struggling in 1955, the consequent future-Marty, who, once born, regains his freedom to make his choices anew, may choose *not* to befriend Doc or travel back in time, thus compromising his own existence in 1955. Due to the constant openness of the future and the persistent freedom of those who came back to life in 1955, Marty's time-travel establishes a condition in which every new choice affirmed in the past spawns a new future in 1985, generating and corrupting one yet-to-be universe after another, ceaselessly spawning people and situations in and out of existence in a realm yet to come. But while this occurs, the choices of those who inhabit that future-realm, even if their existence is limited to a short interval of time before it is undone by another unexpected occurrence in the past, are themselves capable of *changing* the past. At any moment, some version of Marty or Doc may travel back to the past and change it, thus contributing to the chain of production and decomposition of various future-worlds. Thus, not only is any expected future liquified because its existence is ceaselessly compromised by the changing past, but the past too undergoes the same fate and is constantly changed by those who are heading towards it from the future and for whom that past *becomes a potentiality of the not-yet*.

In other words, as soon as the original Marty travels back, he brings about the ultimate time-paradox: the liquidation of both future and past into a ceaseless flux of appearing and disappearing worlds. The present then only exists as a residue of whatever past/future shortly flickers into existence before it is, by virtue of its own existence, instantaneously replaced by another variant. While difficult to imagine, this state is best comparable to those moments when, in dreaming, a scene occurring in some definite place and situation is abruptly replaced by another, often with no logical transition or continuity. Despite this disruptive transition, everyone partaking in it, including the dreamer, changes along *with* the transition and is embedded in it as if this situation has been developing continuously without any interruption. In analogy to this image, Marty's first journey back in time would condemn the universe to remain stuck in an eternal sequence of dreamlike transitions from one possible world to another.

The connection with the dream is particularly interesting because, upon Sartre's assessment, the dream represents a state of consciousness being enclosed entirely in the mode of imagination.[2] The dreamer does not perceive but rather *imagines*; the dream world is an imaginary world, and even the dream-subject is an imaginary "object I" in which the dreaming consciousness condenses itself. But more importantly, imagination is not only the fundamental category of the dream, it is also the main source of our ability to relate to the future. To the extent that in imagination consciousness relates to something that is given as an irreality rather than a reality, our ability to relate to something that is not yet existent is rooted in imagination. When I commit myself, for example, to the project of building a time machine, my project is guided by the time machine as imaginary, as not yet existent, and it is by drawing the unreal entity closer to the present—and simultaneously reaching *out* of the present and *toward* what does not yet exist—that I finally merge with the imagined possibility that is lacking in the given world.

With this in mind, it becomes clear why Marty's journey "back" in time leads to the total collapse of the universe. While the freedom of those who live in 1955 and after modifies the future, those who live in that modified future can themselves modify 1955 by relating to it as something *to be changed*, in other words, something *not yet* changed. Thus, by traveling to the past and reanimating the freedom of past consciousness, the past shape of the universe becomes dependent on the choices of those who *themselves* result from the choices made in this past. In other words, not only those in 1955 relate to an open future, but those time travelers who, in 1985, *result* from that relating, themselves *also* relate to 1955 as an open future. Thus, all that exists now are different modalities of the future, different modalities of irreality or pure possibility that, having permanently lost their unchangeable past, have no solid actuality to stabilize the present. The resulting paradox entails the transformation of the universe into a pure possibility, a constant self-regeneration of the now-moment, consisting of a series of worlds that flicker in and out of existence, without any coherent trace to what preceded it or anticipation of the next moment. In this kind of universe, Doc "disintegrated Einstein" after all.

Notes

1. What follows is based on what Sartre develops in the first part of *Being and Nothingness*. See Sartre, Jean Paul. 1956. *Being and Nothingness*. Barnes, Hazel E. (trans.). Philosophical Library.

2. See Sartre, Jean Paul. 2004. Part IV, "The Imaginary Life"; Part IV, "The Dream." *The Imaginary: A Phenomenological Psychology of the Imagination*. Webber, Jonathan (trans.). Routledge.

"*Nobody* calls me chicken"
How Should Marty Respond to Insults?

Jon Robson

Marty McFly is the recipient of quite a range of insults in the *Back to the Future* films, from Biff Tannen calling him "butthead" to Biff calling him a "loser" to Biff calling him "butthead" again (Biff's not the most imaginative guy). However, there's one insult that's guaranteed to get his blood boiling ... *nobody* calls him chicken!

A key point in the trilogy's narrative is his susceptibility to being goaded into all sorts of foolish, inadvisable, and sometimes downright illegal actions merely to avoid the label of "chicken" (or its 19th-century variant: "yellow"). This is a rather idiosyncratic trait which most readers of this essay are unlikely to share—though, if you do, I'll remind you that only chickens refrain from sending me large sums of money—and it is also clearly presented as a flaw to be overcome. Indeed, Marty overcoming his susceptibility to this kind of pressure is an important part of his character arc in the films. Still, there is something surprisingly relatable at the heart of it. Most of us are unlikely to be needled (if you'll excuse the pun) into committing financial malfeasance as a result of mere name-calling, but reassuring childhood rhymes notwithstanding, words really do hurt, and we're often unwilling to let even the smallest of insults go unchallenged. Should we be, though? Philosophers have had a lot to say on this question.

Have Some Respect for Yourself!

Aristotle famously thought that anger—as with other human emotions—is a fitting response in certain circumstances and that the virtuous person isn't one who *always* refrains from feeling anger. Rather, the virtuous person feels anger to the appropriate degree in the appropriate circumstances. Our emotions, like our beliefs, represent the world as being a certain way, and these representations can be more or less fitting. Marty's fear of a holographic shark is inappropriate—since it poses no threat to him—but fear of an actual shark would be entirely reasonable. Similarly, feeling anger at a genuinely undeserved harm is fitting in a way that being angry at a kind gift wouldn't be. Further, Aristotle takes one of the most common objects of appropriate anger to be "those who laugh, mock, or jeer at us."[1] Indeed, failing to be angry at unprovoked mockery and jeering would show that someone failed to have proper respect for themselves. This is something which, in Aristotle's view, is just as much a failing as having an overly inflated self-regard. This all sounds like good news for Marty. After all, the various members of the Tannen family he encounters (and their associated hangers-on) are hardly averse to laughter, mockery, or jeering. So, should we conclude that Marty's response to being called chicken is—the apparent message of the films aside—an appropriate one?

Not so fast. Of course, feeling angry at a perceived slight isn't always appropriate. Griff is clearly enraged at (who he believes to be) Marty Jr. refusing to assist with his criminal schemes, but this is inappropriate as he had no legitimate claim to such support. And insults themselves are sometimes perfectly apt.[2] When old Biff tells his younger self that he sounds "like a damn fool" when he mangles his arboreal idioms, his response may well elicit some chagrin from young Biff but ... the old guy has a point. If, then, Marty was genuinely a coward, then that would be one reason to deny that he can reasonably be angry at the various insinuations that he is one. Yet, Marty is hardly a coward. He is, it's clear, not quite the bold and fearless risk taker he believes himself to be, but, throughout the trilogy, he regularly faces dangers which many of us would blanch at. Why is it, though, that Marty reacts so violently to being called a chicken when he's able to brush off being labeled as a loser or a butthead (alongside ridicule of the apparently nautical theme of his attire)? Again, Aristotle offers us some clues here. He notes that we are often inclined to feel the greatest anger at those who "show contempt for us, in connection with the things we ourselves most care about: thus those who are eager to win fame as philosophers get angry with those who show contempt for their philosophy; those who pride themselves upon their appearance get angry with those who show contempt for their appearance and so on."[3] And the films not only make it clear that Marty values being courageous but also give us a clear explanation as to why this is the case.

George McFly—or, at least, the original version of George we meet prior to Marty's time traveling antics—is, as he rather charitably describes himself, "just not very good at confrontations." Others, less charitably inclined, might use some less restrained words (perhaps alongside some poultry-based sound effects). And it is abundantly clear from the start that Marty wants to distance himself from his father. In the first few minutes of the original film, we already see Marty being chastised for being too much like his father, and we hear him repeatedly express his desire to be as different from George as possible (which is hardly unreasonable within the context of the film). We see a young George being chastised by Goldie Wilson that "if you let people walk over you now, they'll be walkin' over you for the rest of your life," and the parallels between his past and present interactions with Biff are hardly subtle. Once again, then, it starts to seem like Marty's position may well be justified. Yet, all of Aristotle's views on appropriate anger rely on the idea that insults (or at least insults of a certain kind) are, in some way, injurious to us. However, some philosophers are inclined to deny this.

Worse to Call Someone Chicken Than to Be Called Chicken

The Stoic philosopher Epictetus would maintain that Biff no more injures Marty merely by calling him a "butthead" than he would damage a rock by belittling it. Rather, suffering any genuine harm requires cooperation on your part. "Remember that it is not he who reviles you or strikes you, who insults you, but it is your opinion about these things as being insulting. When then a man irritates you, you must know that it is your own opinion which has irritated you."[4]

That is, Epictetus maintains, we are only harmed by insults if we allow them to disturb our tranquility. The virtuous person would not, however, choose to let them do so, and so is not harmed by insults.[5] And since insults do them no harm, the virtuous person would feel neither anger nor the need to provide any kind of rebuttal. Indeed, the Stoics often went much further than claiming that insults couldn't harm the virtuous person, and echoed Socrates' famously perplexing thought that nothing can.[6] It's not merely words that cannot hurt the virtuous person, sticks and stones also fail to do so. The thought here isn't that the virtuous person can't suffer physical injury. Being virtuous wouldn't stand in for Doc's bulletproof vest or render flesh and blood sharks as harmless as the holographic variety. Rather, the claim is that virtue is, in some sense, sufficient for someone's life to be going well for them. Anything external to virtue (including the most extreme physical suffering or death) just has no impact on the well-being of the virtuous person. We are harmed by acting viciously but not by having others act viciously toward us.

An extreme view of this kind has, however, tended to be regarded by subsequent philosophers as about as plausible as someone claiming to have made a time machine out of a DeLorean. There are almost certainly some petty or trivial things that trouble the rest of us which wouldn't concern the fully virtuous person, but the risk of serious physical injury, and still more injury to others, doesn't seem to be one of these. Let's assume, then, that even the virtuous person will regard being shot in a showdown with Buford "Mad Dog" Tannen as a genuine harm. This doesn't mean that they should see his calling them "yellow" in the same light. A Stoic might criticize Marty's reactions to provocations of this kind as showing that he's more concerned with his reputation, something far more trivial than his physical safety, than with virtue. Courage is, of course, a virtue, but Marty's concern doesn't seem to be with being courageous as such but with being *seen* as courageous. And, certainly, many of us will be inclined to think that Marty is too concerned with maintaining his reputation as a non-coward. Still, it hardly seems fair to dismiss someone's reputation as a trivial thing which the virtuous person would show no regard for. How we are seen by others makes a huge difference in our ability to navigate the social world. It plays a significant role in determining our prospects for friendship, career advancement, romantic endeavors, etc. Yet, if we think both that the stoics go too far in dismissing insults and that Marty isn't willing enough to dismiss them, is there a happy medium?

A Gentleman Wouldn't Call Me Chicken!

Frederick Douglas is often reported as maintaining that "a gentleman will not insult me, and no man not a gentleman can insult me."[7] The thought being, roughly, that a virtuous person wouldn't stoop to insulting others—or at least not those who are undeserving of it—and that the negative opinions of those who lack such virtues aren't worth the dignity of being insulted by them. The first part of this claim is certainly open to question. Even the best of us should admit that there are some respects in which they're open to legitimate criticism and also that they might themselves occasionally stoop to making the odd unmerited jab at others. Let's focus on the second part, though.

Biff (along with his fellow Tannens) is hardly likely to be regarded, by Douglas or anyone else, as either a virtuous person or as a gentleman. He is rude, entitled, quick tempered, violent, dishonest, and in dire need of urgent lessons on the importance of consent. Douglas might reasonably question, then, why Marty should have any regard for Biff's opinion. He is hardly a good judge of character or someone whose opinions would carry weight with those who are. Indeed, we might think that earning approval from someone of Biff's character would itself be a stain on our reputation.

Once again, this is an area where Aristotle's views part company with those of the Stoics. The Stoic Seneca found it ridiculous to take offense at the insults of those as distant from virtue as Biff. Rather, he believed that the wise person "is quite justified in treating the affronts which he receives from such men as joke."[8] The Tannens of this world are to be laughed at, ignored or—for those in a charitable mood—educated, but their words are never to be taken as a serious affront. Aristotle, by contrast, claims that "we feel particularly angry with men of no account at all, if they slight us" and appears to suggest that such a response is an apt one.[9]

How should Marty react to insults then? Certainly, he shouldn't let them goad him into acting rashly. They shouldn't spur him to embezzle money or take part in street racing. I'm confident that all of the philosophers discussed—both ancient and modern—would be on Jennifer's side there. Beyond that, though, the answer isn't an easy one. Some insults may, if left unchallenged, cause serious damage to your reputation in ways that can severely curtail your options for navigating the social world. Others are merely insignificant or laughable. How do we tell the difference? Well, that's heavy.

NOTES

1. Aristotle. 2010. *Rhetoric*. W.D. Ross (trans.). Cosimo, 63.
2. On this I disagree with Daly when she suggests that insults always express a lack of due regard. Daly, H.L. 2018. "On insults." *Journal of the American Philosophical Association*, 4(4), 510–524.
3. *Ibid.*, Aristotle.
4. Epictetus. 2012. *Enchiridion*. G. Long (trans.). Dover, 8.
5. Some, such as Roy Sorensen, adopt a stronger interpretation where the virtuous person literally cannot be insulted. Sorensen, R. 2018. "Stoic Silencing of Insults." *Oxford Studies in Normative Ethics*. Oxford University Press. 8, 274–96.
6. As revealed in Plato's *Apology*.
7. The quote itself may well be apocryphal. For a more nuanced discussion of Douglas' view on insults, see Brewton, V. 2005. "'Bold defiance took its place'—'Respect' and Self-Making in 'Narrative of the Life of Frederick Douglass, an American Slave.'" *The Mississippi Quarterly*, 58(4), 703–717.
8. Seneca. 2020. *On the Firmness of the Wise Man*. A. Stewart (trans.). Montecristo. Book 12.
9. *Ibid.*, Aristotle.

VIII

Doc Brown and the Philosophy of Science and Technology

Doc Brown's Paradox and Dr. Frankenstein's Plight

JOHN P. IRISH

In the opening passage of George Gipe's 1985 novelization of *Back to the Future*, Marty McFly is depicted suffering through his U.S. History class where the students are viewing a documentary detailing the bombing of Hiroshima and Nagasaki. As the narrator describes the monumental historical impact of these events, Marty struggles to stay awake. The vivid imagery of catastrophic annihilation permeates the screen, culminating in a solemn caution: "You have just seen how this mighty force can utterly destroy a society unprepared for its use."[1] Steeped in forewarning, the scene underscores the potential for science to deviate into perilous territories.

This cautionary note embodies the "Frankenstein Effect"[2]—a term that captures the unintended and often perilous outcomes arising when scientific inventions or discoveries, initially pursued with benevolent aims, spiral beyond the control of their creators. Originating from Mary Shelley's 1818 seminal work, *Frankenstein: or, the Modern Prometheus*, this concept is epitomized by Dr. Victor Frankenstein's experiment, which, though conducted with the noble intention of conquering death, ultimately leads to catastrophic consequences as his creation becomes an agent of destruction and sorrow. Similarly, in *Back to the Future*, Doc Brown's foray into time travel stems from his benign curiosity about the future. However, his naive optimism regarding the consequences of traversing time quickly spirals into a series of events that disrupt the fabric of multiple timelines.

Through the lens of both *Frankenstein* and *Back to the Future*, we are presented with a vivid exploration of the double-edged sword that is scientific innovation. These narratives serve as a stark reminder of the fragile boundary between groundbreaking discovery and unforeseen disaster. As we delve deeper into the ethical dilemmas and moral responsibilities that accompany scientific exploration, these stories urge us to ponder the true cost of tampering with the natural order. They challenge us to consider whether the pursuit of knowledge, however well-intentioned, justifies the risks of venturing into realms that perhaps are best left unexplored. In doing so, they encapsulate the essence of the "Frankenstein Effect," highlighting the timeless relevance of caution in the face of human curiosity and ambition.

The Shadows of Genius and the Birth of Frankenstein

Mary Wollstonecraft Godwin (1797–1851),[3] later known as Mary Shelley, was born into a family of radical intellectuals, the daughter of feminist pioneer Mary Wollstonecraft (1759–1797)[4] and anarchist philosopher William Godwin (1756–1836).[5] Her early life, overshadowed by her mother's death shortly after her birth and complicated by her father's remarriage to a distant stepmother, drove her to educate herself using her father's library, drawing heavily on her mother's works. This self-education, coupled with her exposure to her parents' revolutionary ideas, profoundly shaped her intellectual and literary development. Facing societal opposition and personal tragedies such as financial difficulties, the suicides of close family members, and the loss of three children, Mary's life changed dramatically at seventeen when she eloped with the poet Percy Bysshe Shelley (1792–1822). Despite these challenges, their intellectual and emotional partnership spurred Mary's creative growth. Though Percy's death in 1822 left her a widowed mother, Mary's resilience enhanced her literary contributions and secured her the status of an icon.[6]

During the notably cold and stormy "year without a summer" in 1816, Mary and Percy, along with John Polidori and Lord Byron, were confined near Lake Geneva, near the eerie Frankenstein Castle. The inclement weather led them to read German ghost stories,[7] inspiring Byron to challenge each to write a superior horror story.[8] After days of thought, Mary conceived *Frankenstein* from a vision of a scientist horrified by his own creation—a story that not only won her the challenge but also became a seminal Gothic novel. Brian Aldiss, a significant figure in science fiction history, argued in *Trillion Year Spree: The History of Science Fiction* (1986) that *Frankenstein* marked the birth of the science fiction genre by combining legitimate scientific research, a vision of future scientific advancements, and a critique of the ethical and societal impacts of scientific endeavors, thus paving the way for future science fiction literature.[9]

Unintended Consequences of the DeLorean's Journey

Both *Frankenstein* and *Back to the Future* illustrate the complex ramifications of scientific exploration, driven by a relentless curiosity and ambition to transcend conventional limits, which can precipitate unintended outcomes. Although the outcomes may be unintended, the absence of rigorous discipline in practice does not absolve the scientist of responsibility.

In Shelley's narrative, Dr. Victor Frankenstein, son of a distinguished lineage of physicians, becomes consumed by an infatuation with the enigmatic threshold between life and death. This fixation is catalyzed by his mother's demise—a pivotal tragedy that propels him into a grim quest for forbidden knowledge. Initially, Frankenstein's intentions are noble, aimed at conquering mortality itself, yet his endeavors swiftly escalate beyond his control. The being he engineers and then disavows rebels against its creator. Left to grapple with an existential quandary, devoid of any moral guidance from Frankenstein, the creature questions its very existence and purpose, "I saw and heard of none like me.... I [was] then a monster, a blot upon the earth, from which all men fled, and whom all men disowned,"[10] embodying Rousseau's concept of innate virtue corrupted by society.[11]

Confronted by his creation, Frankenstein faces an ultimatum: "Make me happy, and I shall again be virtuous."[12] Fabricate a mate for the monster, ensuring its departure from human society, or face its wrath. Despite initiating the creation of a female counterpart, Frankenstein destroys her, apprehensive of the ramifications. This act incites the monster's vengeance, leading it to systematically annihilate Frankenstein's loved ones. In a poignant irony, the very creature birthed from Frankenstein's endeavor to conquer death, upon facing rejection, becomes the harbinger of mortality for Frankenstein's circle. Frankenstein, in his bid to protect his loved ones from the clutches of death through his scientific creation, inadvertently subjects them to the fate he sought to avoid.

Similarly, *Back to the Future* navigates the terrain of unintended consequences born from scientific curiosity and the human urge to transcend our limitations. Doc Brown, much like Dr. Frankenstein, is driven by an insatiable curiosity and a desire to achieve what has never been done: time travel. His invention of the time machine, while initially seeming like a triumph of human intellect and a boon to mankind, quickly reveals the potential for disastrous outcomes. Marty's journey through time underscores how even the smallest changes to the past can have profound effects on the present, illustrating the fragile nature of the temporal continuum and the ethical quandaries involved in meddling with it. The film, though lighter in tone than Shelley's novel, shares the theme of scientific advancement pursued with noble intention—Doc's desire to explore the unknown and Marty's attempts to improve his family's circumstances—yet both face consequences that challenge their initial aspirations.

Marty finds himself grappling with the unintended repercussions of his time travel adventures in *Back to the Future*. Paramount among these is the threat to his own existence, as his mother inadvertently falls in love with him instead of his father, setting off a chain reaction that risks erasing him and his siblings from existence; Doc's warning "Anything you do can have serious repercussions for future events" begins to come true. Throughout the majority of the film, Marty navigates a complex web of challenges, striving to mend the timeline he has disrupted. His efforts culminate in successfully recoupling his parents, George and Lorraine, thereby securing his place in the future.

While Frankenstein's creation culminates in his own demise and the ruin of those he holds dear, Doc's invention sets Marty on a path toward potential destruction. However, Marty ultimately manages to alter his fate. This presents an intriguing contrast: whereas Frankenstein meets his end, Marty successfully evades his.

Crossing Boundaries with the Flux Capacitor

Both stories question the ethical limits of scientific exploration. Both Dr. Frankenstein's act of playing God by creating life and Doc Brown's manipulation of time challenge the boundaries of ethical science. These narratives suggest that just because something *can* be done scientifically does not mean it *should* be done. Neglecting philosophical and ethical considerations in science, thereby creating a discipline devoid of moral guidance, heralds a path toward potential disaster.

Frankenstein's daring quest to transcend the boundaries between life and death embodies a profound transgression against natural and divine laws, culminating in tragedy and personal ruin. His endeavor, marked by a desire to unlock the mysteries of existence, veers into the realm of the unethical on multiple fronts. Initially, Frankenstein's pursuit is fueled by a voracious appetite for knowledge deemed forbidden, as it encroaches upon territories traditionally reserved for the divine. The essence of life and the moment of its inception are considered sacrosanct, beyond the reach of human interference, thus positioning Frankenstein's experiments as a challenge to the natural order.

The philosophical underpinnings of his scientific exploration are similarly tainted, drawing upon ancient and esoteric theories that dabble in the metaphysical and the occult. Despite the Enlightenment's emphasis on reason and scientific inquiry, Frankenstein finds himself disillusioned with the limitations of contemporary science. In seeking wisdom from antiquated and mystical sources, he is met with scorn and derision from the academic community.

> Every instant that you have wasted on those books is utterly and entirely lost. You have burdened your memory with exploded systems and useless names. Good God! In what desert land have you lived, where no one was kind enough to inform you that these fancies, which you have so greedily imbibed, are a thousand years old, and as musty as they are ancient?[13]

Highlighting the chasm between his ambitions and the ethical standards of his time, his professor's rebuke underscores the folly of his reliance on discredited systems of thought, emphasizing the futility and danger of his obsession.

Moreover, the procurement of materials for his creation ventures into the macabre, as Frankenstein resorts to desecrating graves and plundering charnel houses—a clear violation of legal and moral codes. These actions not only underscore the illicit nature of his experiments but also reflect a profound disrespect for the sanctity of life and death. As Frankenstein's creation comes to life, the catastrophic consequences of his actions unfold, leading to the annihilation of his family and ultimately, his own demise at the hands of the very being he brought into existence.

Doc's groundbreaking invention of the time machine in *Back to the Future* is not without its own ethical and legal quandaries. To power the flux capacitor, the core component that "makes time travel possible," an immense energy output of 1.21 gigawatts is required. In the context of the 20th century, such power necessitates the use of nuclear energy. In a morally questionable maneuver, Doc obtains his plutonium by deceiving Libyan terrorists into thinking he will construct a nuclear bomb for them. Rather than fulfilling this perilous endeavor, he repurposes the plutonium as fuel for the time machine and delivers to the Libyans only a shoddy bomb casing full of used pinball machine parts. This act of deception not only involves the illegal acquisition of nuclear materials but also carries significant risks of nuclear proliferation and terrorism.

Furthermore, Doc's approach to experimentation raises serious ethical concerns, particularly his decision to use his dog, Einstein, as the inaugural time traveler. This choice prompts questions about the welfare and treatment of animals in scientific research, as Einstein had no ability to consent to the experiment and was unwittingly exposed to unknown risks. When Marty raises concerns about this, Doc swiftly reassures him that Einstein was never at risk. However, Doc's minimal testing does not ensure the dog's safety.

Additionally, there are insinuations that Doc financed his extravagant scientific pursuits by depleting his family's inheritance, suggesting a reckless disregard for financial stewardship and personal responsibility. The implication is that he diverted significant sums, meant for other purposes, to fund the development of his time machine. Together, these actions paint a picture of a brilliant but ethically compromised inventor whose pursuit of scientific achievement comes at the cost of moral integrity and legal standing.

Both Dr. Frankenstein and Doc Brown are depicted as morally compromised and hazardous, posing risks not just to themselves but also to those in their vicinity. Frankenstein, who clings to archaic and darkly mystical concepts, receives explicit cautions about the peril these ideas entail. However, he disregards these warnings because they conflict with his desired results. Similarly, Marty is cautioned by Mr. Strickland about the dangers of "hanging around with Dr. Emmett Brown," emphasizing that any involvement with him could lead to perilous consequences for both himself and others.

The Hubris of Redefining Boundaries

There is an element of hubris in both Dr. Frankenstein and Doc Brown. Frankenstein's ambition to conquer death and create life, and Doc's desire to master time, reflect the age-old theme of human hubris in the pursuit of knowledge and the need for humility in scientific endeavors. Their knowledge, perceived as superior and enlightening, illustrates that science, devoid of humility, can be hazardous and lead to downfall.

Frankenstein's relentless pursuit to unveil the mysteries not meant for human understanding is a quintessential example of hubris. This excessive pride and overconfidence detach him from the reality of his limitations and the moral implications of his actions. In his quest to conquer death and animate the lifeless, Frankenstein embodies the classical theme of hubris, a critical flaw that precipitates the downfall of many protagonists in Greek tragedies. His actions signify a profound disrespect for the natural boundaries and a challenge to the cosmic order, mirroring the defiance of ancient heroes against the decrees of the gods. This defiance inevitably attracts grave repercussions, underscoring the timeless narrative that such arrogance leads to ruin.

Frankenstein's creation of his monster stands as a monumental act of hubris, a vivid illustration of overreaching ambition that breaches the bounds of natural order. Upon witnessing the life spark in his creation, Frankenstein is immediately struck by the gravity of his transgression, recognizing the monstrousness of his deed: "I seemed to have lost all soul or sensation but for this one pursuit."[14] However, his response to this realization is marked not by accountability, but by cowardice: he abandons his creation, leaving it to fend for itself in a hostile world, naively wishing for its natural demise.

Confronted later with the consequences of his abandonment, Frankenstein is tempted to amend his initial error by granting the creature's demand for a companion, thereby hoping to mitigate the loneliness and suffering he has inflicted. Yet, as he nears the completion of this second being, he is beset by a vision of further calamity that might arise from introducing another such entity into the world. In a moment of panic and moral quandary, he destroys the unfinished mate before its animation, an act which irrevocably seals his fate and that of his first creation.

This decision sparks a relentless vendetta, with the creature vowing retribution, which culminates in a harrowing chase to the desolate reaches of the Arctic. There, the creator and the creation confront the ultimate consequences of Frankenstein's hubris. In the icy wilderness, both Frankenstein and the monster face their demise, entwined in a tragic end that underscores the profound costs of human overreach and the irrevocable loneliness borne from reckless creation and abandonment. This chilling conclusion serves as a stark reminder of the perils inherent in playing God and the moral responsibility that accompanies the act of creation. In *Frankenstein*, Shelley illustrates the dangers of unchecked ambition and the catastrophic outcomes of assuming powers beyond human entitlement, offering a cautionary tale about the perils of hubris that resonates as much in contemporary times as it did in her own.

Doc Brown, unlike Frankenstein, seems resistant to fully acknowledging the lessons presented by his own brush with catastrophic outcomes. Throughout the *Back to the Future* trilogy, despite repeatedly acknowledging the perils introduced by the time machine—vowing its destruction to prevent further misuse—Doc never follows through on this resolution. His actions betray a persistent temptation to tamper with the timeline, underpinned by a belief in the potential for positive change, yet overlooking the chaos that often follows such interventions.

In *Part II*, Doc's decision to transport Marty and Jennifer into the future to rectify their family's issues only serves to spiral into further calamity. This intervention sets off a chain of events that not only jeopardizes the well-being of their children but also inadvertently facilitates a darker timeline. Biff Tannen's acquisition of the time machine, followed by his journey to the past in 1955, armed with a sports almanac, fundamentally alters the course of history, enriching his family and transforming Hill Valley into a dystopian landscape under his control.

Part III concludes the trilogy with a reaffirmation of the series' central motif: the unpredictable and often hazardous nature of altering time. Despite the ongoing turmoil caused by their time-traveling escapades, it is only when the DeLorean is finally destroyed by a train upon Marty's return to 1985 from 1885 that there seems to be a chance for normalcy to resume. The destruction of the time machine symbolizes a potential end to the disruptions in the temporal continuum, offering a momentary sigh of relief that the chaotic manipulations of past and future might cease, allowing the characters (and audience) to envision a return to a stable reality.

However, this sense of resolution is short-lived. In a twist that reignites the saga's core intrigue, Doc re-enters the scene aboard a locomotive converted into a new time machine, accompanied by his family. This revelation underscores his unwavering commitment to exploring the realms of time, despite the previous disasters his inventions have precipitated. With the introduction of the time-traveling train, the narrative suggests that the allure of manipulating time is too compelling to resist, even when faced with the potential for calamity.

Doc's continued forays into time manipulation highlight a recurring theme of unintended consequences that resonate with Frankenstein's initial transgression. However, where Frankenstein is tormented by guilt and seeks to escape the repercussions of his actions, Doc's character arc is one of stubborn optimism in the face of potential disaster. His refusal to abandon time travel, despite its proven danger, underscores a complex interplay between hubris and hope—a desire to harness scientific breakthroughs for the betterment of mankind, yet frequently blinded to the hazards such meddling incurs.

The Moral Compass of Creation and Consequence

In both narratives, the creators are confronted with the repercussions of their actions. Dr. Frankenstein's monster, seeking understanding and companionship, becomes a figure of tragedy, reflecting the dangers of creation without responsibility. Doc and Marty's escapades in the *Back to the Future* trilogy reveal the perils of altering time, highlighting the theme that science and its practitioners must be mindful of their ethical responsibilities. Both stories serve as cautionary tales about the hubris of surpassing natural boundaries and the moral obligation of creators to foresee and mitigate the effects of their inventions. Frankenstein's tale of horror and the adventurous narrative of *Back to the Future* converge on the critical insight that scientific exploration, while a testament to human creativity and resolve, requires a balanced approach guided by ethical considerations and an awareness of potential future impacts.

VIII. Doc Brown and the Philosophy of Science and Technology

NOTES

1. Gipe, George. 1985. *Back to the Future.* Berkeley Books.
2. The term "Frankenstein complex" was introduced by Isaac Asimov in his series about robots, describing the apprehension surrounding mechanical beings.
3. Mellor, Anne K. 1996. "Shelley, Mary (1797–1851)." *British Writers.* Charles Scribner's Sons.
4. Mary Wollstonecraft's seminal work, *A Vindication of the Rights of Woman*, published in 1792, stands as a cornerstone of feminist philosophy. In it, Wollstonecraft argues for the equality of the sexes, advocating that women are not naturally inferior to men but appear so only because of a lack of education. She contends that both women and men should be treated as rational beings and proposes that the education of women should be of a serious nature, suggesting that women should be educated alongside men and receive the same breadth and depth of knowledge. This, she argues, would enable women to become virtuous and independent, contributing to society in the same capacity as men. Wollstonecraft's ideas were revolutionary for her time, laying the groundwork for future feminist movements by challenging the prevailing notions of female inferiority and advocating for women's rights in education, society, and politics.
5. William Godwin, an influential philosopher of the late eighteenth century, is renowned for his foundational contributions to anarchist thought. He argued against the necessity of government, arguing that rational individuals, capable of moral judgment and empathy, can self-regulate without the coercion of state power. Godwin believed in the inherent goodness of humanity and maintained that social injustices and corruption stem from the institutions of government and private property. He advocated for a society based on equality, reason, and mutual aid, where individuals freely cooperate without the imposition of laws or authority. His vision of a decentralized and non-hierarchical society laid the groundwork for later anarchist theory, emphasizing the importance of education, free thought, and the gradual abolition of centralized political structures.
6. Bomarito, Jessica. 2006. "Shelley, Mary Wollstonecraft (1797–1851)." *Gothic Literature: A Gale Critical Companion.* Gale.
7. For interested readers, two modern English translations exist for the anthology of ghost stories from which they drew inspiration. Hale, Terry (ed.). 1992. *Tales of the Dead: The Ghost Stores of the Villa Diodati.* The Gothic Society. Day, A.J. (ed.). 2004. *Fantasmagoriana: Tales of the Dead.* Fantasmagoriana Press.
8. John William Polidori (1795–1821) was a distinguished British author and doctor, celebrated for his ties to the Romantic movement and often regarded as the pioneer of the vampire genre in fantasy literature. His seminal piece, written alongside Shelley's *Frankenstein*, "The Vampyre" (1819), stands as the first modern vampire story to be published.
9. Aldiss, Brian. 1986. *Trillian Year Spree: The History of Science Fiction.* House of Stratus.
10. Shelley, Mary. 2008. *Frankenstein; or, the Modern Prometheus* (The 1818 Text). Oxford University Press.
11. Jean-Jacques Rousseau argues that humans, in their natural state, are inherently good and peaceful, with society and its constructs leading to corruption and inequality. He argued that in nature, humans live in harmony, guided by instinct and empathy, without the artificial hierarchies and possessions that characterize modern life. Rousseau believed that societal progression, marked by the introduction of property and social stratification, distorts human behavior, fostering competition and diminishing innate moral values. His work suggests that education should nurture this inherent goodness while equipping individuals to navigate societal structures, significantly impacting modern views on education, ethics, and human nature.
12. *Ibid.*, Shelley.
13. *Ibid.*
14. *Ibid.*

Great Scott!
The Logic of Certain Scientific Discovery
KEITH BEGLEY *and* AADIL KURJI

In the first act of *Back to the Future*, Doc Brown asks Marty to meet in the parking lot of the Twin Pines Mall at 1:15 a.m., because Doc has made a major breakthrough and requires Marty's assistance. When Marty arrives, Doc reports that his latest experiment "is the big one, the one I've been waiting for all my life!" This statement takes on a new significance later in the film, when we learn that Doc had indeed been working toward *this very experiment* for thirty years! As we shall see, the meaning of "working toward" shifts throughout the series. To understand this, we must first investigate the separate timelines of the first film, before considering elements of the beginning of *Part III*.

A Red-Letter Date in the History of Science

The first timeline split has its origin in Doc's initial demonstration of the time circuits in the parking lot at Twin Pines Mall. He picks some famous dates from history and enters them as potential time travel destinations: the signing of The Declaration of Independence; the Birth of Christ; and what he calls "a red-letter date in the history of science, November 5th, 1955." Here "he pauses, realizing something—as if something suddenly makes sense to him."[1]

> DOC: Yes, of course. November 5th, 1955!
> MARTY: What? I don't get what happened.
> DOC: That was the day I invented time travel. I remember it vividly. I was standing on the edge of my toilet, hanging a clock. The porcelain was wet. I slipped, hit my head on the edge of the sink, and when I came to, I had a revelation, a vision, a picture in my head, a picture of this [points

to the flux capacitor]. This is what makes time travel possible. The flux capacitor.
MARTY: Flux capacitor?
DOC: It's taken me almost 30 years and my entire family fortune to realize the vision of that day.

This is not as unusual a story as it may seem. Many scientists have had similar *Eureka!* moments, moments of revelation in which they come to realize something about the universe that had not previously been known. *Eureka!* is said to have been what Archimedes shouted as he leapt out of his bath upon realizing the connection between displacement and measurement of volume, solving a problem for King Hiero II.

For further examples, consider some of Doc Brown's own scientific heroes, of whom he has portraits hanging in his living room. Isaac Newton was inspired to develop his theory of gravity after seeing an apple falling from a tree and connecting this phenomenon with a question regarding how the Moon stays in its orbit. Albert Einstein, aged just 16, imagined chasing and catching up to a beam of light, which would have to appear static yet be oscillating. This contradiction later influenced the development of his special theory of relativity, which makes a connection between velocity and the rate of the flow of time.

These *Eureka!* moments are characterized by a "flash of insight," some event that inspires the thinker to see the world in a new light and forms a theory in their mind. With Archimedes, the change in the water level of the bath provided this trigger; with Newton, it was the fall of the apple. We should note that this isn't the only part of those moments, otherwise any moment of insight would be a *Eureka!* moment, even those that do not end up being borne out.[2] That is, there is also some confirmation of the theory, through observed phenomena, as well as the inspiration, though the fully-developed theory would come later. The philosopher of science, Hans Reichenbach called these the "context of discovery," the context where the theory is initially thought of, and the "context of justification," the context in which the theory is supported by the evidence.[3] For Archimedes and Newton, these are both immediate and part of the event; with Einstein, it was different. For the 16-year-old Einstein, the vision and context of discovery predated, by quite some time, both the development of the theory it inspired but also any confirming observations and experiments, the context of justification.

What suddenly made sense to Doc about the 5th of November 1955? Was it just that he remembered the date he invented time travel, or was it that he realized that this was the moment he had set everything in motion? There are many things we cannot know about *Back to the Future*, including whether this was the "first" timeline (there seem to be reasons for and against this idea). Doc and Marty meet at Twin Pines Mall, but when Marty gets sent back to the future, it has become Lone Pine Mall, because he knocked down a pine while escaping Old Man Peabody's farm in 1955. However, although Goldie Wilson is already Mayor of Hill Valley at the beginning of the film, we learn that he seems to have gotten the idea from Marty mentioning this eventual state of affairs back in 1955.[4]

As Doc elaborates in *Part II*, when a time traveler alters events in the past, they effectively bring a new timeline into existence from the point they travel to, with the previous timelines erased entirely, save for their memory. What is really interesting, for our purposes, is what happens to Doc's *epistemic state*, that is, his knowledge set, when these various new timelines are triggered by meeting Martys and the like in 1955.

The changing timelines affect the moments and notions of scientific discovery involved with Doc Brown's *Eureka!* moment. To understand this, there are three Doc Browns whom we should consider:

Doc^1: The original Emmett Brown who conceives of time travel on November 5th, 1955, and doesn't meet Marty until the 1980s.
Doc^2: The Emmett Brown whom Marty visits on November 6th, 1955, to get help going *Back to the Future*.
Doc^3: The Emmett Brown who remeets Marty in 1955 shortly after sending him back to 1985, at the end of *Part II* and the beginning of *Part III*.

Returning to Doc^1's story, after his *Eureka!* moment he is so sure of his inspiration that he goes on to spend the next thirty years working on the time machine, dedicating his life and his family's considerable fortune to the dogged pursuit of confirming his theory. Allan Franklin called this the context of pursuit, the context in which a scientist or community deems a theory worthy of further investigation and experimentation.[5] For Doc^1, his theory of time travel was discovered in the bathroom, following his fall, pursued over a thirty-year period until finally being justified. A second "red-letter date in the history of science" to be noted is surely a date on which this confirmation happens: early on October 26, 1985, when Doc successfully sends his dog, Einstein, through time in the remote-controlled DeLorean.

It Works!

When Marty dives into the DeLorean to avoid the Libyan terrorists and accidentally activates the time circuits, they are already set to November 5, 1955, so this is the date to which he travels back. The next day, he finds Doc^2 and is able to convince him that he is from the future in part by repeating the story about how Doc got the bruise on his head and came up with the idea for the flux capacitor (which makes time travel possible). Marty then takes him to where he's hidden the DeLorean. Doc² shows Marty the picture he drew of the flux capacitor after hitting his head; the context of discovery hasn't changed. Marty then shows Doc² the actual flux capacitor, which lights up and pulses. To this, Doc² exclaims, "It works, [laughing] it works! I finally invented something that works!" Here Doc² receives the first confirmation that his time travel device will eventually work. We also see that the Doc is not exactly a successful inventor in 1955 and only really finds his forte in time travel some time after hitting his head on the sink.

What makes the situation with Doc² interesting is that he meets Marty on November 6 and, due to this interaction, comes to know that not only is his underlying theory correct, but that he will successfully create a machine that uses this theory in practice, in thirty years' time. That is, this meeting of Marty and the DeLorean put Doc² in the context of justification. These facts differentiate him from Doc¹ epistemically speaking, that is, with regard to their knowledge. Oddly, the confirmation of the theory is presented to Doc before he has had time to flesh out the details; the context of pursuit is still the following thirty years. Instead of his theory being confirmed by the first test drive of the DeLorean on October 26, 1985, some thirty years later, he is convinced by Marty within twenty-four hours on November 6, 1955. More direct confirmation of the time circuits in action appears on November 12, 1955, the day of the Enchantment Under the Sea dance and the lightning strike on the clock tower.

Something to Shoot For

This is an odd situation for a scientist to be in. Typically, scientists have some hypothesis or theory that they must develop and eventually test against reality through some means. Hypotheses allow scientists to make predictions about the world. For example, the Newtonian laws of motion, and their successors, predict that if I let go of an apple, it will accelerate and reach a certain velocity before hitting the ground. That is, if the theory is true, then the prediction should also come true. If the prediction turns out to be false, all other factors considered, the hypothesis is falsified.[6] That is, because it made a false prediction, we infer that the hypothesis must itself be false. This is based on a standard logical principle called *Modus Tollens*, or "denying the consequent." The consequence of believing the hypothesis, the prediction it made, is false, so the hypothesis must be false.

We say "all other factors considered" because some other factor, some auxiliary assumption of the situation could have influenced the outcome. We are never testing a theory or hypothesis on its own, as there are always other assumptions and particular circumstances. For example, there could be something funny going on with the apple: perhaps it has a magnet in it, or the air through which it was falling was moving upwards, etc. In such cases, it is more tricky to work out whether the hypothesis should be falsified or whether merely one or more of these many attendant auxiliary assumptions is to blame and should be taken as being the "bad apple" instead.[7] That is, if from the theory and what we think we know of the actual world, we make a prediction that turns out to be false, then either the theory or one or more of those many other items must be incorrect. Further, even if the prediction turns out to come true, all that the scientist knows is that the theory wasn't falsified on *this* occasion, not whether the theory is actually correct for all cases or all future predictions. There could also be another, as yet unknown, more powerful theory, which explains more and makes more predictions. That such a prediction comes true does not always provide enough information to resolve such an issue.

In the case of Doc^2, his future self has effectively tested his hypothesis for him and sent the results back to the past for him to view with his own eyes. From Doc^2's perspective, all he has had is an idea which he has not had an opportunity to test yet. He doesn't even know *how* to go about testing it, yet he knows that it is correct insofar as it will allow someone to travel back in time. This is liberating for him to know but also provokes a certain expectation in him that he will be able to figure out how to bring it about merely from the starting point of having the idea.

Later, when back in his workshop viewing the videotape of the experiment in 1985, Doc learns that it will take 1.21 gigawatts of power to travel through time. Since plutonium isn't readily available in 1955 to generate the necessary electrical power, Doc and Marty hatch a plan to channel a lightning bolt directly into the flux capacitor on a night when they know that one will strike the clock tower. Doc spends much of the next few days setting this plan in motion and getting everything set up, while Marty is enjoying some quality family time.

On the night of the lightning strike, before Marty goes back to the future, Doc tells Marty that he has given him a great motivation in life, as he knows that he is going to succeed.

> You know, Marty, I'm going to be very sad to see you go. You've really made a difference in my life; you've given me something to shoot for. Just knowing that I'm going to be around to see 1985, that I'm going to succeed in this! That I'm going to have a chance to travel through time! It's going to be really hard waiting thirty years before I can talk to you about everything that's happened in the past few days. I'm really going to miss you, Marty.

Would Doc have been able to do this without Marty's help? It seems clear that he is not exactly a successful inventor. In fact, he ends up using most of his family's wealth on his scientific endeavors. Nevertheless, he *must* have been able to do it in order for Marty to have been sent back in time at all. What impact might this have on the pace of his scientific investigations and the degree of commitment to the underlying theory?

The danger of such a long project is always that one has embarked upon what is known as a *degenerating research programme*.[8] That is, a program of scientific research having the same hard core of theoretical proposals over time, which ends up making no novel predictions that don't get refuted. In short, it's an idea that isn't going anywhere fast. If we opt for this more moderate view of scientific endeavor, then we don't immediately throw out our favorite theory merely because something it predicted turned out to be false. Such theories can hang around for a long time, even thirty years or more. However, if they stop providing us with new tests or predictions, or continually fail every test possible, it may be wise to start abandoning the hard core of the theory; this is the core of the context of pursuit. For Doc^2, this might be something like abandoning the claim that time travel is possible at all. However, with Marty's help, Doc^{2}'s theory is in better stead. Even if every test were to fail for thirty years, and no new test were to arise until the DeLorean is outfitted for its first test at Lone Pine Mall in 1985, Doc^2 would still know that he need not abandon the hard core of his theory. This is a tremendous advantage in the face of a potential thirty years of recalcitrant evidence, an unwavering context of pursuit. Further, as luck would have it, the Doc did not have to wait that long to see Marty again.

A Schematic from the Past

At the end of *Part II* and the beginning of *Part III*, we see Doc^3 in 1955 just after he has successfully sent Marty back to 1985. A slightly later version of Marty comes running down the street just after seeing 1985-Doc disappear in the flying DeLorean because it was accidentally struck by lightning. Marty also received a letter that Doc sent to him in 1885 informing him that he was still "alive" in a four-dimensional sense. Doc^3, who had just sent Marty back to the future using the lightning strike at the clock tower, did not expect to see Marty so soon, and faints from the shock. Marty takes Doc home to recuperate. When they wake up, Marty shows Doc^3 the letter that Doc^2 sent to him from 1885, in part to convince him of what has happened, and Doc^3 learns that the DeLorean will eventually fly! Here is an excerpt from the letter.

The lightning bolt that hit the DeLorean caused a gigawatt overload which scrambled the time circuits, activated the flux capacitor, and sent me back to 1885. The overload shorted out the time circuits and destroyed the flying circuits. Unfortunately, the car will never fly again. I set myself up as a blacksmith as a front while I attempted to repair the damage to the time circuits. Unfortunately, this proved impossible because suitable replacement parts will not be invented until 1947. [...] I have buried the DeLorean in the Delgato mine adjacent to the old Boot Hill Cemetery, as shown on the enclosed map. Hopefully it will remain undisturbed and preserved until you uncover it in 1955. Inside, you will find repair instructions. My 1955 counterpart should have no problem repairing it, so you can drive it back to the future.

The "suitable replacement parts" that Doc refers to here are the early tube-like point-contact transistors invented at Bell labs in 1947. When they find the hidden DeLorean in the mine there is another letter inside.

As you can see, the lightning bolt shorted out the time circuit control microchip. The attached schematic diagram will allow you to build a replacement unit with the 1955 components, thus restoring the time machine to perfect working order.

Doc³ then uses the schematic to build a unit that he calls the "time circuit control tubes," which he straps to the DeLorean. So, in addition to gaining motivation and the certainty of knowledge of success, Doc³ also gains a schematic for the time circuits and their connection to the flux capacitor. He then has an opportunity to build (at least) a part of the time circuits and test his part by sending Marty back to 1885. Although Doc³ is then left without a DeLorean in 1955, he has gained a lot of knowledge about how to build his time machine after twice working with the complete machine, obtaining a schematic, and successfully building part of it.

Interestingly, Doc³ has the exact same *Eureka!* moment as the Docs of the other timelines. The slip and fall while hanging the toilet clock gives him the inspiration for the flux capacitor. That is, the context of discovery once more is the same. However, the gap between theory and confirmation radically shifts, as now he actively builds time circuits and sees Marty off into the time stream once more in late 1955, fixing the context of justification in 1955, like that of Doc². Having received the schematics, and merely working off the efforts of others (even if they are Docs Brown from different times/timelines) Doc³ is relegated to more of a knowledgeable machinist/engineer, having not had the time to develop the underlying theory that is needed to understand and build the time-traveling DeLorean. He receives a literal cheat sheet for his own discovery. This yields an interesting twist to the notion of the development of time travel from the perspective of Doc³. While he has the plans to build certain parts of the machine, he still needs to figure out the rest. Crucially, this includes the details of the underlying theory, that is, the context of pursuit stretches before him though, with a research program that is less degenerating or perhaps even *progressive*.

Unfortunately, we don't have a clear notion of what the time between Doc^3 sending Marty back to 1885 and the (assumed) development of time travel in 1985 was like, as Marty and Doc's adventures in the remainder of *Part III* would have triggered the creation of yet another timeline. Also, at the end of the film, Marty has barely returned when the steam train time machine appears, and the final scene occurs. The only real indication of this timeline is the ravine, now renamed to "Eastwood Ravine." We do know that there were certain general scientific developments that were needed for the time machine to be built in 1985, the stainless-steel bodied car and availability of plutonium at the very least. Despite having the cheat sheet, it is plausible that Doc^3 wouldn't have been able to build the time machine sooner, even if he tried. From a discovery standpoint, Doc^3 has an interesting set of scientific activities available to him. He has the same paths as the other two Docs did, but he also has the ability to rebuild the time circuits and reverse engineer his theory from the working parts, or indeed use the *already proven successful* device for all kinds of experimentation that would not have been available to his "predecessors." In a sense, Doc^3's forays into temporal science are much more like scientific rediscovery.

Scientific discovery is littered with *Eureka!* moments, where a scientist has a flash of insight, triggered by an event that leads them to understand the way the world works in some *new* way; at least the rudimentary theory "clicks." These moments are accompanied by the moments of confirmation and the development of the fully-fledged theory. These together are the context of discovery and the context of justification. As we have seen through Doc Brown's scientific idols, these moments can be temporally close, or much further apart. What's interesting is that the insight they inspire leads to a clear idea of the theory, such that the scientist works toward sorting it out, which is the context of pursuit. For all of the Doc Browns, this took thirty years until he had the moment of confirmation, made possible in part by the availability of necessary parts for the final confirming experiment, a plutonium powered stainless-steel time machine, the DeLorean.

Notes

1. This is a quote from the original script.
2. Laukkonen et al. illustrate this point nicely by relaying that John Nash believed that aliens were recruiting him because the ideas came to him in the same way as his

mathematical insights. Laukkonen, R., et al. 2020. "The dark side of Eureka: Artificially induced Aha moments make facts feel true." *Cognition* 196, p. 1.

3. Reichenbach, H. 1938. *Experience and Prediction*. University of Chicago Press. pp. 6–7.

4. It's possible that this helps explain the changes to Hill Valley at the end of the first film, as it may have encouraged Goldie to "clean up this town" years earlier than he would have if he didn't meet Marty.

5. Franklin, A., and Fischbach, E. 2016. *The Rise and Fall of the Fifth Force: Discovery, Pursuit, and Justification in Modern Physics*. Springer.

6. Karl Popper called this process "falsification," which was a central element of his method of *conjecture and refutation*. Popper, K. 1959. *The Logic of Scientific Discovery*. Routledge.

7. This is known as the Duhem thesis, after Pierre Duhem. Duhem, P. [1914] 1954. *The Aim and Structure of Physical Theory*. Princeton University Press, p. 187.

8. This was part of a philosophy of science put forward by Imre Lakatos. Lakatos, I. 1978. *The Methodology of Scientific Research Programmes* (Philosophical Papers: Volume 1). J. Worrall and G. Currie (eds.), Cambridge: Cambridge University Press.

Doc Brown's Techno-Ethical Journey

KENNETH R. PIKE

As a time travel story, the *Back to the Future* trilogy is (perhaps inevitably) beset by paradox. But equally labyrinthine are the under-explored moral intuitions of the time machine's creator (and self-appointed regulator), Emmett "Doc" Brown. Despite the fantastical nature of his invention, Doc's moral journey gives viewers a front row seat to some of the real ethical challenges raised by scientific inquiry and technological innovation. Why do we innovate? What are the ethical boundaries of experimental inquiry? Does the possession of knowledge or capacities others lack imply an obligation to benefit the less gifted? What if that benefit can only be bestowed by impacting people's autonomy in paternalistic ways? In short: is it ever okay to change the course of history?

Time Travel for Truth

Today, the acquisition of knowledge and the development of new technology are commonly treated as a single pursuit, with "STEM" (science, technology, engineering, and math) a major focus of education and industry the world over. However, history's earliest natural philosophers (i.e., "scientists," as we call them today) would find our blending of science and technology a bit vulgar. Ancient philosophers were engaged in a search for truth and regarded the truth as its own reward. For instance, Aristotle famously reports that Thales, after being taunted concerning the apparent uselessness of philosophy, applied his knowledge to secure a monopoly on olive presses in advance of an abundant growing season—"proving that it is easy for philosophers to be rich if they choose, but *this is not what they care about.*"[1]

Though the natural philosophers of ancient Greece recognized the *instrumental* value of knowledge, practical considerations were not what drove them to ruminate on the nature of reality. Rather, they were motivated by a love of the truth, which they regarded as *intrinsically* valuable.

Early in the *Back to the Future* trilogy, Doc's perspective on inquiry seems to echo that of the ancients. When his good friend, Marty, tries to bring a sports almanac from 2015 back to 1985 in order to "place a couple bets," Doc explains the motive behind his innovation: "I didn't invent the time machine for financial gain. The intent here is to gain a clearer perception of humanity. Where we've been, where we're going, the pitfalls, the possibilities, the perils, and the promise. Perhaps even an answer to that universal question: *why*?" Doc is expressing an idealized view of science as the pursuit of knowledge for its own sake, unsullied by practical considerations. Technology, on this view, can be instrumental to the discovery of truth, but should not be employed to venal ends. When Doc reveals that he's spent thirty years and his "entire family fortune" developing the time machine, which he intends to put to no other use than satisfying his own academic curiosity, he is demonstrating his commitment to an ancient and arguably noble ideal. This would be a bit like Elon Musk giving away Tesla automobiles for free, on the grounds that electric vehicles exist to reduce carbon emissions, *not* to make people rich.

Sometimes, however, Doc's idealism can seem dangerously naïve (e.g., when it inspires him to acquire plutonium by double-crossing a terrorist organization). Clearly, the pursuit of knowledge can have practical consequences, even when it is not driven by practical aims. This is one reason why, even when it seems likely that researchers have the best of intentions, government agencies, institutional review boards, ethics committees, and other regulatory bodies are often put in place to approve and monitor research and innovation. Even Plato, who regarded the pursuit of truth as fundamentally divine, believed that an ideal government could permissibly impede inquiry and even lie to the citizenry in furtherance of a community's overall good.[2] Given Doc's own concern that the time machine could potentially destroy *the entire universe* (or possibly just our own galaxy), it is difficult to imagine any regulatory body approving of the project.

Perhaps this is why, or at least *one* reason why, Doc submits his work to neither democratic regulation nor academic oversight. Something Thomas Sowell famously observed concerning economics is also true of scientific inquiry: "there are no 'solutions' but only trade-offs."[3] While oversight and regulation ideally mitigate risk, they accomplish this in part by impeding innovation—inspiring some scientists to declare that ethicists need to "get out of the way."[4] Today, we enjoy the benefits of many labor-saving, pain-alleviating, life-prolonging technologies, so we might plausibly worry that anything slowing the development and implementation of new technologies is directly responsible for unnecessary drudgery, suffering, or even death. Perhaps most famously, medical research and technology that could be saving lives *now* sometimes instead languishes in interminable approval processes imposed by government regulators. One very real risk of curbing innovation is that we hamper our ability to *do more good*.

But when regulators *do* get out of the way, or when innovation outpaces the ability of regulatory bodies to anticipate it, this does not free innovators from the demands of ethics—it just makes scientists themselves the *de facto* regulators of their own work. To no one's surprise, innovators favor innovation! Doc Brown recognized the destructive potential of his time machine and built it anyway. Inquisitiveness so zealous as to overlook risks of such magnitude seems like *precisely* the sort of thing oversight committees exist to mitigate. But oversight also implies disclosure, and disclosure comes with risks of its own. What if Doc disclosed his research to someone who stole it or used it to harm to others? Perhaps, in a world where everyone undertook scientific inquiry in a perfectly Platonic way, such concerns would be unwarranted. In reality (and in film), however, these are not questions innovators can long afford to ignore.

Time Travel for Power

As the golden age of Athens receded into the past, philosophy moved beyond Platonic idealism. Two thousand years after Thales, Francis Bacon laid the groundwork for what we now call the scientific method—and is often attributed with authorship of the aphorism that "knowledge is power."[5] This is not a complete repudiation of Plato; one needn't deny the intrinsic value of knowledge to recognize that its instrumental value is also tremendous. But Bacon believed that the growth of human knowledge would eventually give birth to a scientific and political utopia. Rather than pursuing knowledge for its own sake, as the ancients proposed, Bacon suggested we pursue knowledge in order to improve ourselves and the world. His speculative fiction on the matter has proven so prescient, one might wonder whether he received visitors by DeLorean.

Doc Brown's ethical outlook, too, evolves away from ancient Greek ideals as his practical experience with time travel increases. After succumbing to the temptation to read Marty's timely letter of warning, Doc wears a bulletproof vest to the DeLorean's inaugural run. He then travels to 2015, where he has the DeLorean upgraded with flight capabilities and a Mr. Fusion power system. Doc also gets a few upgrades of his own, replacing organs, enhancing his appearance, and adding "30 or 40 years" to his life. Then he decides to improve the future-of-the-future by intervening in the 2015 arrest and incarceration of Marty's son, Marty Jr. These are not strictly the activities of a Platonist seeking truth; these are exercises of power that directly benefit Doc and his friends.

Technological innovation often works this way. Academic curiosity births a new technology, which eventually disrupts people's lives—even if, arguably, for the better. In the process, innovators (or those who control innovators, for example, through patronage) are enriched. The inventive, their wealthy benefactors, and their cronies gain increased access to existing resources, including an increased ability to direct the activities of the brightest minds of the rising generation. This, in turn, shapes the future for everyone, no time machine necessary. For example, the cryptocurrency, Bitcoin, was invented by political anarchists seeking to create an unregulated, anonymous currency.[6] Early adopters instead became wealthy when the technology was overrun by speculative investment, and "Bitcoin millionaires" became a significant source of venture capital directed toward further technological innovation.

But not every kind of knowledge makes the world a better place, and even presumptively beneficial changes are not always welcomed, particularly when they are imposed by others. The word "Westernization" is sometimes used to describe the process by which traditional activities and ways of life are undermined, not necessarily by literal colonization, but by the supernormal stimuli furnished by globalized market competition between highly incentivized innovators.

Naturally, the first victims of technological Westernization were those Westerners who had their pastoral lifestyles eradicated by technological advancement without so much as an "if you please." These changes did not pass unresisted, but reactionary movements like Romanticism and Luddism have never convincingly succeeded in stalling the march of (putative) progress. One reason may be that technological progress is a kind of cultural superweapon; the cost of innovation, however steep, is often exceeded by the cost of letting someone else get there first. Concerns of this nature are often expressed in connection with atomic weaponry[7] but apply just as well to any technology with the potential to change the course of history.

Initially, this is not something Doc seems to fully appreciate about his time machine. But after a handful of misadventures in 2015, he suggests that he should simply destroy the DeLorean. He tells Marty, "The risks are just too great ... and I was behaving responsibly! You can imagine the danger if the time machine were to fall into the wrong hands." Doc's remorse is good evidence of ongoing character development! But it's not the *machine* Doc needs to worry about—it's the *knowledge*. What Doc accomplished, others might also accomplish. Preventing others from discovering time travel and possibly using it to change Doc's preferred version of history will likely require Doc to wield his own power over history. To what extent does his *power* to accomplish this underwrite a *responsibility* to do so?

Time Travel for Justice

The *Back to the Future* movies often evade questions of responsibility by using accidents as a plot device; in particular, the DeLorean's "time circuits" appear shockingly fussy. But after creating a device that *twice* spares him from certain death, allows him to exploit beneficial technologies inaccessible to his contemporaries, and wins him the love of a woman simultaneously old enough to be his grandmother and young enough to be his daughter, Doc declares to Jennifer Parker that "your future hasn't been written yet. No one's has." Even if we disregard the animated series into which Doc's train subsequently delivers his anachronistic family, he's not being particularly truthful. The 1985 in which Marty and Jennifer remain at the end of the *Back to the Future* trilogy is not the 1985 Marty left. It's a 1985 in which George McFly is a successful author and Biff Tannen is the family's fawning lackey. It's a 1985 in which Marty retains the ability to play the guitar. Perhaps most importantly, it's a 1985 in which Doc wore a bulletproof vest to the DeLorean's inaugural run. Not a bad ending for Doc and his friends, but far from the future 1955's Biff once wrote for himself. It would not be unreasonable for someone like Biff to conclude that the "wrong hands" into which the time machine has fallen are *Doc's*.

Naturally, Biff's role is written to elicit no sympathy for his plight, but we don't need a villain-centered deconstruction of the trilogy to notice that Doc's circumstances are not unique to time travel. Our best understanding of physics is that humans can never alter our own past, but the actions we take in the present clearly influence the future, including the identities of future humans. What obligations, if any, arise from the power innovators wield over the shape of our lives and the direction of history?

The question can be difficult to answer in part because of something the philosopher Derek Parfit calls the "non-identity problem." The non-identity problem is complex, but one interesting thing about it is that Parfit thinks it (that is, the *existence of the non-identity problem*) may need to be kept secret, at least from policy makers.[8] His reasoning is that when our actions change the future, this doesn't harm anyone, even when it causes certain hypothetical people to never come into existence. The people who exist in the future are simply different people than those who would have existed otherwise. So, as long as their lives are worth living, we haven't harmed them by bringing about a future in which they exist. We also haven't harmed the people who didn't come into existence, because they do not exist and so cannot be harmed. But *believing* this could lead policy makers to discount the interests of future humans in objectionable ways, so Parfit suggests the problem might need to be concealed.

That Parfit makes this suggestion in a now-famous and influential work of philosophy is a bit like the inventor of a time machine deciding that it ought to be destroyed. Ultimately, Doc's time-traveling DeLorean *is* destroyed, not by choice but by chance. Marty can't rebuild it, and Doc is stuck in 1885. "Just like you wanted," Marty says to his absent friend. But shortly after (from Marty's perspective), Doc returns in a time-traveling train, bedecked with future technology and carrying passengers. Here, the audience is left to draw their own inferences, but clearly, Doc has changed his mind about the existence of time machines. His partial explanation is "I had to come back for Einstein, and I didn't want you to be worried about me." But this could have easily been accomplished without first taking the train into the future, so Doc's intentions remain somewhat opaque. Is it possible that he returned to 1985 to ensure that the DeLorean was in fact destroyed, thus monopolizing his technological power over the course of history?

Here, it may be useful to pose a somewhat obvious question: if you had a time machine, what would you do with it? Popular answers, like revisiting past mistakes or meeting (or assassinating) major historical figures, fail to grasp the scope of what it means to transcend cause and effect. Provided they are not being thwarted by accidents or agonizing over ethical implications, clever time travelers would be wise to seek extension of their own lifespan and improvements to their time travel technology— which is exactly what Doc does. This is because a person with sufficient time, unfettered by the laws of cause and effect and unopposed by rival time travelers, is suitably equipped to make of the *entire history of the world* whatever they care to make of it—so long as they can also avoid paradoxes that unmake themselves, their time machine, or their home galaxy. A utilitarian like John Stuart Mill could manipulate events to ensure that the greatest number of beings experience the greatest aggregate happiness.[9] An egalitarian like John Rawls could tweak history to ensure the moral and political equality of all.[10] A sufficientarian like Harry Frankfurt (or myself) might work to ensure that everyone always had *enough*.[11] To ponder what one would do with a time machine is, eventually, to ponder what one would do were one to ascend to quasi-omnipotent godhood.

What can we infer about his apotheosis from the terminus of Doc's moral journey? Unwilling or unable to abandon either his friends or his ideals, Doc ultimately appears to adopt an attitude of benign nonintervention.

Marty—as Doc's friend and first disciple—is permitted to retain the modest favor of living in an optimized 1985. Beyond that, however, Doc's assurance to Jennifer that the "future hasn't been written yet" might best be taken as an assertion that Doc is the sort of time-god who favors autonomy. Rather than maximizing utility or equality, Doc appears to align himself with the contractualist philosopher T.M. Scanlon, who writes that we "generally have good reason to want what happens to [us] to be affected by the choices [we] make under appropriate conditions."[12] A world in which external forces optimize our lives along some other metric is a world of diminished autonomy. As Sheila Jasanoff observes, "Only if we acknowledge technology's power to shape our hearts and minds, and our collective beliefs and behaviors, will the discourses of governance shift from fatalistic determinism to the emancipation of self-determination."[13]

Time Travel for Everyone

Meanwhile, back in our own 21st century, we find ourselves beset by a veritable army of godlings—innovators whose influence over the future is more constrained than Doc's, but no less real for that. How much of what happens to us is a product of the choices we make, rather than being a product of the technological innovations of others? Many, perhaps most innovations begin where Doc began, with curiosity about the world around us. But such "pure" inquiry is often derailed by the twin temptations of profit and power, and those who resist may nevertheless find their funding cut or their DeLorean misappropriated. Thus, it behooves aspiring innovators to be not only clever but wise. The first and most important regulator of new technology is not a government agency or institutional review board, but innovators themselves, scientists and researchers, inventors and engineers, natural philosophers all. Perhaps, as Plato and Derek Parfit suggest, some things should be kept secret—though how this might be accomplished in the Information Age is difficult to imagine. Perhaps Doc should have eschewed autonomy in favor of a world of utility, equality, sufficiency, or some other overriding value. Whatever the case, it is not something to decide *post hoc*, but to consider at every step along the way. So concludes the parable of Emmett "Doc" Brown: to change the future is to assume responsibility for whatever comes next.

Notes

1. Aristotle. 1944. *Politics*. Harris Rackham (trans.). Harvard University Press. 1259a15.
2. Plato. *Republic*. 414a–415a.

3. Sowell, Thomas. 2011. *Basic Economics: A Common Sense Guide to the Economy*, 4th ed. Basic Books. p. 593.

4. Pinker, Stephen. 2015. "The Moral Imperative for Bioethics." *The Boston Globe*.

5. In fact, Bacon did not author the aphorism. The Latin phrase "scientia potentia est" apparently first occurs in print in the 1668 edition of Thomas Hobbes' *Leviathan*. That said, Hobbes was Bacon's secretary for a time, and there can be no doubt that Bacon endorsed the aphorism's underlying sentiment.

6. Magnusson, William. 2020. *Blockchain Democracy: Technology, Law and the Rule of the Crowd*. Cambridge University Press. pp. 9–40.

7. Devereaux, Bret. 2022. "Collections: Nuclear Deterrence 101." *A Collection of Unmitigated Pedantry*.

8. Parfit, Derek. 1984. *Reasons and Persons*. Oxford University Press. p. 373.

9. Mill, John Stuart. 1861. *Utilitarianism*. Oxford University Press.

10. Rawls, John. 1971. *A Theory of Justice*. The Belknap Press of Harvard University Press.

11. Pike, Kenneth R. 2025. "The Doctrine of Sufficiency as a Contractualist Principle." *Moral Philosophy and Politics*.

12. Scanlon, T.M. 2018. *Why Does Inequality Matter?* Oxford University Press. p. 61.

13. Jasanoff, Sheila. 2016. *The Ethics of Invention: Technology and the Human Future*. W. W. Norton. p. 267.

The Pinheads

Ben **Almassi** is professor of philosophy at Governors State University on Chicago's far South Side where he teaches environmental ethics, feminist theory, political theory, and practical reasoning. He has written a variety of articles and two books, including *Nontoxic: Masculinity, Allyship, and Feminist Philosophy*. Oh, one other thing: if you guys ever have kids, and one of them when he's eight years old *accidentally* sets fire to the living room rug ... go easy on him.

Keith **Begley** regularly travels to the future and is shocked by what he finds there. Like the DeLorean, he was assembled in Ireland. He holds a Ph.D. in philosophy from Trinity College–Dublin and an M.Sc. in computer science from University College–Dublin. He is turning back the clock by pursuing a second Ph.D. in computer science at Trinity College–Dublin, while continuing to do research in the philosophy of computer science and AI, the philosophy of language and linguistics, the history of philosophy, and computational philology.

Taylor W. **Cyr** is associate professor of philosophy at Samford University. His main interests lie at the intersection of metaphysics and ethics, especially issues surrounding free will and moral responsibility, and he also sometimes writes about the hypertime model of time travel. He would ask you to please excuse the crudity of this model. He didn't have time to build it to scale or paint it.

Silence, Earthlings! My name is Darth Jeremy C. **DeLong**! I am an extraterrestrial from the planet Vulcan! During my time on Earth, I serve as associate professor of philosophy at Fort Hays State University, stationed at one of their Chinese partner institutions (Sias University). While my research interests primarily focus on ancient Greek philosophy (especially Parmenides), I also enjoy writing about philosophy in film. Representative publications respectively include: "Unifying the Poem: A Divine-Modal Reading," *Inquiring into Being* (2024); "Star Trek: Into Darkness—Ethical Impartiality, Partiality, and the Need for a Male/Female Synthesis," *Film & Philosophy* 19 (2015).

John M. **DePoe** is headmaster at Kingdom Preparatory Academy in Lubbock, Texas, and he also teaches undergraduate classes in the philosophy department at Texas Tech University. His research mostly examines topics in epistemology, the metaphysics of mind, and philosophy of religion, which can be found in more than 15 peer-reviewed journal articles and a co-edited book. When he can get the requisite plutonium from the Libyan terrorists, he likes to pursue his density of building a time traveling DeLorean.

Nikk **Effingham** is professor of philosophy at the University of Birmingham and a research associate at the University of Johannesburg. He studies metaphysics, the philosophy of time (mainly time travel) and the philosophy of religion. He is the author of *Time Travel: Probability and Impossibility*, in which he argues that Doc Brown is correct that time travel is dangerous and its risks are just too great.

Ryan **Falcioni** is a professor of philosophy at Chaffey College, in Southern California. He received his Ph.D. from Claremont Graduate University in 2011 and specializes in the philosophy of religion, ethics, the philosophy of language, cultural theory, and philosophical anthropology. Other interests include the ethics of storytelling, tribalism, conspiracism, and the rise of Christian nationalism. When not philosophizing, Ryan enjoys Brazilian jiu-jitsu, punk, reggae, and riding his hover board to the 7-Eleven to hone his *Wild Gunman* skills.

Don **Fallis** is a professor of philosophy and computer science at Northeastern University. In the past, he has published several highly-cited articles on lying and deception, including "What Is Lying?" in the *Journal of Philosophy* and "The Epistemic Threat of Deepfakes" in *Philosophy & Technology*. There is also information—based on his travels through time—that he won't tell you about his future lest it screw up the space-time continuum.

John **Garcia** is a professor of philosophy at Harper College, where he teaches critical thinking, symbolic logic, philosophy of religion, and non-western philosophy, among other courses. He received his Ph.D. in philosophy from Loyola University–Chicago. He has also been involved in the Intercollegiate Ethics Bowl for the last twenty years as a coach and organizer. He has frequently been called a "slacker who will never amount to anything," by friends, teachers, and Principal Strickland.

Catherine Villanueva **Gardner** is a professor of philosophy and women's and gender studies at the University of Massachusetts–Dartmouth. Her primary research interests are in the recapture of neglected historical women philosophers. In her spare moments, she is building a time machine from a kit. Thus far, her experiments with time travel have not been successful. If anyone finds a puzzled-looking German Shepherd dog by the name of Mileva, please return her, preferably to 2025.

In the current timeline, Zack **Garrett** completed a PhD in philosophy from the University of Nebraska–Lincoln in 2020 and then took up a job as a high school philosophy and logic teacher. But, once he gets his hands on a time machine, he will be spending the future living lavishly with his gambling winnings. Don't worry, though, his chapter will still appear in this book. Money or no money, Zack likes to write about philosophy.

Richard **Greene** is a professor of philosophy and the director of the Richard Richards Institute for Ethics at Weber State University. He is the author of *Spoiler Alert: It's a Book About the Philosophy of Spoilers* and *Conspiracy Theories in the Time of Coronavirus*. One book project was supposed to be completed in 2015, but like all his projects, it is way behind. Anyone traveling from 1985 to obtain this will want to aim for 2030 or so.

All right guys, listen, this is an author bio in Garamond; watch me for the changes and try and keep up, okay? Joshua **Heter** is an associate professor of philosophy at Jefferson College in Hillsboro, Missouri. He's the co-editor of a number of pop-culture and philosophy books including *Punk Rock and Philosophy: Research and Destroy* (2022), *Post-Punk and Philosophy: Rip It Up and Think Again* (2024), and *The Godfather and Philosophy: An Argument You Can't Refute* (2023).

John P. **Irish** is an independent researcher specializing in 19th-century American thought. His Ph.D. dissertation explored the ideas of Fitz-James O'Brien, the Irish-American "Poe." He is interested in the intersection of pop culture and philosophy, contributing articles to *Philosophy Now* and essays to *Asimov's Foundation and Philosophy* and *The Witcher and Philosophy*. He ran out of time trying to think of a funny author bio because his computer requires 1.21 gigawatts of power, and his local corner drugstore is all out of plutonium.

David Kyle **Johnson** is a professor of philosophy at King's College (Pennsylvania) and produces lecture series for *The Great Courses*, such as *Sci-Phi: Science Fiction as Philosophy* and *The Big Questions of Metaphysics*. He's contributed to around 30 philosophy and pop culture volumes, edited (or co-edited) a few others (for example, on *Black Mirror, Inception*, and *The Orville*), and is also the editor-in-chief of *The Palgrave Handbook of Popular Culture as Philosophy*. His latest project is a crazy wearable mind-reading contraption, but so far, the damn thing doesn't work at all.

Leonard **Kahn** is a professor of philosophy and the dean of the College of Arts and Sciences at Loyola University–New Orleans where he roams the halls in search of slackers with real attitude problems. His most recent work is on just war theory and the ethics of technology. His primary areas of research are moral theory and applied ethics, and his teaching interests include political philosophy, the philosophy of mind and action, and both decision and game theory.

Justin **Kitchen** teaches philosophy at California State University–Northridge, and is the co-founder of the Los Angeles Stoics, a non-profit promoting the study and practice of philosophy among the general public. His work centers on virtue ethics and virtue epistemology, drawing from Stoic philosophy and Indian Buddhism. After years of experience, he believes that if you put your mind to it, you can accomplish *anything* ... as long as you have a Mr. Fusion and a tank full of gasoline.

S. Evan **Kreider** is a professor of philosophy at the University of Wisconsin–Oshkosh. He received his Ph.D. from the University of Kansas. He has made numerous contributions to pop culture philosophy anthologies and is the co-editor of *The Philosophy of Joss Whedon*. He has also been known to steal razor-scooters from small children, rip their handles off, and race away on them like skateboards. In his defense, he does return them to the children. Usually.

Aadil **Kurji** is an assistant professor of philosophy at Durham University where he teaches logic to philosophers and ethics to budding data scientists. Channeling his inner Doc Brown, he has been rocking a yellow coat since 2015. He has taught courses on the philosophy of logic, the philosophy (ethics) of data and AI, the philosophy of language, the philosophy of mathematics, and logic, dynamic logics, and modal logics.

Elad **Magomedov** is an FWO (Research Foundation—Flanders) postdoctoral fellow at the Husserl Archives, KU Leuven. Having attained all his degrees (including a Ph.D.) in Leuven, he is somewhat like Doc and Marty in Hill Valley: no matter where he is on the timeline, he always ends up close to home. His research examines the relation between the imaginary and temporality within the context of authoritarian propaganda. His most recent publication is titled "Sartre's Break with Heidegger in L'être et le néant" (2024).

Daniel **Malloy** teaches philosophy at Aims Community College and writes about the intersections of popular culture and philosophy. He is a visitor from the future. Or the past? Maybe a different timeline? It's hard to keep straight. Regardless, he's pretty sure he doesn't belong here. Unfortunately, his time machine was impounded. Or has ceased to exist. Or never existed in this timeline. Maybe it was stolen? Or lost? Again, hard to keep straight.

Kristie **Miller** is professor of philosophy at the University of Sydney and director for the interdisciplinary Centre for Time. She has published widely on the metaphysics of personal identity, persistence, and the nature of time, including her recent books *Out of Time* and *Does Tomorrow Exist?* Her latest book project, *Life in Four Dimensions*, defends the block universe theory of time, because *we finally invented a theory of time that works!*

Kenneth R. **Pike** is an associate professor of philosophy and law at Florida Institute of Technology. When he's not writing on pop culture, he researches moral and political philosophy, law, and technology. If you want to read something that really cooks, he once published an essay blending the contractualism of T.M. Scanlon with the sufficientarianism of Harry Frankfurt. Well, you might not be ready for that yet ... but your kids are gonna *love* it.

Casey **Rentmeester** is a professor of philosophy at Bellin College. He is co-editor of *Heidegger and Music* and author of *Heidegger and the Environment*, as well as numerous peer-reviewed essays and articles on philosophy. When he was a kid in the '80s, *Back to the Future* was a staple VHS tape in his home—and though he dreamed of becoming a skateboarding musician à la Marty McFly, he had no talent for either pursuit, so he settled for academia.

Leigh E. **Rich** will finish her chapter tonight, and she'll *run it on over* first thing in the morning, all right? Not too early; readers sleep in on Saturday. Oh hey, your shoe's untied! She is a professor of health sciences at Georgia Southern University in Savannah, GA. A medical anthropologist, former journalist and radio host, and former editor of the *Journal of Bioethical Inquiry*, she teaches courses in bioethics, health law and policy, and special topics such as "Literature and Medicine," "TV's Take on Medicine," and "Medicine at the Movies."

Michael N. **Robinson** received an MFA in playwriting from the University of California–Riverside and creeps—as if he has a DeLorean with a flux capacitor—toward a Ph.D. in English/media studies at Claremont Graduate University. He's authored a bewilderingly disconnected artifacts—plays, short fiction, poetry and esoteric academic pieces on Chaucer, August Wilson and whoever wrote "Awyntyrs off Arthure" in the late 14th century (again, a DeLorean with standard F/C would be handy)—yet remains (halfway) convinced a throughline exists.

Jon **Robson** is an assistant professor in philosophy at the University of Nottingham in the UK. He has research interests in a number of different areas including aesthetics, epistemology, ethics, metaphysics, and the philosophy of religion. He has previously contributed to *Veronica Mars and Philosophy* and *LEGO and Philosophy*. He is the author of *Aesthetic Testimony* and co-author of *A Critical Introduction to the Metaphysics of Time*. He's yet to invent anything that works.

Kate C.S. **Schmidt** is an assistant professor of philosophy at Metropolitan State University–Denver. She holds a Ph.D. in philosophy-neuroscience-psychology from Washington University in St. Louis. Her research interests include ethics, epistemology, and moral psychology, and she has published essays and articles on related topics in a variety of books and journals. She wrote her essay for this book using her head as well as her heart.

Grace **Scott** graduated with her bachelor's in philosophy from Samford University in 2025. Building a career in tech, she endeavors to tinker, to go with the flux capacitor, and to always remember the eternal words of Doc Brown: "Your future hasn't been written yet ... so, make it a good one!"

Joe **Slater** is a lecturer in moral and political philosophy at the University of Glasgow. He is interested in research related to moral theory and applied ethics. He's not afraid of asking the big questions, like whether Marty is an inadvertent killer (in this volume) or, in recent publications, how much we ought to donate to charities, or whether we should get rid of juries. As such, *nobody* calls him chicken!

Dennis M. **Weiss**, up until recently (whenever that was), was a professor of philosophy at York College of Pennsylvania where he taught courses and wrote essays on philosophy of technology, pop culture, film, and the posthuman. But then he retired. And moved. And now he is intimately familiar with the flux-series of time, both as a scholarly topic and a lived experience. He is the co-author of *Designing the Domestic Posthuman*.

Xuanpu **Zhuang** is a ZJU100 young professor in the School of Philosophy at Zhejiang University. He earned his Ph.D. in applied philosophy from Bowling Green State University. He works mainly in ethics, political philosophy, and social philosophy. Research interests also include topics in PPE, epistemology, metaphysics, and the history of philosophy. If you'd like, you can drop him a line (at xuanpuzhuang@zju.edu.cn) at any point in the future (or the past, if you have a time traveling DeLorean).

Index

Aldiss, Brian 223
Archimedes 232
Aristophanes 133, 134
Aristotle 117, 118, 119, 120, 122, 180, 181, 182, 183, 184, 185, 215, 216, 217, 219, 239
Augustine 83

Back to the Future 1, 2, 4, 12, 13, 14, 16, 18, 19, 20, 22, 23, 24, 26, 27, 29, 30, 31, 32, 33, 34, 37, 40, 41, 42, 46, 47, 49, 50, 51, 52, 54, 61, 66, 67, 68, 81, 83, 85, 86, 87, 89, 91, 96, 106, 107, 109, 110, 111, 112, 123, 124, 126, 127, 128, 129, 132, 133, 136, 139, 142, 143, 144, 146, 148, 149, 150, 151, 152, 153, 154, 157, 158, 160, 161, 168, 170, 174, 178, 180, 181, 184, 188, 195, 198, 201, 203, 205, 206, 208, 215, 222, 224, 225, 226, 228, 229, 231, 232, 233, 239, 240, 243
Back to the Future Part II 4, 6, 7, 10, 16, 18, 24, 32, 33, 46, 47, 49, 50, 52, 53, 60, 61, 65, 66, 77, 83, 86, 89, 93, 94, 96, 101, 124, 135, 137, 142, 144, 146, 147, 151, 153, 154, 155, 156, 159, 160, 164, 167, 170, 228, 231, 233, 237, 238
Back to the Future Part III 18, 24, 46, 61, 135, 136, 137, 144, 146, 147, 151, 153, 155, 159, 164, 167, 231, 233, 236, 238
Bacon, Francis 241
Baines, Sam 4, 42, 43, 162, 202, 204, 205
Baines, Stella 205
Baines, Uncle 155
Berry, Chuck 19, 81, 112, 130
Berry, Marvin 81, 112
Bok, Sissela 83, 84
Bornstein, Kate 143
Brod, Harry 165
Brown, Doctor Emmett 4, 5, 6, 7, 8, 11, 12, 13, 14, 15, 16, 18, 19, 20, 24, 26, 27, 29, 32, 33, 36, 37, 39, 40, 42, 46, 47, 48, 49, 50, 51, 52, 54, 60, 61, 62, 63, 72, 73, 74, 76, 77, 79, 82, 83, 86, 89, 91, 92, 93, 94, 95, 96, 108, 114, 116, 117, 121, 125, 126, 127, 132, 133, 134, 135, 136, 137, 138, 139, 142, 144, 147, 149, 151, 152, 153, 155, 156, 157, 158, 161, 162, 163, 167, 170, 173, 184, 190, 191, 199, 202, 205, 208, 209, 210, 211, 213, 214, 222, 224, 225, 226, 227, 228, 229, 231, 232, 233, 234, 235, 236, 237, 238, 239, 240, 241, 242, 243, 244, 245
Byron, Lord 223

Carson, Thomas 83, 84
Chisholm, Roderick 83
Chomsky, Noam 21
Clayton, Clara 134, 136, 137, 138, 139, 147, 158, 162, 167
Conee, Earl 41, 42

Darth Vader 128, 154
Darwall, Stephen 74
deliberative freedom 54
DeLorean/time machine 5, 8, 9, 10, 11, 14, 15, 16, 29, 31, 32, 36, 51, 53, 61, 79, 81, 85, 86, 89, 92, 114, 126, 151, 156, 157, 163, 173, 201, 206, 209, 210, 218, 229, 233, 234, 236, 237, 238, 241, 242, 243, 244, 245
Descartes, Rene 61, 62, 63, 64
determinism 18, 19, 20, 25, 27
Deutsch, David 85
Douglass, Frederick 218

"Earth Angel" 23
Eastwood, Clint 164
Eastwood Ravine 238
1885 11, 15, 16, 18, 24, 61, 74, 77, 147, 155, 157, 158, 167, 229, 236, 237, 238
Einstein (dog) 5, 73, 79, 125, 127, 149, 163, 190, 191, 214, 226, 232, 233, 244
Einstein, Albert 232
Eisenstein, Alex 39
Eisenstein, Phyllis 39
Enchantment Under the Sea dance 130, 145, 234

256 Index

Epictetus 138, 217
ethics 117, 122

Flea, 129
flux capacitor 8, 26, 32, 63, 79, 124, 126, 157, 205, 210, 226, 232, 234, 235, 237
Fox, Michael J. 142, 144
Frankenstein 222, 223, 224, 225, 226, 227, 228
Frankfurt, Harry 244
Freud, Sigmund 152, 157, 198, 199, 200, 201, 202, 203, 204, 206

Gale, Bob 1, 67, 161, 167
Generation X 106
Gilligan, Carol 152, 153, 154, 155, 156, 157, 158
Gipe, George 222
Glover, Crispin 119
God 22, 87, 107, 225, 226, 228
Goddu, G.C. 39
Godwin, William 223
Gottschall, Jonathan 20, 21, 22, 27, 28
Grandfather Paradox 126
Grays Sports Almanac 72, 96

Heidegger, Martin 181, 182, 183, 184, 185
Held, Virginia 154, 156
Hill Valley 1, 5, 34, 45, 48, 60, 64, 76, 80, 89, 91, 92, 94, 96, 103, 108, 130, 153, 154, 157, 161, 162, 167, 202, 204, 228, 233
Hilldale 8, 16, 57
The Hitchhiker's Guide to the Galaxy 87
Hitler, Adolf 13, 188
Hobbes, Thomas 154, 189
The Honeymooners 151, 155, 171, 195
Huey Lewis and the News 61, 151
Hutcheson, Francis 106, 107, 108, 111
hypertime 13

Jocasta 2, 126, 198, 199

Kant, Immanuel 76, 78, 100, 101
Kennedy, John F. 29

Langer, Susanne 106, 111
Lewis, David 29, 32, 33, 39, 51, 84, 108, 129, 151
Libyans 11, 19, 93, 151, 153, 156, 226
Locke, John 190, 191
Lockwood, Michael 85
Lou's Café 112

Marcus Aurelius 138
A Match Made in Space 128
McFly, David 19, 23, 99, 101, 102, 119, 145, 155, 171, 178, 188

McFly, George 8, 11, 19, 31, 42, 46, 47, 50, 51, 74, 75, 76, 77, 78, 79, 80, 86, 89, 90, 114, 115, 116, 117, 118, 119, 120, 121, 122, 126, 128, 129, 133, 134, 135, 136, 144, 145, 146, 149, 152, 153, 154, 155, 157, 158, 161, 162, 163, 164, 165, 166, 171, 172, 173, 174, 177, 180, 181, 182, 183, 184, 185, 186, 187, 188, 189, 190, 192, 193, 194, 195, 202, 203, 204, 205, 209, 211, 216, 217, 222, 225, 243
McFly, Linda 19, 23, 92, 93, 119, 155, 162, 171, 188, 206
McFly, Lorraine 19, 31, 33, 42, 43, 50, 51, 78, 86, 89, 91, 110, 114, 115, 116, 117, 118, 119, 121, 126, 128, 129, 134, 135, 145, 146, 147, 149, 153, 154, 155, 157, 158, 162, 163, 165, 166, 171, 172, 174, 177, 180, 181, 182, 183, 184, 185, 186, 187, 188, 194, 195, 199, 201, 202, 203, 205, 206, 209, 211, 225
McFly, Maggie 147, 157
McFly, Marty 2, 4, 5, 6, 7, 8, 11, 12, 14, 15, 16, 18, 19, 20, 23, 24, 27, 29, 31, 32, 33, 34, 36, 37, 39, 40, 41, 42, 43, 46, 47, 48, 49, 50, 51, 53, 55, 56, 57, 59, 61, 62, 63, 64, 65, 66, 67, 68, 72, 73, 74, 75, 76, 77, 78, 79, 80, 81, 82, 83, 85, 86, 87, 89, 90, 91, 92, 94, 95, 96, 99, 101, 107, 108, 109, 110, 112, 114, 115, 116, 117, 118, 119, 120, 121, 124, 125, 126, 127, 128, 129, 130, 133, 134, 135, 136, 139, 142, 143, 144, 145, 146, 147, 148, 149, 151, 152, 153, 154, 155, 156, 157, 158, 159, 161, 162, 163, 164, 165, 166, 167, 170, 171, 172, 173, 175, 176, 177, 178, 180, 181, 182, 183, 184, 185, 186, 187, 188, 189, 190, 191, 192, 193, 195, 198, 199, 201, 202, 203, 204, 205, 206, 208, 209, 210, 211, 212, 213, 214, 215, 216, 217, 218, 219, 222, 224, 225, 226, 227, 228, 229, 231, 232, 233, 234, 235, 236, 237, 238, 240, 241, 242, 243, 244, 245
McFly, Marty, Jr. 6, 7, 18, 77, 155, 216, 242
McFly, Seamus 157
McTaggart, John 29, 30, 31, 35, 124
Meiland, Jack 38
Men in Black 82, 84
metaphysics 43
Mill, John Stuart 100, 104, 166, 244
mimesis 113
Mr. Fusion 157, 241

Needles 33, 76, 78, 80, 92, 146, 147, 164, 165
Newton, Isaac 125, 232
1955 4, 5, 11, 12, 14, 15, 16, 19, 32, 36, 43, 61, 72, 73, 74, 75, 77, 81, 83, 85, 86, 89, 91, 94, 96, 108, 114, 115, 116, 120, 121, 126, 130, 136, 144, 145, 146, 149, 153, 154, 157, 158, 161, 165, 170, 172, 173, 174, 177, 180, 186, 188, 191, 192, 199, 201, 202, 204, 205, 209,

Index 257

210, 211, 212, 213, 214, 228, 231, 232, 233, 234, 235, 236, 237, 243
1985 4, 6, 7, 8, 11, 12, 14, 15, 19, 32, 33, 36, 39, 53, 57, 59, 74, 76, 78, 83, 86, 89, 96, 114, 120, 136, 145, 146, 147, 149, 151, 154, 155, 156, 157, 162, 165, 166, 170, 171, 172, 173, 177, 178, 180, 182, 184, 187, 199, 201, 202, 203, 204, 205, 209, 210, 213, 214, 222, 229, 233, 234, 235, 236, 238, 240, 243, 244, 245
nostalgia 113

Oedipus 2, 157, 198, 199, 200, 201, 202, 203, 204, 206
Olson, Randy 21, 22, 28

paradox 19, 28, 66, 126
Parfit, Derek 43, 75, 191, 192, 243, 244, 245
Parker, Jennifer 7, 8, 12, 14, 15, 16, 52, 53, 54, 55, 56, 57, 59, 60, 73, 77, 83, 96, 120, 121, 128, 129, 146, 147, 152, 153, 155, 157, 158, 162, 172, 201, 206, 219, 228, 243, 245
Peabody, Old Man 16, 202, 233
Plato 106, 108, 109, 110, 111, 132, 133, 137, 138, 241, 242, 245
"The Power of Love" 51, 129, 151
Presley, Elvis 112

Rawls, John 244
Reagan, Ronald 204, 206

Sartre, Jean-Paul 209, 211, 212, 213
Scanlon, T.M. 245
Schechtman, Marya 193, 194
Schick, Ted 63, 64
science fiction 142, 223
Seneca 138, 219
Shelley, Mary 222, 223, 224, 228, 230
Shelley, Percy Bysshe 223
Ship of Theseus 189
Sider, Theodore 41, 42, 123, 124, 126, 127, 128, 130
Silvestri, Alvin 50
Singer, Marcus 73
Socrates 132, 133, 134, 136, 137, 217

Sophocles 198
Southworth, Jason 68
Star Trek 66, 82, 84, 85, 86, 87, 192
stoicism 138
Stoltenberg, John 164, 165
Strickland, (Mr.) Stanford 51, 126, 152, 154, 171, 184, 202, 227

Tallman, Ruth 67
Tannen, Biff 8, 9, 11, 12, 13, 14, 15, 16, 18, 20, 24, 33, 34, 46, 47, 49, 50, 61, 72, 73, 74, 75, 76, 77, 78, 79, 80, 86, 89, 90, 91, 92, 94, 96, 98, 99, 100, 101, 102, 103, 110, 114, 115, 116, 118, 119, 120, 121, 144, 145, 146, 147, 153, 154, 155, 157, 162, 163, 164, 165, 166, 171, 180, 181, 182, 183, 184, 185, 186, 187, 188, 191, 192, 194, 195, 202, 203, 204, 205, 215, 216, 217, 218, 219, 228, 243
Tannen, Buford 11, 15, 18, 74, 77, 80, 147, 164, 218
Tappolet, Christine 48
Thales 241
Tronto, Joan 165
Twin Pines Mall 77, 231, 233
2015 6, 7, 8, 9, 14, 16, 28, 52, 53, 54, 55, 59, 60, 78, 79, 83, 89, 96, 147, 154, 164, 240, 241, 242

utilitarianism 99

Van Halen 163
Van Halen, Edward 129
Verne, Jules 134, 167

Wasserman, Ryan 39
Western Union 11, 15, 16
Wilson, Goldie 19, 80, 112, 116, 130, 204, 217, 233
Wittgenstein, Ludwig 21, 22
Wollstonecraft, Mary 163, 166, 223

Zemeckis, Robert 1, 31, 65, 67, 161, 167
Zeus 133
ZZ Top 129

www.ingramcontent.com/pod-product-compliance
Lightning Source LLC
Chambersburg PA
CBHW032035300426
44117CB00009B/1067